Lady Blackrobes

Missionaries in the
Heart of Indian Country

Irene
Mahoney
O.S.U.

Fulcrum Publishing
Golden, Colorado

Library of Congress Cataloging-in-Publication Data
Mahoney, Irene.
  Lady Blackrobes : missionaries in the heart of Indian country /
Irene Mahoney.
    p. cm.
  Includes bibliographical references and index.
  ISBN-13: 978-1-55591-617-6 (pbk. : alk. paper)
  ISBN-10: 1-55591-617-1 (pbk. : alk. paper) 1. Ursulines--
Missions--Montana. 2. Cheyenne Indians--Missions--
Montana. 3. Indians of North America--Missions--Montana.
4. Missions--Montana. 5. Montana--Church history.
6. Montana--History. I. Title.
  BV2803.M9M28 2006
  271'.9740786--dc22
                                                        2006021326

Printed in the United States of America by Color House Graphics
                    0 9 8 7 6 5 4 3 2 1

                    Editorial: Kay Baron, Katie Raymond
                         Design: Patty Maher
Cover image: Sister Ursula Marie Johnson and Mrs. Gone to War in front
of her lodge. Courtesy of Ursuline archives, Great Falls, Montana

                        Fulcrum Publishing
              4690 Table Mountain Drive, Suite 100
                      Golden, Colorado 80403
                   800-992-2908 • 303-277-1623
                      www.fulcrumbooks.com

For Colette Lignon, O.S.U.,
whose admiration for the Montana missions initiated
and encouraged *Lady Blackrobes*

Contents

Acknowledgments

My first word of gratitude must go to the Ursulines of Toledo, Ohio, especially to Sister Mary Rose Krupp (recently deceased), who initiated me into the untold story of the Ursuline missions in Montana. The Ursuline convent in Toledo became my home as I made my first foray into their archival treasures.

In addition to the Ursulines of Toledo, I found a whole household of archivists, both here in the United States and abroad, who opened their treasures and responded tirelessly to my never-ending requests. I owe special gratitude to the following archivists, who made their materials available with unfailing generosity and graciousness:

Mark Thiel, Special Collections, Marquette University,
    Milwaukee, Wisconsin
David Kingma, Jesuit Oregon Province Archives,
    Spokane, Washington
Stephanie Morris, Sisters of the Blessed Sacrament,
    Bensalem, Pennsylvania
Marie Andrée Jégou, Ursuline Roman Union
    Generalate, Rome, Italy
Julianne Ruby, Ursuline Roman Union, Western
    Province, Great Falls, Montana
Francis Xavier Porter, Ursuline Roman Union,
    Western Province, Great Falls, Montana
Rosemary Meiman, Ursuline Roman Union, Central
    Province, St. Louis, Missouri
Marie Marchand, Ursuline Canadian Union, Province
    of Québec, Québec, Canada

Shirley Teasdale, Ursuline Canadian Union, Province
of Trois Rivières, Trois Rivières, Canada

Christine Kroesel, Archdiocese of Cleveland,
Cleveland, Ohio

Dolores Brinkel, Archdiocese of Helena, Helena,
Montana

The staff at the archives of The Catholic University of
America, Washington, D.C.

Gratitude, too, to the staff at Fulcrum Publishing, especially to Kay Baron, who believed in *Lady Blackrobes* from the beginning, and Katie Raymond, who guided it (and me) through publication.

My greatest debt of gratitude, however, is to Irene Kutsky, O.S.U., who spent her summers in Montana poring through dusty boxes of tattered photographs, finding the ones that were "just right." Her enthusiasm never flagged, and her artist's eye found value where I saw only blurred images. If this were all, it would be a great deal, but beyond this was the unremitting task of living in graceful patience with the author throughout the manuscript's long months of gestation. *Lady Blackrobes* is her book as well as mine.

Introduction

Soon after I started work on *Lady Blackrobes*, a friend asked me as we had lunch in the local diner, "Isn't it a strange time to write about missionaries now, when all that stuff is so discredited?" The question was no surprise to me, but it got my hackles up, partially because I—like the missionaries I was writing about—am a member of the Ursuline Order, but also for some less personal and more substantive reasons.

Certainly, I would agree that missionary activity as it was practiced in the nineteenth century (and later) looks to us now, with our contemporary perspective, as, at best, a flawed enterprise. Yet what motivated these religious men and women was little different from the mind-set of the general populace. The Native Americans had not disappeared, had not slipped away into some unknown existence as an earlier generation had hoped. They were still there, pushed from east to west by hunters, government soldiers, and settlers. Since they had not gone away, they had to be dealt with, and by the mid-nineteenth century, two methods were in vogue: exterminate them or assimilate them. At face value, it seemed far more humane to assimilate them, although, as one critic charged, assimilation was simply a more subtle form of extermination.

When in January 1884 six Ursuline nuns left their convent in Toledo to travel to eastern Montana to establish a mission school for the children of the Northern Cheyenne, their goal, of course, was to assimilate them. How they would do this seemed to them fairly straightforward. They would gather the children into a boarding school and teach them basic skills: to read, to write, to cipher in the English language. In time, they learned from the Jesuit priests, who had already established missions in the Montana region, that it was essential that children be separated from their families as much as possible, that all Indian customs be forbidden, and that they must never be permitted to speak their native languages. Only with such draconian measures could assimilation be assured.

But for these religious missionaries, this was only the periphery; the real purpose of their activity was to bring these "pagans" into the comfort of the kingdom of God. The god they had in mind, of course, was the god of Christianity, and the religion was that of Roman Catholicism. Both nuns and priests had an unswerving belief that they possessed the one and essential truth, and that outside this truth, there was no salvation. To save poor ignorant souls from the fiery pit of hell was a powerful motive that enabled the missionaries to endure lives of heroic hardship.

In order that the Native Americans be brought into the family of Jesus Christ, their culture, with its rituals, myths, and languages, had to be destroyed. Missionaries accepted this without a pang. To lead these people from darkness into light was a goal that could not be questioned.

It is, of course, precisely this absolutism that today we question and deplore. Our theology of "mission" has changed radically. The goal of "missionaries" today is a far different affair—not destroying but enabling people to live fuller lives within their own culture.

Some time ago, I listened to a group of historians discussing their craft. "History is a crippled discipline," one of them ruminated. "It can't really get at the truth." I found the statement comforting as I tried to sort out what these Ursuline missionaries thought and accomplished, knowing that however hard I worked, I would never be able to get at the truth. Hindsight prevents me. I live in another world with another perspective, another set of assumptions.

So what then are we to say of those Ursulines who so single-mindedly strode off into the plains and mountains, the gullies and buttes of Montana? Whatever their limitations (and there were many), they lived lives of almost unendurable hardship, unswervingly faithful to the only vision available to them. Perhaps our best explanation is found in the words of that perceptive novelist Henry James: "We work in the dark; we do what we can. The rest is the mystery of life."

—Feast of St. Angela, January 27, 2006

Chronology
Ursuline Missions in Montana
1884–1972

Of the eight missions where Ursulines served, it was St. Labre's—the poorest and most problematic—that has perdured and flourished. Today, St. Labre's is known nationwide as among the finest schools for Native Americans in the United States.

St. Labre's Mission to the Northern Cheyenne Nation

1884—Founded by the Ursulines from Toledo

1917—Destroyed by fire but rebuilt

1926—Capuchin Fathers assumed administration

1933—Ursulines withdrew. They were replaced by the School Sisters of St. Francis.

St. Peter's Mission to the Blackfeet Nation

1859—Founded by the Jesuits

1862—Relocated to permanent location

1890—Ursulines began girls' school

1898—Jesuits withdrew

1912—Fire destroyed main building

1917—Second fire occurred. The mission closed.

St. Paul's Mission to the Gros Ventre and Assiniboine Nations

1884—Founded by the Jesuits

1887—Ursulines began school

1931—Mission buildings partially destroyed. School continued.

1936—Ursulines withdrew. They were replaced by the School Sisters of St. Francis.

St. Francis Xavier's Mission to the Crow Nation

1887—Founded by the Jesuits

1887—Ursulines began school

1921—Ursulines withdrew

1921—Mission school temporarily closed

St. Ignatius's Mission to the Flathead and Kalispel Nations

1854—Founded by the Jesuits

1864—Sisters of Charity of Providence opened girls' school

1890—Ursulines opened a kindergarten

1922—Fire destroyed Ursuline buildings

1924—Ursuline school rebuilt and reopened

1962—Boarding school closed. Land returned to Indian tribes.

Holy Family Mission to the Blackfeet Nation

1884—Founded by the Jesuits

1890—Ursulines opened girls' school

1941—Mission closed

St. Charles's Mission to the Crow Nation

1890—Founded by the Jesuits

1890—Ursulines opened school

1898—School closed

St. John Berchmans's Mission to the Flathead Nation

1889—Founded by the Jesuits

1890—Ursulines opened school

1897—School closed

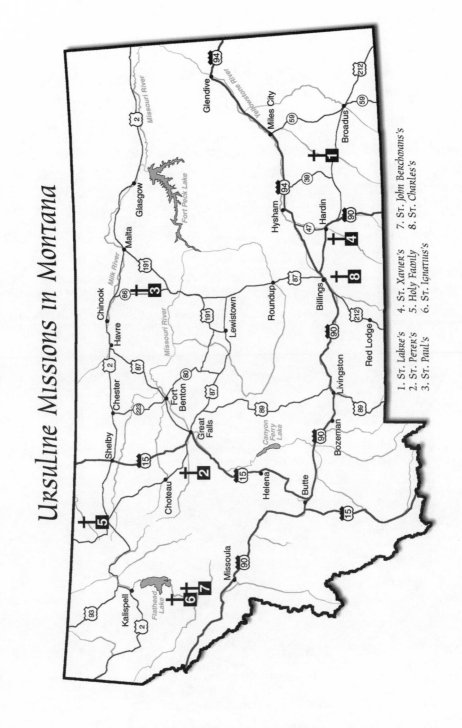

Ursuline Missions in Montana

1. St. Labre's
2. St. Peter's
3. St. Paul's
4. St. Xavier's
5. Holy Family
6. St. Ignatius's
7. St. John Berchmans's
8. St. Charles's

Chapter One

There was once a bishop who loved us.
—*Cheyenne chief*

In the spring of 1879 in Miles City, Montana, a group of school-children and their teacher watched as remnants of the Cheyenne nation were brought to Fort Keogh under military guard. It was a frightening sight.

A half century later, one of those children, Laura Zook, wrote in her memoirs:

> A terrible sight to remember, one hundred sullen, vicious
> looking Indians, fresh scalps dangling at their belts, with the
> squaws trailing in the rear. They had fought their way from
> the Indian Territory, had killed men, women and children, in
> order to get back to what they considered their home, the
> Lame Deer country. The soldiers had met them at Fallon and
> were bringing them in. Little wolf himself, sitting erect on his
> pony, and with the most ferocious look on his face, was
> ordering the crossing of the squaws over the pontoon bridges,
> while the bucks swam their horses across the swollen river.[1]

It is a description more illustrative of the attitude of the white settlers toward the Cheyenne than it is historically accurate. The lurid reference to "fresh scalps" is far from the mark. Hungry and weary, the Cheyenne had been harassed for months by soldiers, who gave them no respite. If they appeared "sullen" and "vicious," it was their final effort to maintain dignity in the wake of their humiliating defeat.

No nation had endured more or been subjected to more injustice than the Northern Cheyenne. Often referred to as "the race of sorrow," the title was apt. In 1876, weary of false promises and broken treaties, the Cheyenne joined the Sioux in the Battle of the Little Bighorn and toppled the famous General George Custer. The Cheyenne paid dearly for their victory, however. Seven years later, reduced to a remnant of their original nation and displaced from their ancestral lands, they waited despondently for the government to implement its promise to assign them a reservation.

At Fort Keogh, however, where they were housed under ambiguous status—neither prisoners nor free—they found an advocate. A young soldier, George Yoakum, angered at the injustice of their situation, contended that their lot would be improved if the Cheyenne could be provided with a mission school. Although not Catholic, he suggested to Father Eli Washington John Lindesmith, the military chaplain, that a group of sisters be asked to come to minister to these neglected people. Thus, in the summer of 1883, John Baptist Brondel, recently appointed bishop of the Montana Territory, was made aware of this small portion of his extensive domain.

While a schoolboy in Bruges, Belgium, Brondel had determined to follow in the footsteps of his hero, Father Peter De Smet, founder of the Jesuit Rocky Mountain Mission. Two years after Brondel's ordination, he sailed for Canada, arriving in Vancouver in 1866. Years of working in a poor and isolated community on Puget Sound gave him a compassionate understanding of the pastoral needs in the lonely reaches of the New World. Even after being appointed bishop, he maintained his original thrust that had impelled him to the Pacific Northwest: to work with those most in need. A month after his appointment as apostolic administrator of Montana, he recognized the need for additional help and wrote to Richard Gilmour, bishop of Cleveland, Ohio, begging for help:*

---

*There is no explanation as to why Gilmour was singled out, except perhaps because his diocese had a remarkable number of flourishing congregations.

> I am newly appointed here and have one priest whom I can
> call my own in the Territory of Montana. The Territory extends
> from east to west over an area of 800 miles. The Jesuit Fathers
> are among the different Indian Tribes but cannot spare a
> Father to reside with the Cheyennes who are in number 600.
> ... Please assist me if you can in getting a good stirring priest
> ... Excuse my boldness, but the love of souls makes me so ... [2]

Gilmour immediately presented Brondel's request to the religious of his diocese in a letter published in the diocesan newspaper *The Catholic Universe*. "Who of our young priests will volunteer their services for these children of the forest? Who of our female religious will devote themselves to the care and education of these pagan children?" he pleaded.

> Here are the Cheyennes—a tribe of 800 souls most anxious for
> a priest and Sisters to come and preach to them, and teach their
> children. Without means themselves they beg of those who
> have the means to help them. ... Priests or religious willing to
> devote themselves to those Cheyenne Indians can communi-
> cate with the Rt. Rev. John B. Brondel, Helena, Montana, or
> with the undersigned, who will be willing to help in this work
> as far as lies with his power. R. Gilmour, Bishop of Cleveland.[3]

It is hard to know how much the religious of Bishop Gilmour's diocese knew of the plight of the Cheyenne. Cleveland was far from Montana, and although the Indian question (the conflict with whites, the efforts to assimilate native people into American culture) was a subject of general conversation, the plight of the native people themselves was far from the average citizen's understanding (or interest). Cruelties wrought upon white settlers—rather than injustices wrought upon the Indians—were uppermost in people's minds.

It says much, therefore, of the temper of Ohio's Catholics that within weeks, Gilmour had a positive reply to his appeal. In 1883, the diocese of Cleveland had a rich source from which to draw: four-teen congregations of religious sisters, half of which were engaged in education.[4] It was, however, from a congregation relatively new to the diocese that the final choices were made.

In 1850, at the invitation of Bishop Amadeus Rappe, five Ursuline nuns arrived in Ohio and settled in his episcopal city of Cleveland. Their numbers increased rapidly, and four years later, again at Rappe's request, they were able to send five Ursulines to establish a new house in the small city of Toledo, situated on Lake Erie in western Ohio. They flourished quickly, building two new con-vents (one each on Cherry and Erie Streets), establishing an academy, and staffing several parochial schools. By the time Richard Gilmour replaced Bishop Rappe after his death in 1870, the Ursulines were well known and admired.[5]

At the time of Bishop Brondel's request for missionaries, the Toledo Ursulines numbered some forty sisters, and according to legend (documents are lacking), thirty sisters responded to Bishop Gilmour's letter. Such enthusiasm should have come as no surprise: the Ursulines had already proved themselves as missionaries, having established a school for the native population in Québec as early as 1639, thus becoming the first women religious on the North American continent.

Gilmour replied at once to the generous response, and on October 24 he wrote to the current superior, Mother Stanislaus Duffey:

D[ea]r Child,
  I have today written to Rt. Rev. John B. Brondel, Helena, Montana of your offer to go to the Indian Missions and in time will hear what he has to say. I will be glad to let a colony go for such purpose and will give them my God-speed with all my heart rejoicing that the diocese is blessed in its off-spring. We may need as many as eight, so as to form two [groups] ... but of this farther on.[6]

Needless to say, Brondel was delighted, and at once Gilmour set about determining his choices from the list, of volunteers. According to Mother Amadeus Dunne's ornate narrative, the selection took place during a solemn and sacred ceremony. The occasion was one of prayerful reflection, and the bishop had requested Exposition of the Blessed Sacrament to signalize the sacredness of the moment. While the community knelt in adoration "before the Silent Source of Inspiration," as Amadeus described it, the bishop saw each sister in turn. Before the day was out, the choices had been made.

> Mother Amadeus Dunne, born in Akron, Ohio, in
> 1844, professed in 1864
> Sister Ignatius McFarland, born in Cleveland, Ohio,
> in 1852, professed in 1873
> Sister Holy Angels Carabin, born in Peru, Ohio, in
> 1849, professed in 1874
> Sister Sacred Heart Meilink, born in Toledo, Ohio, in
> 1850, professed in 1877
> Sister Francis Seibert, born in Adrian, Michigan, in
> 1850, professed in 1879
> Sister Angela Abair, born in New Baltimore,
> Michigan, in 1856, professed in 1881[7]

To no one's surprise, Amadeus Dunne was chosen as superior, a role she had fulfilled successfully at Toledo. She was intelligent and quick (too quick for some), with a ready charm that cloaked a natural impatience and a tendency to march ahead of the group. She was a woman of spiritual vision and passionate dedication. In modern parlance, she was charismatic. She was beautiful as well. She had just passed her fortieth birthday, and her forty-first year found her eager and energetic. Who could hold a candle to her?

With his selection made, Gilmour again published a letter in *The Catholic Universe*, on December 13:

Some weeks ago we made a call for a priest and a colony of Sisters to go out to care for the Cheyenne Indians. The answer was prompt. Rev. J. Eyler offered his services, as did also a colony of Sisters from the Ursuline Convent of Toledo.

By direction of Bishop Brondel, who has late been appointed to the spiritual care of Montana Territory, the above-named parties will leave for their new home immediately after the New Year. They will need help to take them on their journey, as also help for the establishment of schools, and such other needs as the opening and founding of a mission among the converted Indians necessarily means. ... Books will be needed, also chapel and altar furniture, besides the necessary house furnishing for the Sisters and the priest, who for long days to come will have but little of the comforts of civilized life.[8]

When the news reached Brondel, he responded with exuberant gratitude, and on the last day of the year he wrote to Gilmour, saying that his message "sounded like the song of the angels and was heard

Six foundresses—Front: Ignatius McFarland, Amadeus Dunne, and Sacred Heart Meilink; Back: Angela Abair, Francis Seibert, Holy Angels Carabin, 1884. Courtesy of Ursuline archives, Toledo, Ohio

from the East to the West of America. Your arrangements are perfect," he continued, "and I will do my best to cooperate and make it a success here with the grace of God."[9]

At once, Brondel entrusted the practical arrangements to Father Lindesmith, the army chaplain at Fort Keogh whose persuasive advice along with that of Yoakum had initially encouraged Brondel to undertake the project.

Born in Ohio and ordained to the priesthood in 1855, Lindesmith had spent the next twenty-five years serving in various Ohio towns before receiving Gilmour's request to serve as chaplain to the military at Fort Keogh. Named for the prophet Elias, for the father of his country, and for the evangelist St. John, Lindesmith took all his names as symbols of his destiny. Coming from a deeply religious and military family, he considered his position as an army chaplain in the distant territory of Montana as the very apogee of destiny. Perhaps nothing provides a clearer insight into his character than the photograph of which he was so proud: Lindesmith stands tall, western hat in hand, dressed in the buckskin garb of a Montana hunter.

Although in his mid-fifties, he adapted to his new role with an energy and sensitivity that won him universal acclaim. He immediately recognized needs beyond his duties at the fort and soon established himself as the pastor of the small Catholic population of Miles City, some two miles distant. Nothing was beyond his zeal. He traveled to the railroad towns of Glendive and Forsyth, rode to outlying ranches for baptisms and funerals, established catechism classes for both old and young. Small wonder that a contemporary noted that no preacher was ever more zealous than Eli Lindesmith.[10]

In addition to his responsibilities for the soldiers, Lindesmith's position at Fort Keogh brought him into contact with the Northern Cheyenne, who remained under the continued jurisdiction of General Nelson Miles. Miles, although a rigorous military man, was unusually understanding of the Cheyenne's position.

Officially "prisoners," many Cheyenne acted as scouts or in similar capacities, thus permitting them free range at the fort and at nearby Miles City.* Their status, however, remained problematic. Although no longer considered enemies, yet they remained homeless. Once again, the government assured them that by the following spring, 1884, a reservation would be legally established in their old territory, along the Rosebud River, some eighty miles west of Miles City. It was this possibility that encouraged Lindesmith in the proposal that if sisters could be found to educate and Christianize these victimized souls, a new life would be open to them.

By the beginning of 1884, Gilmour had informed Lindesmith that six sisters would arrive in mid-January at Miles City—the closest railroad depot to the proposed Indian reservation—and Lindesmith set about locating temporary housing for the new arrivals.

In Toledo, the nuns had little more than a month to assemble all their necessary supplies, a task made more difficult because of their ignorance of what they would need: warm clothes, surely, and sturdy boots for the outdoors. In addition to their personal necessities, they had to gather materials to equip a school for children who not only knew no English, but who, because their language was still only in oral form, had no concept of reading and writing. Yet excitement rather than anxiety was the overriding emotion. Young and zealous, they were moved by the sense of being divinely chosen for the work of spreading the Gospel. There could hardly be a more empowering motive.

Lindesmith, delighted by the speed with which things were moving, informed Gilmour that he had secured temporary lodging for the sisters in a rooming house run by an Irish widow, Bridget McCanna. (Although Miles City boasted a number of hotels, it is significant of their quality that Lindesmith never considered housing the Ursulines in any of them.)

By the end of December, Gilmour had completed their travel arrangements. Father Joseph Eyler, a priest of the diocese of Cleveland, offered himself to accompany the sisters and remain on

---

*At this time, Miles City was, strictly speaking, not a "city." It was not established as such until 1887.

as chaplain once they were established on the Cheyenne reservation. On December 31, Gilmour wrote to Mother Stanislaus, "I have arranged with Rev. Father Eyler that the sisters will leave Toledo on the 15th January. He will reach Toledo on Monday and all can leave at 11am Tuesday."[11]

Their route brought them west into Chicago, where they boarded the Northern Pacific, taking them northwest into Minnesota. At St. Paul, the state capital, they had a short stopover before continuing northwest through the Dakotas, and then across into Montana Territory, and finally into Miles City.

Nothing had changed life in the West so dramatically as the advent of the railroad. By the mid-1880s, the two great railroads (the Northern Pacific and the Great Northern) had been completed. In September 1883, the golden spike of the Northern Pacific, indicating the "wedding of east and west," was driven in near Garrison in central Montana. Of that glorious moment, a contemporary wrote histrionically, "At last, Oh people of Montana, the hour of your deliverance draws nigh."[12] The Northern Pacific, chartered by Congress at the end of the Civil War, followed a more southernly route from Minneapolis across Dakota and into central Montana. Had the nuns attempted the trip a few years earlier, they would have been subjected to endless and uncomfortable days on the stagecoach or the much slower travel of the Yellowstone steamboat. Even by train, it was a long journey, but one that was reasonably direct and relatively safe.

Mother Amadeus's memoir, detailed in spiritual aspirations, says nothing of their parting day or of the substantial baggage that accompanied them. Although there is no record, it seems likely that mattresses, tables, and other essential furniture were among the freight they loaded into the baggage car, since they could not count on finding even these essentials at their destination. Bishop Gilmour had collected $281.86 from the Cleveland parishes to enable them to buy school supplies and objects of religious devotion (medals, rosaries, holy cards). In addition, the nuns brought with them several hampers of food, carefully chosen and packed by their sisters, which would sustain them on their travels and into the first days of their unexplored Montana life.

The convent annals are hardly more forthcoming than Amadeus's memoir. "After great preparations and much prayer for the arduous and noble Indian work," wrote the annalist, "the day of departure arrived. Many and holy were the wishes and blessings showered upon the valiant band of missionaries."[13] Virtue abounded, and whatever signs of tears or irresolution there may have been never passed into the unblotted records of the convent annals.

Despite their inevitable anxiety, they found the railroad journey both exciting and comfortable. Mother Stanislaus had arranged for them to have sleepers, and they had sufficient money to enjoy the luxuries of the dining car. Although the Mississippi was frozen over, the cold was not so extreme as they had feared. Sister Sacred Heart later wrote in some detail of the long hours of barren, snow-covered country—a land so deserted that they did not see a house for miles and miles, nor even a tree to break the monotonous landscape. Friday morning, January 18, they crossed into Montana Territory, which had little to distinguish it. Like Dakota, it was cold, flat, and thinly settled, a land ill-suited for vegetation.[14]

By late morning, just ninety-six hours after leaving Toledo, their iron horse pulled into Miles City. Waiting for them on the platform was Bishop Brondel, who had made the 400-mile trip from Helena to be present on their arrival. While the bishop may not have been "weeping with joy," as Amadeus later described, it was, no doubt, an emotional occasion. Along with Brondel and the indefatigable Lindesmith, there was a crowd of onlookers more curious than pious, for Miles City was a small town where even a minor event was sufficient for big news.

Miles City, despite rapid changes, was still considered a cow town. The year before, a visitor from New York had described it as a "typical border town," in an article later published in *The New York Times*:

Cowboys with lariats hanging on their saddles are seen at
every turn, riding on the stout little broncho ponies of the
plains; rough-looking men are loafing on the street corners;
occasionally a 'big Indian' with a squaw or two following
him, stalks across the scene, and on each side of the street are
unnumerable places of low resort, in which the combined
attractions of rum and gambling are openly advertised. These
places are so numerous indeed, that they seem at first glance
to constitute the chief industry of the town.[15]

Yet Miles City, even before the completion of the Northern
Pacific, was growing rapidly. In 1880, the population was less than
600; two years later, it had increased to over 2,000; and by 1884, it
had reached close to 3,000. A directory put out by the publisher of
the *Yellowstone Journal*, Miles City's newspaper, provided a fairly complete account of the town's population and the services offered.
Three doctors (one with no address!), one dentist, and several lawyers
were listed. Seven hotels and forty-two saloons, or "thirst parlors," as
they were sometimes called, provided the prime source of entertain-
ment, along with the "parlor houses," where the ladies of the night
entertained. The First National Bank came into existence in June
1882 to serve the increasing number of businessmen who came into
town from the outlying ranches. New houses tended to be constructed of brick, since the available stone was of poor quality and
wood was in short supply. Grocery, hardware, and haberdashery
stores were all available. A telephone exchange had been constructed
between the town and Fort Keogh, and the central office listed
twenty-five subscribers. Presbyterians, Methodists, and Catholics had
places of worship—although not always churches.[16]

Father Lindesmith's pastoral duties were colored by the atmosphere of the town. The *Yellowstone Journal* described graphically the
subjects of Lindesmith's ministrations: a sick call "to the room of a
Fancy Woman"; a visit to the local jail, where "Jerry the Bum lay
close to death after being bitten by a rattlesnake during a drunken

stupor." Such duties were occasionally balanced by a marriage or baptism or the conversion of one of the "Tainted Lilies."[17]

Despite the obstacles, Lindesmith succeeded in building a small Catholic church, whose main contributors were Miles City's four Jewish businessmen. (The sum collected: $9.50.) The first Mass was offered on Christmas Day of 1881. Even on such an occasion, however, the twelve pews were more than sufficient for the congregation. The sanctity of the church was not free from the general lawlessness of the town, and on one Sunday, the beleaguered pastor had had to forcibly remove a drunken cowboy after he had repeatedly ignored Lindesmith's request for "civil behavior."

Such was the town that welcomed the six Ursulines on that January morning. After the initial greetings, they were taken by carriage along the icy streets (the temperature that morning was twenty-two degrees below zero) to their temporary lodgings. The house of Widow Bridget McCanna was the first—and perhaps the greatest—of many shocks. Mother Amadeus, in her letter to Toledo written the following day, commented bleakly, "I have not language to describe our lodgings with her." Happily, she did find language in a lengthy letter she sent out the following day.

> We drove up in our fine carriage to a whitewashed log cabin
> with a Chinese laundry attached to it, the two cabins forming
> one building. ... The door was ajar so we walked in. ... The
> room was cold; the one window in the room was nearly
> falling out of the frame. The Bishop and I tried very hard to
> fasten the door but could not succeed as the latch was out of
> order, so I backed my chair up to the door to keep it closed.
> Since I did not get pneumonia that day I think I am secure for
> the future since the Bishop remarked it was the coldest day he
> had ever spent in Montana.[18]

It was Sister Francis Seibert, however, who described in vivid detail the events of those first few hours.

[Bridget McCanna] is an old lady of 69 years of age, wears a lace
cap, with a little ostrich tip on the left side near the chin, and has
forty grandchildren. ... We received a hearty welcome from the old
matron and were invited to sit down, but where were we to sit?
We looked around a while and finally by two and three sitting on
a chair we were comfortable in a short time when the door opened
and the Bishop, Father Eyler and Father Lindesmith walked in. You
can imagine the excitement now, the old lady called Jimmy and
Charlie and Robert Emmet to go for chairs. They were brought in a
few minutes, some without backs, others without legs, and we
were again seated in the parlor of Bridget McCanna.[19]

Fortunately, the priests left before dinner—an unappetizing meal
of potatoes, codfish, and jelly roll. Following the meal, the nuns were
shown to their rooms. There was no fire going and snow had blown in
through the windows. It was a bleak prospect made worse by the filth
everywhere. Francis, trying to push aside the straw and feathers that
covered the floor, conjectured that perhaps the widow had used the
room for her chickens. Amadeus, after examining the bed, wrote:

On uncovering of the bed presented a scene it would not be
decent to describe. We hastily dropped the besmeared hay
ticks and coverlets, so we gave up the bed and spread out a
blanket and couched all together wrapped up in shawls and
blankets and Father Eyler's overcoat.[20]

All this might have been endured had it not been for the lack
of privacy. Their lodging could hardly be called a room, for the only
partition separating them from the other roomers—ranchers, cowboys, laborers—were pieces of pink-striped calico stretched across a
series of rods.

Amadeus's decision was immediate: they could not stay in
such a place beyond a single night. By morning, she had determined
that somehow they must find other lodging.

Chapter Two

Everything is far different from what we imagined.

—*Mother Amadeus Dunne*

The presence of the nuns was a subject of immediate interest, and the day after their arrival, the *Yellowstone Journal* announced:

> The west-bound train yesterday brought into Miles City the Rev. Joseph Eyler, of the Roman Catholic Church, and six Sisters of Charity [*sic*]. Father Eyler and three of the Sisters will in a short time proceed to the Rosebud [River] and exert themselves in behalf of God and Christianity by endeavoring to Christianize the unenlightened Indian. This is a hard and thankless task and great praise is due the Catholics for this step taken in this wild country. ... The three remaining Sisters will stay here where they will establish a parochial school, and it is safe to say will point out the path and "bend the twig" for the children whom they will have in their fold.[1]

Such undertakings, however, seemed far distant on that first Saturday morning when the sisters rose before dawn after a cold and sleepless night at Widow McCanna's. There was no need to dress, since they had spent the night hours huddled in all the clothes they had. Their first thought, if Amadeus's memoir is to be credited, was to find their way to the parish church. "Long before dawn," she wrote, "we groped our way through the streets," stopping to gather "bits of frozen wood" in order to light the church fire. Here they waited until

Brondel arrived to say Mass at 7:00 A.M. Even these grim hours glow with the spirit of sacrifice in Amadeus's pious rhetoric: "At four o'clock in the morning it was deadly cold ... but when his Lordship entered for Mass some three hours later he was cheered by the genial warmth of the first Ursuline fire in the Rocky Mountains."[2]

Following Mass and breakfast, Amadeus had time to discuss with Brondel the future of their mission. Their lodgings, she explained, were not appropriate, "not on account of the poverty of the establishment but on account of the promiscuous lodgers." The first work of the day, she made clear, must be to find suitable housing. By early afternoon, she had procured a map of the city, found a "real estate agent," and begun a search for a house. Accompanied by Sister Sacred Heart, she walked along icy streets, guided by the local real estate man. By late afternoon, they had found "a little brown house with five small rooms" that they could rent for $25 a month. Located at the edge of town, it provided them with a little more privacy than the main streets, with their cowboys and thirst parlors. Whatever advantages the house had, it had no source of heat, and the nuns— knowing little or nothing about such things—spent the rest of Saturday afternoon purchasing two stoves, one to heat the front room and a stove for cooking.

This was only the beginning. There were provisions to buy; the provisions they had brought with them would not last forever. Flour ($10 a barrel), eggs (65 cents per dozen), butter, tea, coffee, a quart of milk (10 cents a quart), potatoes, three pounds of bologna, and six pounds of meat (20 cents per pound). They found the prices so high that they bought only small quantities, fearing that their money would not last. Even then, the day was not yet over. "We had to get coal in and set up the stoves and do many other things impossible to describe," Amadeus noted. "We got no assistance from anyone. ... We got no sleep that night—there's the way we began life in Montana.[3]

The furniture that had been freighted ahead of them was clearly insufficient, and they used their ingenuity by improvising with what was at hand. Their kitchen table, Sister Francis wrote in a letter to Toledo, "was a kind of something found in the yard with four legs and on it we put a barn door and covered it with newspaper. It looks grand and we are all very proud of it. ... Our pantry consists of a box found in the same place. It has three shelves well furnished with our bright tins."[4]

The following day, Sunday, all the details of housekeeping—no matter how essential—had to be put aside, since the Ursulines were expected to make their first "public appearance" for Mass in the parish church. The early Mass was said by Bishop Brondel at 8:00 A.M., followed at 11:00 by a High Mass said by Father Eyler. Miles City had never experienced a High Mass before, and the bishop was determined that it be a memorable event. Despite the fatiguing experiences of the preceding days, the nuns collected themselves sufficiently to sing the parts of the Mass—"Dumont's 'Missa Regis' in D minor"— Amadeus noted triumphantly. "The people wept for joy—old and young were beside themselves."

Well, they might have been. Civilization had suddenly swept down on this meager congregation more accustomed to cowboy ballads than the higher reaches of church music. "Sister Sacred Heart accompanied as confidently as though she had been presiding at the organ for years," Amadeus continued. "She and Sister Holy Angels sang at the offertory the 'Jesu dulcis memoria.' All went very well."[5]

It was close to 2:00 P.M. when they arrived home, not yet having broken their sacramental fast. But, no matter: the curious townsfolk "came visiting," eager to explore a "convent," a unique experience for most of them. As the townspeople were leaving, another visitor arrived, this time an Indian, one of the Cheyenne chiefs housed at Fort Keogh, by the name of The Wolf That Lies Down. There could hardly have been a more prepossessing introduction to the Cheyenne tribe. The Wolf That Lies Down was majestic. Over six feet tall, of a light copper color, graceful, and aristocratic, he was the very prototype of the noble savage, that image so popular in the late nineteenth century. But despite his prominent position, he was poorly clad. "[He] wore a thin calico shirt (that longed for a bath) and pants made of some rough woolen material," Sister Ignatius wrote later to Toledo. "His feet were covered with moccasins, and a buffalo skin fell from his shoulders to his knees and was fastened around the waist by a kind of girdle." Perhaps as a symbol of his station, his ears were pierced with gold rings, and he wore a slouched felt hat with a cord and tassel.

He was all their romantic spirits could have imagined, and his positive response when, through an interpreter, they assured him that they had come to instruct his children and teach them the way to heaven, lifted their weary spirits. "He stayed with us this Sunday afternoon about an hour, and after refreshing himself with part of our dinner, shook hands, made a low bow and departed," Ignatius concluded.[6] With the visit of The Wolf That Lies Down, the sisters felt they had truly entered into their missionary call.

In the following months, they continued to welcome their Indian visitors, who walked three miles from Fort Keogh to satisfy their curiosity about the "Lady Blackrobes," whom they were told had come to set up a mission for them. Both men and women wandered in at any hour, sitting on the chairs, the table, the floor, saying nothing but waiting to be offered some food. The nuns had little enough for themselves, and the best they could do was a piece of bread or some mush, sweetened with a little sugar. Their pious explanations, enhanced by a crucifix, of how Jesus came to earth and suffered a cruel death to save all souls from hell seemed less alluring to their visitors than did the food they sought.

While the mission to the Cheyenne was the nuns' primary work, it was determined that three nuns would remain in Miles City, which would function as a sort of base camp. Here, they would conduct a school for the children of white settlers, a school that they hoped would provide some income toward their mission work. Although Miles City had already opened what one of its pupils later described as a "genuine school, a real honest-to-goodness brick building with blackboards, assembly rooms, grades and everything," there were no provisions for boarders, and this, Amadeus determined, would be the unique contribution of the Ursulines.[7] It is hard to imagine how she planned to accommodate such students, since space was so limited that beds had to be folded up and stored away during the daytime.

Within a month of their arrival—despite all obstacles—school was in session. They had alleviated the space problem by renting a room on the second floor of a nearby house, and here Ignatius had her class of eight children who had been transferred by their parents from the small public school. In addition, Francis had a "primary department" with seventeen children, while Sacred Heart taught vocal and instrumental music. "Poor children," Francis wrote. "They think all the nuns are saints. One of my little girls was so surprised to think I had never seen or spoken to God."

At the beginning of March, they accepted their first boarders: Lulu, Lottie, and Maimie Price, whose father was stationed at Fort Keogh. A few days later came Lizzie and Nellie Wyman, whose father was the Indian agent at the Crow reservation—some 200 miles distant. Prunetta and Clara Bishop brought the tally to seven. Their tuition was fixed at $20 per month, or $25 with the inclusion of music lessons. "For many months," Amadeus wrote later, "we suffered real poverty as we slept on the floor in cramped quarters ... our food was so scarce and insufficient that the dear nuns ... lovingly pretended to one another that they were not hungry as the poor, sparsely filled dishes were passed around. ... "[8]

As Amadeus and Bishop Brondel began drawing up plans for a more adequate building, the mission to the Cheyenne was uppermost in the minds of Sisters Angela, Ignatius, and Sacred Heart, the three whom Bishop Gilmour had chosen as the initial pioneers. Sister Sacred Heart, the oldest of the group, was its appointed superior. Although better educated than most women of their day, their education was circumscribed by the atmosphere of a convent boarding school. Until they boarded the train for Miles City, none of the three had ever traveled far from their birthplaces. They were, of necessity, naive in the ways of the world.

It is unlikely that the sisters knew much of the government treatment of the Indians, of the way in which treaties had been reduced to "executive orders," leaving no room for response or objection. They may not have understood, either, the consequences of the reservation system by which Indians were reduced to being the children of a dominant white father and wards of the government. Their dignity, their independence, their native culture was, in every case, inevitably eroded. It is equally doubtful that the nuns knew much of the history and the actual conditions of the Northern Cheyenne. That Bishop Brondel had singled them out as the tribe most in need in the whole of the Montana Territory was sufficient to win their compassion.

What had touched their hearts was the image of a people to whom the word of salvation had never been preached. Their mission was unambiguous: to "save souls" from eternal damnation. Faithful to the theology of their day, they were certain that souls could be saved only through the sacrament of baptism administered according to the Roman Catholic ritual. In this light, they could imagine no more imperative duty than to lead a godless people along the path of salvation and save them from the fires of hell. Along the way, they would teach the elements of literacy, enabling a primitive people to be assimilated into a white civilization. That such assimilation would at a future date be interpreted as a kind of genocide was beyond their imagination.

By late February, the snow melted sufficiently for Father Eyler, accompanied by Richard Toner, a well-known carpenter and a devoted Catholic, to make an exploratory trip to the Cheyenne, temporarily situated on the Rosebud River, some eighty miles southwest of Miles City. When they returned, a week or so later, it was with the good news that they had been able to purchase several former ranch buildings on the Tongue River. These would be sufficient as a beginning. When the school was a reality, Father Eyler assured them, they would be able to build more satisfactorily. Bishop Brondel had already given them $1,000, which he expected would be enough to construct a small house for Father Eyler, a convent for the sisters, leaving enough money to buy whatever was needed for the school. Amadeus was dubious that so much could be accomplished with so little, but she said nothing.

While the snowmelt gave them hope of spring, it also caused disastrous flooding. As the ice broke up in the Tongue River, the streets of Miles City filled with water. The sisters' yard was awash in eighteen inches of water, and with the help of some neighbors, they lugged and lifted their trunks out of the cellar into drier rooms. For a while, they kept watch, fearful that they might be forced to move. "The danger is over," Ignatius wrote in relief the following day, February 16. "Immense blocks of ice are sitting majestically across the street and we see and hear distinctly the overflowing water of the Tongue rushing into the far-famed Yellowstone. ... Thanks be to God, we did not have to leave our 'little brown cottage.'"[9]

Shortly after the flood receded, they received precious boxes of freight from Toledo: pillows, chairs, carpets, household utensils, maps, blackboard, pictures; but preeminent was the arrival of a piano. Ever since their arrival, they had longed for this—a precious means of special lessons that would earn them some essential income. "Now I hope we will be able to get some good music pupils," Amadeus wrote in satisfaction.[10]

The same letter, however, announced the imminent separation of the community. "This day is a sad one in our little convent, a real heart-breaking day. Poor Sisters, how grieved we all are at the separation. We know what this word means; you have no idea what it comprehends. ... Everything out here is far different from what we imagined it—there is a sacrifice of some kind awaiting you at every step you take," Amadeus wrote in a rare moment of acknowledging the suffering of her heart.[11]

Not least of their sufferings was the uncertainty that surrounded them. It seemed that every plan in this primitive territory had to be made and remade. On March 12, Father Eyler left for the reservation, able to travel along the Tongue River, hoping to have the

sisters follow him by March 19. But March 19 found the rivers flooding, and another week passed before there was any hope of travel. On
March 27, the weather seemed hopeful and Father Lindesmith
arrived from Fort Keogh to say Mass and see the travelers off. But
once again, the Tongue River betrayed them and they were told that
there was no possibility of crossing. Two days later, they were ready
again, but even as they were setting out, they were warned that they
still might find the Tongue too turbulent to cross. It was a peril they
would face when they met it. Fortunately, the government was providing army wagons to transport their baggage and an "ambulance,"
a covered wagon drawn by mules, to transport the sisters. An army
escort would accompany them with a sergeant to direct the route.

On the afternoon of March 29, they departed at last after a
festive dinner, completed by a fruitcake brought with them from
Toledo two and a half months before. Amadeus had decided to
accompany them to assure herself of their situation, leaving Sisters
Francis and Holy Angels at home to mind the school.

So far, their experience of Montana was of flat land, extending
endlessly, with hardly a tree rising along the landscape, but once they
passed Fort Keogh and started south, they began to experience a less
temperate side of Montana's strange geological structures. A good portion of the land between Miles City and Ashland was covered with
those unique formations called buttes—hills rising suddenly, then flat-
tening out into a table before descending precipitously. It could hardly
have been a more difficult terrain for mules to negotiate with their
heavy wagons. "Rough riding over the roughest roads that can be
imagined," Amadeus wrote. "Steep gullies descend eight feet in a distance of twelve feet and ascend in the same proportion. [We are]
pitched from one corner of the ambulance to the opposite one and
shaken and jarred till we think there is no life left in us."[12] Their fears,
however, were allayed by the skill and courage of their driver with his
four pet mules: Pink, Blue, Pet, and Baby—their feminine names amus-
ingly at odds with their rugged, imperturbable strength that enabled
them to cross hills and washouts without a moment's hesitation.

In the four days it took them to complete the eighty miles from Miles City, the nuns received nothing but courtesy and generosity from their army escort. At night, the soldiers raised the nuns' tent, put up their camp beds, carried whatever they needed from the wagons, and brought them their supper in their tent to ensure that their cloister be maintained. Meals followed an unchangeable pattern: fat bacon, fried potatoes and onions, washed down by coffee that even virtue could not stomach. "Imagine a pail of water dipped from [the muddy river] and boiled with the taste of coffee added. We put in condensed milk and tried to settle it, but all we had was mud," Sister Meilink later wrote.[13]

Their second day was even more difficult, and they came close to losing a wagon full of their precious possessions.

> We were well into the Buttes again, at one time on the summit, then in the valley, when the road led quite suddenly around the side of a hill and we were asked to alight and walk as there was danger of the ambulance falling into a gulch on the lower side of the road. We did so, and the men before they would venture to drive the teams across went to work with pick and shovel to level the road. The ambulance and first wagon with great care and dexterity were gotten safely over, the second wagon coming a little near the end, and the ground, a loose clay, giving way, we saw the wagon sliding down the embankment dragging the mules after it. We were terrified but the soldiers after a glance at the debris … went to work to extricate [the mules]. The poor animals were not injured and after being released had a good roll on the grass and commenced grazing as though nothing had happened. Fortunately army transports are very strong; only the tongue of the wagon was broken and as extra ones were provided, in three hours we were ready to continue our march.[14]

On the evening of the second day, they made camp close to an encampment of Cheyenne. Although the sisters left no record of conversing with the Indians, they observed them with fascinated curiosity. Sister Ignatius later wrote to Toledo expressing shock and disapproval at the way Indian women were treated. To them fell the burden of the work (gathering wood, erecting the tepees, making the fire, etc.), while "those great strong men" did nothing.

After two more days of near misses (a wagon mired in quicksand, the necessity of building a corduroy bridge, crossing a turbulent river on horseback), at noon on Tuesday, April 2, the fourth day of their travels, they arrived. "A greater length of time to travel ninety miles than it took us to come the 1600 from Toledo to Miles. Thanks be to God we are here in safety. One who has never traveled over the mountains has a very faint idea of the difficulties and dangers," Sister Sacred Heart wrote.[15]

Six miles from their destination, they found Father Eyler waiting to welcome them "home." His three lonely weeks as a missionary had changed him. "He had grown so thin you would scarcely recognize him, and then he was so brown and sun-burned," wrote Sister Sacred Heart. It was a presage of ill health that would soon cut short Eyler's missionary aspirations.

Their lodging was a three-room cabin ("what they call a shack," observed Sister Sacred Heart) built on the banks of Otter

St. Labre's Mission, original cabins, 1884. Courtesy of Ursuline archives, Toledo, Ohio

Creek and Tongue River in sight of the Indian dwellings. This was to be the school, the chaplain's quarters, and the convent. If their hearts sank as they explored their new home—one clearly unoccupied for a long time—they had no time to indulge the feeling. The cabin had to be cleaned and the wagons unpacked so that the army escort could begin their return trip. That afternoon and into the night, the nuns worked, helped by the men.

> [They] unpacked the wagons, made an altar of rough boards, a kitchen table, and a few stools to sit on. The box that the organ came in was transformed into a cupboard for our china and tinware. Some of the men mended the old stove that we found in the shack, brought water from the river, made fire wood, while the others made a path to the river bank so we could get down without falling ... The altar was fixed and calico curtains for the sanctuary were made. The No. 8 stove was cleaned, and the plank floor was mopped. It was nearly morning by this time, and we lay on the floor for a little rest. ... Mother Amadeus left two days later for Miles City in an Indian wagon with White Bull and his girl, Yellow Stocking. How Mother fared, she never would tell. She only said, "God knows!"[16]

The mission that the three nuns were to establish had already been named by Bishop Brondel in honor of St. Joseph Labre, a beggar saint whose poverty and spirit of sacrifice had seemed to the bishop an emblem of what this mission would be. Certainly, St. Labre was an appropriate patron for a tribe that had been despoiled of their rights again and again. Originally from central Minnesota, the Cheyenne had been pushed westward, first by other Indian tribes and then by the whites—gold prospectors and ranchers—eager for more land. At some time, the tribe divided: the Southern Cheyenne found land in Oklahoma while the Northern Cheyenne settled near the Tongue River in eastern Montana.

Although originally not a hostile nation, their part in the Battle of the Little Bighorn won them lasting enmity. As punishment, they were removed from their ancestral lands and force-marched south to Indian territory in Oklahoma, where they found themselves aliens in an arid and inhospitable land. Hundreds died due to starvation and a climate to which they could not adjust. In 1878, a portion of the tribe evaded their guards and started the long trek back to their motherland in Montana. It was this group that ultimately found a temporary refuge at Fort Keogh while they waited for the government to fulfill its promise of a reservation. By the spring of 1884, they had begun to drift to the land promised them on the Tongue River, but it was not until November 26 of that year that an executive order was issued by President Chester A. Arthur:

> It is hereby ordered that the following described country,
> lying within the boundaries of the Territory of Montana,
> beginning at the point on the 107 Meridian of West
> Longitude ... be and the same is hereby, withheld from sale
> and settlement as a reservation for the use and occupation of
> the Northern Cheyenne Indians now residing in the Southern
> portion of Montana Territory. ... [17]

Although the final paragraph made clear that none of this land could be occupied by settlers, even those who asserted prior claim, this did little to alleviate the conflict between whites and Indians concerning land. Nor did it provide sustenance for a starving population. With the deliberate destruction of the buffalo—their source for food, clothing, and dwellings—the Indians had been reduced to abject poverty and dependence. The buffalo had been their life.

This was the atmosphere in which the sisters began their school. Within a short time, they had thirteen little girls in their schoolroom—a space only twelve feet square, with no fireplace and only a dirt floor. The first lessons were a simple process of trying to learn each others' languages by pointing to objects and listening to how they were identified. The Cheyenne language did not yet have a written form, and so the nuns could do nothing but try to approximate the strange sounds their children made.

Although they had no room to accept boarders, the Indian parents expected that their children would receive food, so the nuns were required to provide two meals a day. They soon discovered the peculiarities of Indian diet: the children would eat no vegetables but expected meat at every meal. Fat bacon was all that the nuns could provide, along with bread made with white flour mixed with cornmeal, so that it would last longer. In their first desire to win the Indians' trust, they gave away food imprudently, leaving themselves without even necessities. "We were eighty miles from Miles City and it was not easy to obtain anything even with money to pay for it. ... We had not foreseen these difficulties," Sister Angela wrote later in a memoir describing these early months.[18]

Their first summer was spent in hard labor: attempting to improve their "shack" to make it more habitable for the winter and planting a vegetable garden to augment their meager food supply. The nuns did not yet have a government contract for their school and consequently received no government assistance. The full burden of providing for their children fell on them. The attitude of the Cheyenne did not help. They were constantly at odds with the Indian agent, an arbitrary man who often withheld or shortchanged the Indians' rations. All of Bishop Brondel's efforts to receive some government help had, so far, come to nothing. He wrote indignantly to Charles Lusk, then secretary of the Bureau of Catholic Indian Missions (BCIM):* "All I can say is that the three sisters there are living in a mud cabin and that the Indians want to see a decent building up, but I cannot build it because I have no money."[19]

---

*The Bureau of Catholic Indian Missions was established in 1874 to promote and administer Catholic missions. It became the primary channel for distributing funds to the missions.

By the beginning of June, the nuns' situation became even more precarious. The mission had hardly opened before it was clear that Father Eyler's health was in decline. The climate, the food, the constant excursions to visit the Indians in their crude tepees, but perhaps most of all, the loneliness, had undermined his energies. In April, Sister Ignatius wrote, "He looks quite sad and discouraged at times; he is astonished at our courage and cheerfulness."[20]

Two months later, Father Eyler became seriously ill, and Sister Sacred Heart wrote an anguished letter back to Toledo:

> A new and heavy cross. Father Eyler who is in very poor
> health from his lungs has left. ... He thinks he has quick
> consumption and fears that if he doesn't go now he will not
> be well enough to make it to Miles City and perhaps to Ohio.
> He cried bitterly this morning. ... We are alone now, yet not
> alone, the Blessed Sacrament is with us. Father Eyler said he
> could not leave us alone without it, but when we will have
> Mass, Communion, Confession again, God only knows ...
> how very strange it all is. Will light ever come? Yellow Horse

St. Labre's Mission, Amadeus Dunne, sisters, and two Cheyenne women. Courtesy of Ursuline archives, Great Falls, Montana

is upset about Father Eyler's departure and asked if we were
also going. He was very happy when I assured him we would
stay. Do not feel troubled for us, dearest Mother, it is remarkable how God sustains us, how we keep up cheerful hope.[21]

Bishop Brondel, well aware of the problem of getting a priest
to accept this difficult assignment, was less sanguine when he heard
the news that Father Eyler had left the mission. Determined that the
mission continue under any circumstances, Brondel wrote to
Amadeus, "It will be a great disaster if it fail and the Sisters have to
return to Miles City ... in Toledo they are in great distress and offer
to have the Sisters return to Miles City, but I would not advise that
till all fail."[22]

Even as the sisters' spiritual resources were being tested, they
were learning firsthand the animosity the white settlers felt not only
for the Indians, but for anyone helping them. Since a reservation had
not yet been formally established, ranchers continued to hope they
might have the Indians moved and thus acquire their land. On May 5,
a letter from a sympathetic white man went to John Mullan, a
member of the BCIM, protesting the conduct of the Indian agent,
whom he described as "one of the boys who takes in the town
o'nights—women, wine, cards ... and lo, poor Indians on short rations
in mid-winter with no game on the range." His letter further inveighed
against the fact that white ranchers let their cattle roam with
impunity through Indian land. "There is presently running on the
Cheyenne Reservation not less than 200,000 head of stock," he
noted, adding that, by contrast, any Indian accused of stealing a
single steer could be shot dead—no questions asked.[23]

Sister Ignatius was particularly sensitive to the incursions of
the white ranchers:

The state of the Indians living in the valley of the Tongue
River is very unsettled from the fact that the whole valley is a
fine grazing country and much coveted by the stock-men of

Montana. ... The stock holders have taken decisive measures
to have the Indians removed from their present situation—
removed from the Territory, if possible, or at least to the Rose
Bud Valley (about 18 miles west of us). ... Mr. Scott, one of
the wealthiest Cattle Kings of this section, has gone to
Washington, and it is the general opinion that he will succeed
in getting the Indians off the Tongue River. Poor Indians! I
fear they will be the victims of advancing civilization. ... The
buffalo, deer, mountain sheep, game of every variety that
about four years ago thickly inhabited this region have now
disappeared—the buffalo was shot by the thousands, the rest
took flight. ... Again the soil is little adapted to agriculture,
and even if it were, farming implements and knowledge of
their use are wanting.[24]

It was a remarkably perceptive appraisal from someone who
had been living less than a month among the Cheyenne.

Amadeus, learning of these episodes through an article in the
Yellowstone Journal, wrote to the nuns at St. Labre's, concerned for their
safety. Sister Sacred Heart answered at once. "Let me put you at ease
about our personal danger," she assured, explaining that both whites
and Indians treated them with deference. They also had as protection
Richard Toner, who had accompanied them from Miles City to help
with the work. "Mr. George Yoakum is also around but is in poor favor
with the whites. He is a poor simple-minded man who means well but
who rather injures than promotes the cause of the Indians." [25]

St. Labre's Mission, first buildings. Courtesy of Ursuline archives, Great Falls,
Montana

The same month brought news they had been praying for: Bishop Brondel had at last found a priest to be their chaplain. "A priest, a Jesuit, a missionary!" Sacred Heart wrote ecstatically toward the end of June. The priest who was to fulfill these expectations was Peter Barcelo, who had briefly visited the Cheyenne the preceding year. Born in Mexico in 1838, he had entered the Society of Jesus and completed his seminary studies at Santa Clara, California. Eight years after his ordination, his desire to work in the western missions was granted, and he was sent to the Rocky Mountain Province in Montana. Idealistic and passionate for the kingdom of God, he was admired by his brother Jesuits, though they sometimes found his spirit of penance and sacrifice exaggerated. If Peter Barcelo's goal had been to serve at the poorest of the missions, he had succeeded.

At the same time that Brondel was writing anxiously about the situation at St. Labre's, he was writing to Amadeus in Miles City, encouraging her in a further project. "The Jesuit Fathers of St. Peter's Mission are anxious to have sisters. St. Peter's Mission is one days journey from Helena by stage," he wrote, motivating her by enumerating the many advantages of such an enterprise. The Jesuits would give the sisters a farm, two wagon horses (worth $100 each), two milch cows ($120), and $200 worth of provisions (meat, flour, etc.). They would also spend $200 repairing their old house, which they would rent to the sisters for $5 per year. "They want three sisters but it would be even better if they could have four—then the sisters could also teach little boys!"[26]

Although at the end of June the unexpected problems of the missions had left Amadeus so weary and dispirited that she had written to Toledo, "You would not believe what a strange place this is and what a change it has made in us," now Bishop Brondel's letter energized her.[27] In a burst of enthusiasm that characterized her throughout her life, she brushed aside her present problems and wrote at once to Bishop Gilmour, asking him to arrange for at least two more sisters to help them in this projected work. While Gilmour did not hesitate to give his approval, it was an approval tempered by prudence: "I think God is blessing you wonderfully," he wrote, "but you must not seek to run before you have the power to creep."[28] But it was Brondel's insistence rather than Gilmour's prudence that rang in Amadeus's ears.

On August 5, Brondel reiterated his request. "The Fathers at St. Peter's ask when do the Sisters come? ... let them know when you will be ready. Address: Rev. Father Damiani, S.J., St. Peter's Mission, Fort Shaw, Montana."[29]

Although Mother Stanislaus had written from Toledo apologetically refusing the request for two or three additional sisters, Amadeus was not deterred. She had already written to Brondel suggesting some necessary changes in order to establish the school at St. Peter's. Sister Sacred Heart, she explained, would be brought to Miles City as superior; Sister Ignatius could replace her at St. Labre's; and Sister Holy Angels could go there to supervise the music—an essential element for the missions. In the last week of August, Amadeus traveled with Sister Holy Angels to St. Labre's. When she returned to Miles City a few days later, she brought Sister Sacred Heart with her. It was undoubtedly a wrenching separation, especially for those at St. Labre's, whose bonds had been strengthened by days of loneliness and uncertainty. Yet all of them recognized it as a milestone. Miles City had been simply a beginning. Now the horizon was widening. Montana was opening before them.

Chapter Three

We are situated
in a beautiful little valley.
—Mother Amadeus Dunne

The small convent house Sister Sacred Heart returned to at the end of August 1884 had changed dramatically in the five months she had been at St. Labre's. In addition to three Ursulines, they now had two young women who had come asking to be admitted as sisters. Both had been born in Ireland: Bridget Golden was born in County Mayo on August 15, 1864, and Bridget Gahan was born in Carlow on January 6, 1865. There is no record of how long they had been in the United States, but probably they had come with their families during the period of Irish emigration in the years following the potato famine in midcentury.

Now at the ages of twenty and nineteen respectively, they had made the decision to be sisters and missionaries. Amadeus, on her part, did not hesitate a moment in receiving them. They were young, healthy, and enthusiastic, qualities desperately needed to continue the work that was opening before them.

On May 1, Miss Bridget Golden and Miss Bridget Gahan began their apprenticeship as Ursuline postulants. Somehow—hard to imagine—space was made for them in the miraculously flexible convent. They began their religious life with few comforts, even the comfort of time for prayer and reflection. The spirituality that Amadeus fostered was found less in contemplation than in active service to those whose poverty—spiritual and material—she saw all around her. To close oneself off from the needs of others she would have seen as selfishness rather than prayer. It was a spirituality that made her work in Montana eminently successful; that it would also became a source of contradiction to some of her followers was inevitable. Despite her protestations of humility, Amadeus was a woman assured and determined, too single-minded to deal well with compromise. Impelled by a vision that absorbed her life, she was often autocratic and arbitrary in her decisions. Although her charism was unquestioned, it did not always elicit admiration.

As for the new postulants, having very little idea of what the lives of sisters were supposed to be—especially on the plains of Montana—they seemed happy and satisfied with what was offered to them. For Amadeus, their arrival was interpreted as a sign that God was blessing the mission's work, a blessing made even more manifest when, a few days later, the nuns received another request to accept two boarders. Without a second thought, she welcomed them—thus bringing their number to six—crowding them into a single room, presuming that whatever the room's prior use, it could now be transferred somewhere else. Toward the end of May, she wrote to Toledo:

> We now have six boarders but unfortunately of these six only
> one is a Catholic. They are all walking music boxes—the house
> is teeming with music ... Children of eight, nine and ten years
> old sing all the popular songs of the day each accompanying
> herself. They play duets and sing in parts; in fact, we have a
> musical exhibition every night. ... One of them is a prodigy of
> musical talent; her father Mr. Kenneth Price is the U.S. Band
> Master at Fort Keogh, and she inherits the talent.[1]

It is hard to imagine that the small house, "teeming with music," was not often more of a penance than a joy. Small wonder that Bishop Brondel kept encouraging Amadeus to begin building. Although she realized that the combined rent—$25 a month for their inadequate cottage, plus another $12 for the small room where classes were held for the older girls—was draining their limited resources, she was fearful of the responsibility of building. "The Bishop is anxious to have us build, but how can we build?" she wrote to Toledo. "He gave us $100 a few days ago to start a building fund. I have been talking with builders and planning a little but I find the cost of material and labor so high that it is almost impossible to think of building."[2] Despite her best efforts, so far she had collected less than $500 toward the building fund.

Brondel continued to urge her to begin with whatever she had. His advice: "If it cannot be finished because of lack of funds, use it in an unfinished state."[3] Such advice seemed impractical to Amadeus, who could not imagine using a school whose walls were not yet permanent. Desperate, she wrote to Mother Stanislaus in Toledo, begging her to try to arrange a loan.

This was the situation, precarious at best, that Sister Sacred Heart returned to, now with the added responsibility of superiority: little income, no resources, and a convent hopelessly inadequate to house its twelve members.

Amadeus, though still concerned about the future of the Miles City convent, was clearly preoccupied by her next mission. Brondel, urged on by the Jesuits at St. Peter's, wrote impatiently, asking how long they were going to delay; the Jesuits were growing anxious. All through August, Amadeus waited, hoping for a positive response to her request from Toledo to "borrow" two more sisters until the mission was under way. But this time, even Gilmour's influence was unavailing, and on August 30, Amadeus received the answer that she had dreaded: Toledo could spare no one. "I have in my life been disappointed but never so deeply as yesterday," she wrote.[4]

Even with this refusal, she refused to give up the opportunity offered her at St. Peter's. On August 20, Brondel wrote, giving her a ray of hope. A Miss Theresia Yunck had come to him inquiring about entering a religious congregation. She might, he thought, find a place with the Ursulines. She was twenty-four years old, a resident of Helena, "of German parentage but also speaking English, able to read and write, and having other qualifications ... Should you be willing to receive her, let me know and under what conditions."[5] Even sight unseen, Amadeus accepted the new postulant, certain that she would have "the golden qualities of that sterling [German] race."[6]

Earlier that month, she had received word from Father Joseph Damiani suggesting that the Ursuline novitiate be established at St. Peter's rather than at Miles City, as Amadeus had originally planned. She acceded at once, since this meant that she could bring with her Miss Golden and Miss Gahan as well as Theresia. Suddenly, the number of Ursulines available for St. Peter's had grown to four. Additional good news came that fall, when the Ursuline community in Cleveland offered two sisters for the Montana missions: Sister Joseph Steiner and a young postulant, Sister Theresa Henry, who had entered the Cleveland community only two months earlier.

The sisters from Cleveland were slow in coming, however, and Amadeus could not leave before their arrival. Finally, she received word that they would be on the train arriving in Miles City the evening of October 17. Amadeus waited until midnight, without success. Not until morning did they learn that there had been a wreck on the tracks. "The latest news," Amadeus wrote, "is that a bridge gave way near the Little Missouri and a cattle train is wrecked but that the passenger train is all safe and will be in tonight between eleven and twelve."[7]

At last, with the arrival of Sisters Joseph and Theresa, they were almost ready to depart to St. Peter's. There was one more important event to take place, however—this time an event of unalloyed joy: Miss Golden and Miss Gahan, having completed their postulant period (usually of six months' duration, but this time shortened to five), were now ready to become novices. The celebration of this event would take place on October 21, the Feast of St. Ursula.

It was such a ceremony as the rustic parish church of Miles City had never seen. Amadeus, determined to reproduce the traditional ceremony in all its glory, had requested from Toledo two bridal dresses, complete with white veils, along with copies of the intricate reception ceremonial. Bishop Brondel, aware of the importance of the events, made the long trip from Helena to preside at the celebration. Following the ornate ritual of the medieval church, the two young women, dressed in full bridal finery, were presented to the ministers of the church as Brides of Christ, signifying their will to belong to Jesus Christ alone. Following this, they donned the coarse black serge dress and the veil, which would now identify them as "dead to the world." The two novices were also given new names to indicate their new identity: Bridget Golden became Sister Mary and Bridget Gahan became Sister Martha. Like heroines of a fabled event, for a few hours their drab lives in a frontier town were turned into a fairy tale.

The reception that followed the ceremony was joyful and satisfying. Townsfolk made generous contributions: Harriet, a popular black cook, roasted a giant turkey; a former pupil of the Ursulines of Brown County, Ohio, sent "luscious desert"—trays of Charlotte Russe (sponge cake and whipped cream elegantly presented). In addition, the mother of one of their pupils saw to it that the banquet board was stacked with "fruits and dainties."

At the end of the day, nothing remained to do but make final arrangements for the trip to St. Peter's Mission. There would be five of them, Amadeus announced: herself as superior, the two novices (Sisters Mary and Martha), the postulant (Sister Theresa Henry), and Theresia Yunck, who would join them later at St. Peter's. A week later, on October 28, they boarded the westbound Northern Pacific. The trip that a few years before would have taken days could now be made in a day in relative comfort. It was their first trip west of Miles City and gave them the opportunity of seeing the little frontier towns along the way—Forsyth, Laurel, Livingston—that had grown up with the railroad. At Helena, capital of the Montana Territory, they stayed overnight with the Sisters of Charity of Leavenworth, who some years earlier had established a hospital.

The next morning, Amadeus wrote a short note back to Miles City, assuring them of their safe arrival. "Here we are in the heart of the Great Rocky Mountains. On every side, we see them towering around us with their snow-capped tops. In a few minutes, we will start out for St. Peter's mission. Our address for the present will be Ursuline Nuns, Fort Shaw, Montana."[8]

The last lap of the journey, some seventy-five miles, was to be made by stagecoach. While Amadeus said nothing of the rigors, it was an exhausting trip, despite the fact that the October weather spared them the hazards of spring mud and winter snow.

The following day, October 30, at five in the evening, they arrived at last at their new home. It could hardly have been a more beautiful time of year or a more beautiful hour. The vastness of the plains stretched on all sides and the sun was just beginning to set behind the surrounding buttes. After the muddy, noisy streets of Miles City, where they had lived so close to others that they could see into their neighbors' houses, the uninterrupted expanse must have brought a sense of tranquility. Some time later, Amadeus wrote to Toledo:

> We are situated in a beautiful little valley, closed in, surrounded
> on all sides by fine buttes, spurs of the Rocky Mountains. Fish
> Butte rises on the left and resembles an immense sporting
> porpoise or dolphin. Then comes Haystack Butte followed by
> Bird-Tail, Simeon Crown and Square Butte. The latter shuts off a
> view of the outer world, but a charming vista intervenes and a
> valley twelve miles long lies smiling before us.[9]

The Jesuits, true to their word, had prepared their own former residence for the sisters. The three log cabins, although independent in construction, were joined by a porch extending along all three and attached to the small timber church to form an L-shape. They were far from luxurious, but they would do for a beginning: a convent, a school for the Indians, and a school for children of white settlers. Amadeus, with her eye always on the future, already envisioned an additional stone structure as imposing as the one the Jesuits had recently built.

That evening, Father Damiani and his companions were warm in their welcome, even inviting the sisters to join them for supper in the Jesuit refectory—not a usual practice at that time. "It was a real Italian supper," Amadeus commented, "macaroni soup was the opening course and prunes and other dried fruits the closing one, with plenty of substantials in between."[10]

An Italian supper was entirely appropriate, for a large proportion of the Jesuits in the American West were Italian in origin. The turmoil following the process of Italian unification and its accompanying spirit of anticlericalism had left the Jesuits unwelcome in their own country. Banished from their homes, they soon found exciting opportunities for missionary work in the American West along with other European exiles from France, Belgium, and Holland, where politics were increasingly unfavorable toward religion.[11]

The aspiring missionaries were, for the most part, young men, well educated in their own countries, industrious, and passionately devoted to the conversion of the "poor savages." Ignatius, their founder, had trained his men to hardship and sacrifice, and they were not cowed by the primitive conditions under which they were

St. Peter's Mission, original buildings, 1884. Courtesy of Ursuline archives, Great Falls, Montana

to live. For some, however, the greatest hardship came not from their daily privations, but from the difficulties of learning new languages. They found themselves burdened not only with the need to master the formidable tongues of the Indian tribes, but also to master English—a skill they acquired with varying success. Some years later, a German traveler visiting the mission at St. Ignatius noted in a letter to a friend his bewilderment in finding the Flathead children reading admirably but with a disarming Italian accent.

St. Peter's, begun twenty years earlier to serve the branch of the Blackfeet known as Piegans, had a checkered history. By 1870, the Jesuits had at last found a satisfactory location, only to be uprooted by an executive order. President Ulysses Grant, alerted to the venality and corruption among Indian agents, had been urged to devise a plan whereby the missions would be put in the hands of various religious bodies whose members would be motivated by charity rather than greed. It was an admirable concept, but one not easy in the execution. Who was to decide—and on what basis—which church would be assigned to which mission? To their consternation, the Jesuits learned that despite their years of service, St. Peter's Mission would henceforth be under the authority of the Methodists.

Father Camillus Imoda, superior at St. Peter's, wrote indignantly to the secretary of the interior:

> Why an agency, the Indians belonging to which, are in a
> considerable number Catholic, and among whom there is not
> a single Methodist or Protestant Indian of any denomination
> whatever, should be taken from our church and given to a
> denomination of which the Indians know nothing, has always
> been a mystery to me ... a sad comment on the religious
> liberty vouchsafed to all under our noble Constitution.[12]

His objection went unheeded, and for the next six years, St. Peter's struggled on despite little contact with the people they had come to serve.

In 1880, the climate changed when Father Peter Prando arrived to replace the weary and discouraged Father Imoda. Pier Paolo Prando, whom the Indians called "Iron Eyes" because of his metal-rimmed glasses, was a man of immense energy and irrepressible spirit with a remarkable facility for languages. St. Peter's was a perfect fit for Prando's temperament and abilities. He was fearless and he loved a challenge. At the first opportunity, he rode the sixty miles to see the Methodist agent Major John Young in the hope of sweetening their relationship. Prando's powers of persuasion, however, were not sufficient to change Young's anti-Catholic bias. "I have no confidence in these missionaries," he had already written to the commissioner for Indian affairs.[13]

Soon, however, church rivalry was overshadowed by the specter of famine. By 1882, the once powerful and independent Blackfeet nation had been reduced to a pitiful remnant. Once envied for their vast herds of horses and their warlike spirit, the destruction of the bison and the reduction of their lands left them without resources. They disdained the occupations of the white man, and Young's attempts to engage them in farming were met with failure. Cutting up Mother Earth they considered a blasphemy, wounding the spirit that gave them life. By the 1880s, this proud nation had

St. Peter's Mission, nuns with children. Courtesy of Ursuline archives, Helena, Montana

little means of livelihood except for the rations provided by the government. In the winter of 1883, even these resources failed them.

As early as 1881, Young had begun to realize he would need additional rations if the Indians were to survive the winter. He wrote to Congress, outlining his difficulties, but Congress found other issues more important and no action was taken.

By the winter of 1883, the Blackfeet were starving. "There will not be provisions enough to prevent suffering," he wrote to Congress. "Can something be done?"[14]

The bland reply was simply that funds were exhausted; there was nothing to be done. Young had already doled out all the beef he had—even killing the animals used for breeding. Seed potatoes were also gone. The Indians were reduced to eating bark or grass and feeding on the bodies of deceased cattle or rotted bones they found in the fields.

Young continued to write desperate letters, but in vain. The situation was so extreme that word of it even reached George Bird Grinnell, a New York City newspaper editor, who mounted a publicity campaign in July 1884. "Is it the deliberately adopted policy and purpose of the government officials to rid the land of these Indians by penning them up to starve to death?" he asked. But it was Father Lawrence Palladino, S.J., then stationed at St. Ignatius's, who made the most scathing and telling assessment:*

> Whence this desperate and most inhuman state of affairs in a country of plenty. ... The greediness of the frontier man, the dishonesty of Government officials and the cabals of scheming politicians will have to answer for that. By these three combined together, the Blackfeet were confined to a barren country, utterly unfit to support human life. ... The real condition, besides, of these poor wretches was time and again grossly misrepresented to the Department at Washington.[15]

---

*In 1894, Father Palladino published one of the earliest histories on the Catholic Church in Montana: *Indian and White in the Northwest: A History of Catholicity in Montana.*

By the time the situation was alleviated, hundreds of Blackfeet had died from starvation and the inroads of disease. There is no more telling evidence of the state of the survivors than that this warlike, aggressive people did not rise in protest.

Despite the tragic consequences of the Starvation Years, St. Peter's Mission flourished. When Father Joseph Cataldo, the superior of the Rocky Mountain Missions, came to visit in the summer of 1884, he judged that St. Peter's was ready for development. While Prando's approach had been one of direct evangelization—instructing individuals or small groups in their native language—Cataldo was convinced of the primary value of education. If children were educated not only in the faith, but trained in ways that would make them useful members of society, their impact would be much greater. Not only would their own lives be changed, they would influence their tribes as well. Perhaps it was with this in mind that he transferred Prando to work on the Crow reservation in southern Montana, replacing him with Joseph Damiani, a man who shared his views on the importance of education.

St. Peter's, it seemed to them both, was ready for expansion. Damiani, recognizing the importance of educating the Indian girls, suggested that nuns be brought to work with them, asserting that a mission without nuns was no mission at all. On his advice, Cataldo wrote to Bishop Brondel, who contacted the Ursulines in Miles City.

During that summer, the Jesuit mission annalist for St. Peter's noted that through the "generous cooperation of the Bishop," they were expecting a "significant increase" in the mission. The Sisters of St. Ursula would soon join them to begin a school for girls.[16]

August and September came and went while the Jesuits grew anxious to start the new school. It was late October before word came that the missionaries were on their way to Helena. "October 30, 1884, was to be a red letter day in the history of St. Peter's; on that day the first Indian Missionary Ursulines in that part of the country had come," wrote Father Frederick Eberschweiler exuberantly in his short account of St. Peter's Mission.[17]

At first blush, St. Peter's must have seemed to Mother Amadeus the very ideal of mission life. Unlike St. Labre's, where three sisters had borne the full responsibility of establishing a mission, a work about which they knew practically nothing, at St. Peter's Mission, life was already in order. Several Jesuit priests were in residence, assisted by a number of Jesuit brothers. The sisters could be assured of Mass each morning, of confession, of holy days properly observed—even spiritual conferences, should they so desire. It was a far cry from St. Labre's, where the sisters had struggled on for months with no spiritual help.

What Amadeus would learn little by little, however, was that while at St. Peter's, they were spared heavy responsibility; they were also deprived of authority. The pattern of the schools would follow what the Jesuits had already established. Confident in their own methods, they felt no need to depend on the advice or experience of the Ursulines. For a woman of Amadeus's temperament, this was not easy. Her qualities of leadership had been given full rein in Toledo, where she had presided over the Ursuline convent for six years, responsible to no male authority except the congenial and appreciative Bishop Gilmour.

Within a month after arriving at St. Peter's, she had discovered that the Ursulines were to have many tasks beyond those of the classroom. On Sundays and feast days, when the settlers came in from their ranches for Mass, it became the sisters' responsibility to provide food for the women. On December 8, Feast of the Immaculate Conception, she wrote hurriedly to Toledo, "I am setting the table for 12 poor wind-shriven and frost-bitten women that have come over today for Mass and who will not get home before nightfall."[18] Such tasks, though onerous, must also have been pleasant, giving the sisters some contact with other pioneer women.

For other tasks, however, Amadeus had less patience. The tone of her letter written to Toledo shortly before Christmas verges on the caustic:

> Our Novitiate table is piled up with work that must be finished
> before Christmas—Jesuit cassocks, rabbis, birettas, and shirts to

be made. The Fathers and Brothers stockings to be knitted and stockings to be darned and all their clothes, even pants and coats, to be put in order. We have to wash, bake, and mend for the Jesuit household. They believe in the law of compensation.[19]

The Jesuits, impatient for the work to begin, had encouraged Amadeus immediately upon her arrival to begin a school for white girls while they waited for government approbation to open a school for Indian girls. There was never any thought of mingling the two, since the educational needs of whites and Indians were regarded as very different in nature.

Somehow, on November 4, just four days after the nuns' arrival, the school for the daughters of the settlers was opened. How they managed is hard to say, since Amadeus had written home desperately, "We have no ink, paper, nothing in fact as our boxes have not yet arrived."[20]

The Jesuits, faithful to their promise, turned over to the Ursulines the three original log cabins that they had inhabited until their new home—a large, substantial stone structure—had been finished some months earlier. This gave the nuns sufficient space, Father Damiani assured them, to accept twenty pupils.

It was not space that concerned Amadeus, but the burden of work. She had as her helpers two novices and (with the arrival of Theresia Yunck) two postulants, intelligent young women, eager to give themselves to the work of the mission. But much to Amadeus's chagrin, Damiani reminded her that according to church law, no novice could be engaged in teaching; they could do the housework— of which there was plenty—but nothing more. While it was true that in ordinary circumstances, novices led more secluded lives given over to religious instruction and prayer, Amadeus found nothing "ordinary" in the circumstances at St. Peter's. Without the novices, how was the school to function? But Damiani remained adamant. Under these conditions, how was she to open a school for Indian girls? It was beyond her imagination.

In the week before Christmas, she wrote a short, frustrated note to Toledo:

> I am very much pained that I cannot write satisfactory
> letters, and I had hoped to be able to write long letters
> telling you all about our circumstances and surroundings
> here, during Christmas week, but lo! What news comes from
> Father Damiani? I am not to have vacation at Christmas
> week—only two days. I am tied down to the school and the
> novices so as not to have one spare moment. Have pity on
> me and send someone to help teach. I am for the first time
> really overtaxed. ... Things will not succeed here without
> one more professed. Father Damiani will have no novice
> teach for him.[21]

Without additional help, the work could not succeed. All her high hopes were threatened. Her dream had been for the Ursulines to carry the message of the Gospel to the women of the Piegan tribe, to educate them, train them in domestic skills, lead them into a new life. As always, visions energized her, moving her, perhaps impetuously, toward her goal. But as they prepared for Christmas 1884, Amadeus's faith in her dream was severely tested: so far, they had not yet opened the Indian school, and already her energies were spent.

Yet when she took stock of the last twelve months, she had good reason to be encouraged. It was less than a year since they had arrived in Montana, and despite their straitened circumstances, they had accomplished marvels. They had established a school in Miles City, opened a mission for the Northern Cheyenne, and joined the Jesuits in their work for the Piegans. Six nuns had arrived in Miles City; now they were twelve. They had doubled their number within the year—surely a sign that God was blessing their work. As they faced a new year, this was her abiding consolation.

Chapter Four

It is too much
for any human being.
—*Mother Amadeus Dunne*

Christmas at St. Peter's was all the sisters could have asked for. The ceremonies were carried out in full. The church was crowded with ranchers' families as well as the mission children. The Indians, wrapped in their blankets and adorned with feathers and beads, traveled miles to participate, crowding the limited mission quarters for a place to spend the night. For the two novices and two postulants, it was their first Christmas as Ursuline missionaries, and their religious dress and the special duties associated with the great feast elicited a special kind of excitement. Amadeus entered into it as fully as she could, but she was incapable of exorcising her worries, which colored everything. As superior, she was responsible for the convent at Miles City and St. Labre's as well as St. Peter's. The news from Miles City was generally satisfying. Sister Sacred Heart was showing herself to be a capable superior, and construction of their new convent had begun. While they, too, were anxious for additional teachers, Sister Francis and their new member from Cleveland, Sister Joseph Steiner, were proving themselves valuable missionaries.

It was St. Labre's that disquieted Amadeus. Even before leaving Miles City, she had received disturbing news. In late September, the constant friction between ranchers and "Indian lovers" had reached a pitch. One evening, just as the nuns were preparing for bed, they were disturbed by the jingle of spurs and bridles, then the loud voices of men, heavy footsteps outside their door, and, a moment later, a knock. Their one small window was curtained and they could see nothing. They waited, too fearful to open the door. Then the footsteps moved on and there was more knocking—much louder this time—at the second door. This was the schoolroom where George Yoakum, their friend and handyman, sometimes slept on the long table where Indian children studied during the day.

Then came hammering on the door and loud voices. Finally, silence, and the noise of horses and men departing. The three nuns waited a while before opening the door. There was no light anywhere, and they hesitated to light a candle lest it betray them and bring back the intruders. The schoolroom door was open and the room empty. The third door, which led to the priest's room, was also open, and that, too, was empty. Fearful for Father Barcelo's safety, they called his name, but to no avail. Together, in silence, they returned to their room and waited for morning.

Around midnight, they heard a great crashing in the schoolroom, but too fearful to investigate, they waited until dawn to venture out. This time, they found the schoolroom door closed. Sister Angela walked around to the back of the house and peered in the window. There, lying on the table, bruised, terrified, and hardly able to move, was George Yoakum.

The men they had heard were four masked cowboys who had come to the mission house to find Yoakum and teach him what "Indian lovers" might expect. They had forced him out of the house and hoisted him on a horse. At a good distance from the mission, they bound him to a tree and beat him almost senseless. The final warning: leave the mission, stop helping the Indians, or the next time would be his last.

Father Barcelo, when he realized what was happening, had tried to intercede, but a pistol was pointed at his head with a warning of what he could expect. He had watched, helpless, as Yoakum was taken away. For a while, he wandered in the direction of the cowboys in some futile thought of trying to find Yoakum and help to release him; but realizing how foolish this was, he returned to his room. He had not heard the sisters searching for him.

Barcelo and the nuns did what they could to assist the wounded Yoakum. Frightened though he was, Yoakum vowed he would never leave the mission, that he would always be faithful no matter what the cost. It was clear, however, that the hostility he had aroused in the ranchers made him more a danger than a protector, and finally he was persuaded to leave for safer territory.[1]

Although this was their most frightening experience, it was not the only time the nuns were made aware of the hostility of the whites not only toward the Indians, but toward anyone helping them. There was no security they could invoke. They were a good two days' journey from Miles City, even if a wagon and driver could be found to make the trip. Yet they were determined not to be frightened off, and they continued teaching the small group of children who came to them daily. As the days grew shorter and the Montana winter began to settle in, they were often worked to exhaustion. Without Yoakum, they had the full burden of caring for the material concerns of the mission: providing wood, carrying water—a more and more difficult task as the temperature plummeted—as well as providing nourishing food from their scant supply for the hungry Cheyenne children.

Father Barcelo did what he could to help, but it was clear that life at St. Labre's was beyond his capacity. Never robust, he was now in constant pain, unable to eat the rough food, which was all that was available. By December, it was obvious that he was incapable of continuing his mission. In mid-December, he said an anguished farewell and began the journey to Helena, where he could receive medical care.* He left behind three Ursuline sisters who were now alone in the most desolate way they could imagine—desolate beyond poverty, beyond physical hardship, they were bereft of priest and sacraments, that imperative spiritual support on which their religious life was built.

---

*The medical care was insufficient, however; Father Barcelo died in 1888 in Gonzaga College in Spokane.

"Sad news on this merry season," Sister Ignatius wrote to Amadeus on December 23. Father Barcelo, on the recommendation of his superior, had left them on December 15. What his loss would mean for them, she could hardly express. As long as he had been physically able, Barcelo had been their constant helper—working in the garden, assisting with the mowing, and using his gift for languages in translating several hymns into the Cheyenne tongue. He had visited the Indians daily, sitting in their tepees, listening to the old women, and doing what he could to help the children. His loss would be immeasurable. Of course, she continued, there would be no Mass on Christmas Eve or Christmas Day. They did not know what would happen, but they hoped to continue the mission. "It is wrong to be sad on such a day," she concluded, her grief showing clearly between her courageous lines.[2]

In January, Bishop Brondel echoed her concern in a letter to Bishop Gilmour:

> The Cheyenne Indian mission is carried on with the greatest zeal and self-sacrifice by the three Ursuline nuns who write to me that twelve children come daily to school. ... The worst impediment to the mission is that there is no priest. The holy Jesuit priest who was allowed by his superiors to take up when Father Eyler left, is in Helena since my return in December to be doctored as he has all the symptoms of ulceration of the stomach. I waited now a whole month and see no improvement and have no one to send in his place. Shall I have to break up what has been so nobly begun? These sisters are there now for five weeks without priest. Perhaps you could assist me in the matter, hoping so.[3]

Brondel's question was echoed by Amadeus: should she advise closing what had been begun so nobly and so courageously? Ultimately, it was the bishop's decision, but Amadeus recognized that her opinion would bear heavily on his judgment. The nuns at St.

Labre's, however, showed no desire to close the mission. Although they admitted that their log cabin with its mud floor made life uncomfortable when the temperature plunged to forty below, they believed that they were making progress with the Indians, and their spirit prevailed.

On February 5, Charles Lusk, secretary for the BCIM in Washington, D.C., sent a letter to the commissioner of Indian affairs asking for a government contract for the education of thirty Indian children at the boarding school of St. Labre's, asserting that "the school has the proper and necessary buildings and teachers and will give the educational and industrial training requested by your office."[4] The assurance was certainly exaggerated; although there were plans for a new building, the mission was hardly capable of supporting such grandiose promises. Securing government help, however, as they knew, was the only way to sustain the mission.

In mid-February, Brondel made the long trip from Helena to observe firsthand the condition of the mission. He found it more disturbing than he had anticipated. Not only was the nuns' situation precarious, but even the geographical boundaries of the reservation were being reconsidered. Once again, the government was breaking its promises to the Cheyenne. All of this, of course, would affect the mission. If the Indians were moved, it would place the mission some seventeen miles outside the reservation, thus necessitating another land claim, another building, and so on. Not easy when they were struggling for survival.

Sister Ignatius was even more concerned than Brondel, for she was in daily contact with the Indians and could see firsthand the consequences of this projected move. Yet despite the nuns' anger at such injustice, there was little they could do but continue to teach the seventeen children who came to them daily.

Brondel, impressed with what the nuns had been able to accomplish under such difficult circumstances, wrote to Monsignor Joseph Stephan, director of the BCIM, expressing his admiration at the nuns' success. The children were beginning to read and write and cypher and knew their prayers in both English and their own language. When their new building was completed, he assured Stephan, they would easily be able to accommodate forty children.[5]

On March 24, the request asking for a government contract for St. Labre's school was acknowledged favorably, and Brondel wrote from Helena to Sister Ignatius:

> This contract enables you to feed and clothe and instruct and lodge at least 30 children ... for 25 dollars per quarter for each. ... Now begin to clothe and lodge them and teach them in the books, but also industry. The boys to help work on the farm, the girls sewing, etc. ... Courage, courage, courage. Thank God and pray.[6]

At last, they had a firm footing for their work, and Easter, which fell just a week later, was a feast of gratitude. Ignatius had written at once to Lusk, thanking him for his help and telling him that they presently had twenty-eight children (both boys and girls) attending the school. "Had we better accommodations and the means to give food even occasionally we could have had forty children. ... Thanks be to God our zeal has found a field which will, we believe, produce for God a rich harvest of souls."[7]

Her optimism was not without its shadow, however, for they still had no permanent chaplain. During the winter, Brondel had sent them two priests, but one after another had left, finding the mission impossibly lonely and unrewarding. Now the bishop, traveling east on a "begging tour," assured them he would do his best to bring a priest back with him. It was October, however, before a priest, once again a Jesuit, finally arrived.

By then, St. Peter's, too, had experienced a period of dramatic change. The anxiety that Amadeus had experienced at Christmas increased with the grim winter months. For the first time, her determination was not sufficient for the work to be done. Exhausted and frustrated, in March she came down with a cold that quickly turned to pneumonia. Their house provided no adequate heat, and even the heavy buffalo robes were insufficient warmth against the winter cold. No medical help was available, and the four young sisters were terrified as they watched their superior grow more feeble.

Strangely enough, the Jesuits apparently did not suggest moving her to their more comfortable stone house, even though they recognized how ill she was. One of the priests came to administer the sacrament of the dying, frightening the sisters still more, and instructed them to get in touch with the Ursuline superior in Toledo.

On March 17, Mother Stanislaus received a telegram saying that Mother Amadeus was "at the point of death." Immediately, she left for Montana, taking with her Sister Mary of the Angels and Sister Rose of Lima. They were accompanied by Mary Fields, a black woman employed by the Toledo convent. Thus began the legend of "Black Mary."

Fact and fiction are inextricably mixed in the history of Mary Fields. Although the documentation is confusing, it seems probable that she was born a slave in Tennessee in 1832, the daughter of a field hand and a house servant, and later became a servant in the Dunne household in Ohio. Some twelve years older than the child Sarah (later Amadeus), it is probable that the two had become good friends, thus partially accounting for Mary being hired in the Toledo convent after Sarah became a sister there. There, she helped with the housework and kept the grounds. Accepted as part of the household, she had a room on the first floor of the convent, as well as her own place in chapel.

Mary Fields could not be overlooked wherever she was. She was an immense woman, six feet tall and weighing more than 200 pounds. During her days in Montana, she boasted that she could lick any man—and proved it more than once. She was hardly an acceptable convent factotum. She drank (too much), she smoked (cigars), she argued (in questionable language). She wore men's shoes, coats, and hats, but scorned to wear trousers, although—it was said—she sometimes carried a pistol under her apron. But she was loyal, devoted, and generous to the death. Her devotion to Amadeus was a passion. If anyone could bring things right at St. Peter's, it would be Black Mary. Although originally Mother Stanislaus had brought her only temporarily to care for Amadeus in her illness, Mary Fields made it very clear that she was aiming to stay as long as she could help the nuns. When, thirty years later, in 1914, she died in the little town of

St. Peter's Mission, Mary Fields. Courtesy of Ursuline archives, Toledo, Ohio

Cascade, not far from the mission, she had, as the saying goes, become a legend in her own day.

By the end of March, Amadeus was out of danger and able to sit up in bed, but it took weeks before she regained her strength.

Mother Stanislaus, now face-to-face with the rigors of mission life, recognized how desperately help was needed. There was no dearth of sisters at Toledo eager to come; the accounts of mission rigors had only fired their zeal. A few weeks earlier, Stanislaus had written, in some exasperation, to Bishop Gilmour: "There are some who appear quite determined to go to Montana and are giving no little trouble on that account."[8] Although she was more than willing to do what she could, she could hardly be expected to empty the Toledo convent in favor of the Montana missions. Now, however, recognizing their need, she arranged for Sister Mary of the Angels to stay on at St. Peter's and sent word back to Miles City that Sister Francis Siebert and Sister Gertrude O'Reilly, a new arrival from the Ursuline convent in Brown County, Ohio, were to come as soon as possible.

With Amadeus on the road to recovery, Stanislaus left St. Peter's, stopping to visit St. Labre's and Miles City before returning to Toledo. "Both places give great promise of success," she wrote later to Bishop Gilmour. "It is wonderful that so much could have been accomplished in one year," she concluded.[9]

St. Peter's welcomed spring with renewed hope. Amadeus had been able to attend Mass on April 2 for the first time since the beginning of March. From the sisters' windows, they could see the fathers supervising the ploughing for the spring planting.

There were now nine women at the mission (eight sisters and Mary Fields) and an increasing number of children—far more than their housing could sustain. Sister Mary of the Angels wrote home with undaunted cheer: "We have not yet a dormitory but sleep wherever we can find the most convenient corner. Sister Francis's resting place is on the kitchen table, almost on top of the stove. She can arrange the fire in the morning without getting out of bed."[10] They had no chairs; they ate standing, kneeling, or sitting on the floor. It was clear that they needed to build as soon as the weather permitted, for their school was increasing. By October, they had built another log cabin, called Loretto House, which alleviated—but only slightly—their crowded conditions.

Word from St. Labre's and Miles City was also filled with hope. St. Labre's announced that work on the new building had begun. At Miles City, their new convent was under construction, and Sister Sacred Heart wrote that by the end of July they would be able to have Mass and the blessing of the house. The address would be "Ursuline Convent of the Sacred Heart."[11]

At St. Peter's that July, the two postulants, Theresia Yunck and Theresa Henry, completed their initial probation and were clothed in the Ursuline habit with the names Ursula and Santa Clara, respectively. Once again, Bishop Brondel made the demanding trip from Helena and was received by a welcoming procession of both Indians and whites. Although the ceremony had far less fanfare than the one that had taken place in Miles City the year before, for Amadeus, it was an event of prime importance. It set the seal on St. Peter's Mission as the canonical novitiate for the Ursuline missions in Montana. Her dream, of course, was that they would soon be besieged by young women who shared her vision, thus permitting the Montana missions to become self-sufficient, no longer needing to beg Toledo for help.

That time, however, did not come. Despite their increased number, they all remained overburdened by unexpected demands. Several weeks after the novices' reception, Amadeus wrote to Toledo: "We have scarlet fever, malignant form, here in the mission. One of the white boy boarders died yesterday and was buried yesterday evening. By order of General Brooks, Fort Shaw, we are quarantined."[12]

By mid-September, the scare was over, but not before four boys had died. Health, they were beginning to learn, was a persistent problem in mission life.

Hygiene was not an element of Indian life, and the children came to them with all sorts of diseases, primary among them skin diseases, generally the result of the unsanitary conditions in which they lived. Washing either themselves or their clothes was not part of their way of life, and as a result, disease spread like wildfire.

One of the unremitting problems was trachoma, an eye disease that, left untreated, can cause blindness. Repeated infections, left uncared for, scar the inside of the eyelid. Eyelashes turn in, rubbing and scarring the cornea, often causing blindness in later life. Highly contagious, it can afflict a whole tribe. Although science now offers many remedies, for the nuns at St. Peter's, soap and water and an effort to dislodge the inverted eyelashes was all that was available. It was not a bad antidote, however, for even modern medicine admits that so simple a remedy as frequent face washing can prevent, or at least alleviate, the spread of the disease.

In addition to the dreaded disease of trachoma, many of the children suffered from scrofula in various stages. Once referred to as "The King's Evil" and believed to be cured by "The King's Touch," scrofula is now recognized as a form of tuberculosis, the oldest of humanity's infectious diseases, and, like all forms of tuberculosis, is highly contagious. It is often described as TB of the neck, a condition beginning with an infection of the lymph nodes.

What the nuns knew of scrofula beyond its abhorrent manifestations is hard to say. Certainly, they had few remedies for dealing with it. "They are all dreadfully infected with scrofula," Amadeus wrote that summer.

> Glandular abscesses and running sores and matterated [*sic*]
> eyelids are common disorders among these poor, wretched
> Blackfeet children. Their condition requires careful treat-
> ment. The boys are more afflicted than the girls, both
> require medical attention and careful dressing of the parts
> afflicted. We give them a preparation of Cod liver oil with
> hypophosphites of lime and soda and they are improving
> under our regimen.[13]

It was certainly an inadequate remedy for the disease they were treating, but they could do no more. As for the medical attention required, this continued to be a problem in all of the missions. The government doctor, generally connected with the nearest fort, was miles away and ordinarily considered the missions as a subsidiary duty. Only in the gravest situations was he requested to travel the long and dangerous distance to the mission. In some cases, the mission was required to have a resident doctor, paid for by the mission, but the Jesuits found this an outrageous demand and never conceded to it.

In any case, in the summer of 1885, the Ursulines at St. Peter's had neither the knowledge nor the remedies available for the serious health problems of the Indian children. Soap and water was their staunchest ally, and they used it plentifully, combing the girls' hair daily, removing the hundreds of lice—euphemistically referred to as "pearls"—which they drowned triumphantly in a bucket of coal oil.

But all this took time and patience in a life that consumed their energies on every side. In early March, Amadeus was faced for the first time with preparing the monthly report required by the government. It was typical of documents imposed by those who had little experience of mission life, demanding a detailed account of those working at the mission, the scope of their tasks, and so on. Each Indian pupil had to be listed, with her tribe, her age, the number of days in which she was in attendance. It was the kind of work that Amadeus resisted throughout her life. She was impatient with paperwork, impatient with the time spent recording details when she saw so much around her that demanded immediate attention. Such disregard for what seemed to her unnecessary formalities would cause others to misunderstand her throughout her life.

Although they had received three new workers in early spring, on August 12, Amadeus wrote to Mother Stanislaus at great length, outlining their work and begging once again for more recruits, suggesting that if Toledo could not provide them, perhaps Cleveland could:

Our work is rapidly increasing. I think that we will have forty
boarders here next year and we are obliged to teach four
separate schools, white boys, white girls, Indian boys, Indian
girls and we cannot dispense ourselves from taking care of the
Jesuit washing, ironing and mending and sacristy work for two
chapels for four Fathers, since they do so much for us. The
work we do for them is part of our living. The Fathers have all
the farm work done for us gratis. ... Sister St. Mary has charge
of the kitchen, refectory, lamps and chickens. Sister St. Martha
bakes for the mission—for 10 of the Jesuit household, 9
Ursuline household, 20 white boarders (girls) and 20 white boy
boarders, 20 Indian boy boarders, 12 Indian girl boarders
(more on their way) and 10 working men employed at the
Mission, that is for about 100 persons and besides tends to the
milk and buttermaking—too much for any human being.[14]

She continued, reciting the charges of the other sisters: Sister
Santa Clara, who took care of all the washing and ironing ("and a
more incompetent person for this kind of work could not be found,"
she commented in exasperation); Sister Gertrude, who worked with
the Indian children; and Sister Francis, who worked with the white
boys and the Indian children's dormitory.

Although Amadeus recognized that everyone was worked
beyond her capacity, her concern was less for St. Peter's than for St.
Labre's, with its continuing difficulties. Her anxiety was lightened,
however, in mid-October with the news that Father Cataldo was
sending two Jesuits to St. Labre's: Peter Prando and Aloysius Van der
Velden. Father Prando, already famous for his work with the
Blackfeet at St. Peter's, was to work on the Crow reservation situated
west of St. Labre's on the Little Bighorn.

Cataldo was eager to establish a mission for the Crow, and the
irrepressible Prando was a perfect choice. While he reconnoitered, he
made St. Labre's his home base and endeared himself to the nuns,
especially to Sister Angela, who wrote of him, "He was a model of

patience, kindness, gentleness and was very sympathetic to everybody. He had some knowledge of medicine, which is a very great help in missionary work, for we all know that to relieve the body is the first step to the soul."[15]

Father Aloysius Van der Velden, ordained in Holland just a few years earlier, had none of Prando's experience, but he was young, energetic, and determined. With a rudimentary knowledge of medicine and a gift for languages, he was, in his own rather prickly way, a source of life for St. Labre's.

Van der Velden was a realist, not a romantic, and his initial appraisal of the Cheyenne was far from favorable. He found them lazy, dirty, devious, inconstant, but his devotion to them was unflagging. As a missionary, his first goal was Christianization, but he was also sympathetic to their impoverished lives and angered by the injustices inflicted by the whites. When he complained graphically of his terrible bed, which made sleep impossible, he never lost sight of the fact that the Cheyenne had even less.

By the time of his arrival at St. Labre's, the mission was taking care of forty children, with the help of government vouchers. Their new building was progressing and would be finished by the time winter set in. The effort on the part of the whites to have the reservation moved had failed, at least temporarily, and the Indians had quieted down.

Even so, mission life continued, rigorous and often unpredictable. Domestic work filled much of the nuns' days. They had a team of horses by then, and a buckboard, a good saddle horse, and a cow—valuable assets, all of which required extra work.

Sometimes they were able to get the older Indian boys to help, but Indian children were as proud as their parents, and the nuns quickly recognized that they could not be "bossed about," as Sister Angela put it, "but if you say, 'let us do it,' they will do anything most willingly."[16]

The nuns learned, however, that they were not the first authority; authority was the prerogative of the Indian chiefs. "One day when we were at dinner," Sister Angela continued, "a chief came in and asked for a little money, a thing we never gave. He refused the dinner we offered him and turned to the children and said a few words. In an instant, all rose and left the table and went out of the house and the chief followed."[17]

Although that occasion ended happily, with the children's eventual return, there were times when the children were kept from school because of the displeasure of the chiefs. In retaliation, the Indian agent often refused the Indians their rations until the children were returned to school. It was a rancorous situation on both sides, and the nuns were always the losers.

But, as Sister Angela wrote with good spirits, there were joyful times, too. They soon discovered that their pupils were curious and bright. While language was a difficult hurdle, there were other skills at which they excelled. Already accomplished at beadwork, they soon became adept in fancywork (intricate embroidery that was the fashion of the day) and in making their own clothes—but only after they had overcome their initial repugnance at wearing "white man's dress."

Music was their special delight. They sang well and learned to play the musical instruments that the mission had acquired from generous benefactors: two baby organs, an accordion, a zither, and a number of mouth organs. "On Christmas," Sister Angela wrote, "they were able to play and sing the 'Adeste' and 'The Snow Lay on the Ground' for their parents and a crowd of people. The performance was very good."[18]

Health concerns were as serious at St. Labre's as they were at St. Peter's. Although there was less smallpox and scarlet fever (white man's diseases), possibly because the reservation was more isolated, scrofula was endemic. "They came to the mission in the beginning with dreadful sores," Angela wrote. "A number of girls had them from ear to ear, and when these were opened worms were in the decayed flesh and we could see the cords in the neck."[19] Father Prando, with his gentle fingers and skill in medicine, trained the nuns to clean the running sores and alleviate—if not cure—the disease.

In addition to the welfare of the children, the building of the new house brought extra workmen who had to be fed daily. For a few days, while huge stones were being excavated for the foundation, the nuns had to provide dinner for more than thirty men. With no proper kitchen, the task prompted their maximum ingenuity, but there were no complaints as they watched the foundation being laid.

With such needs confronting them daily, schoolroom teaching was but a small part of their work, and Ignatius was concerned that they were not fulfilling the strict government requirements for mission schools. In early October, she wrote to Charles Lusk that she was not prepared to fill out the forms for the required mission statistics, and when toward the end of the month she had not yet received the vouchers for the preceding months, she worried that they might have been revoked. On October 26, she wrote again to Lusk: "I hope you will inform me if the vouchers have been received and how soon we may expect payment for the months of March, April, May, June. On account of our new building we are greatly pressed for money and our creditors are becoming somewhat impatient with us."*[20]

Her fears were unfounded, however; the vouchers arrived, and two weeks later, their house was ready for occupancy.

In the first week of November, they welcomed Bishop Brondel, who had come to bless their new building. During his visit, he wrote a detailed assessment to Bishop Gilmour in Cleveland of the state of the various missions. He was clearly pleased with the "fine building" (two stories high with a separate kitchen and chapel), which had been erected with the funds he had been able to collect on his "begging tour" in the East. With the $1,000 they received quarterly from the government, he explained, the sisters were able to take care of

---

*This lag between the urgent needs of the missions and bureaucratic delay became an endemic problem of mission life.

the Indian children fairly well. As for the Indians themselves, they were often "hungry and starving" because of the treatment by the agent. "I gave them a steer ... and it broke my heart to see their joy." As for the sisters, "they are well physically and religiously."

At St. Peter's, he continued, the sisters have twenty-two Blackfeet girls and twenty-two white girls "from the neighborhood." They clearly need to build, "but the funds are wanting."

At Miles City, the school was full but could have accommodated more pupils if they had another sister. "If two teaching sisters would come to Miles, one of Miles could come here and four sisters at each place would prevent them being overtaxed." But he added a warning: "Sisters are needed of the same spirit as the first six who came from Toledo."[21]

Amadeus, of course, seconded his recommendation, and by the beginning of 1886, it seemed that the convents in both Cleveland and Toledo would answer the requests from Montana. Encouraged by the prospect, in February, despite a winter of poor health, Amadeus started off to visit St. Labre's and Miles City.

In many ways, Miles City was the least demanding of the three houses, and Sister Sacred Heart had proven herself a competent superior: hardworking, creative, a capable manager. With their new house completed, it seemed that their school would flourish. But none of this alleviated Sister Sacred Heart's anxieties.

The year before, she had written to Toledo explaining that she was so busy that it was impossible for her to write often. In the letter, she detailed her duties as superior, which included supervising the building of their new convent, spending six hours in class daily, and teaching her twelve music pupils. While the optimistic Sister Rose wrote enthusiastically about all their improvements—their "nice garden," their new dining room, their ten chickens that were providing daily eggs—Sister Sacred Heart was absorbed by worry. She recognized that the quality of the school was far from satisfactory. Unless they were able to get additional help, they would not be able to compete with the city's growing public school.

It was a legitimate worry, one that Mother Stanislaus had shared when she visited the preceding spring. "Sister Sacred Heart is in need of help," she wrote to Bishop Gilmour. "It will be impossible for her to continue long under the strain that is upon her."[22]

That strain was clearly evident in the letter Sister Sacred Heart wrote to Toledo in July 1885:

> We are busy here trying to make some preparation for the coming year, cleaning house, making comforters, mending our clothing, giving instruction to first communicants, music lessons, etc. I have made inquiries about school furniture which we must have by September 1, but St. Joseph must provide the means as we haven't a penny for these purposes. I have also written a begging letter to my Father for furniture. Then we must have help; I have written to Mother Amadeus and I suppose she has applied to you, as I have not heard from her since I last wrote. It seems selfish in us, Mother, to ask when we know you are taxed at home, yet, you know how our work suffers here ... [23]

When Amadeus had visited Miles City in the fall of 1885, she could offer Sacred Heart no help. Now, however, despite the dangers of travel in midwinter, she was eager to visit again, this time bringing the comforting news that they could expect three additional sisters before the end of February.

Chapter Five

I know not how to tell you.

—Mother Amadeus Dunne

Mother Amadeus's visit to Miles City in February 1886 was not motivated entirely by the desire to bring good news. For several months that winter, she had been receiving disquieting news, none of it specific, but all centered on Sister Sacred Heart. From Sacred Heart herself, she had heard little, except that the sisters had moved to their new house and had more than they could manage to keep the school going. There had, however, been one other letter from Sister Sacred Heart, a letter written in January admitting to Amadeus that she was in "great trouble." But Amadeus had not answered. She had been sick at the time, she later explained, and then the weather had made it impossible to travel. In the midst of so many difficulties, Sacred Heart's plea had been put aside. It was six weeks before Amadeus finally saw her. By then, it was too late.

Although Amadeus would have decried showing favoritism, one would not have to look deep to recognize that of the five sisters she had brought to Montana, it was Sacred Heart who most elicited her admiration and affection. To Amadeus, Sacred Heart seemed the very ideal of religious life. She was gentle, intelligent, modest. She was artistic, well-spoken, musical. In addition, she was physically attractive, even in the confines of black serge and white linen. Even more than that, she was devoted, generous, prayerful, courageous. Amadeus may well have seen in her a second self—and a successor.

But the Sister Sacred Heart who welcomed her to Miles City had lost something of her charm. Although she talked at length with

Amadeus about her concern for the financial condition of the house and the state of the school, when Amadeus attempted to probe the cause of her anxiety, she was met with silence. Sacred Heart was unwilling to explain her distress, except to admit that there was some gossip about her, that Miles City was a mean-spirited little town, and that she hated living there and wished she could return to St. Labre's.

"I asked outright if there was any truth in all the rumors but she refused to give me any answer," Amadeus wrote later in her memoir."[1]

The rumors concerned her relationship with Davíd Toner,* a young man who had lost both his wife and baby in childbirth three years before. A devoted Catholic and respected citizen of Miles City, he was highly regarded by Father Lindesmith, who was instrumental in engaging him to help the Ursulines. It was Toner who had traveled to St. Labre's with Father Eyler to choose a site for the mission. He had remained there to help build the new house and had then been engaged in the construction in Miles City. As superior in both places, Sister Sacred Heart had invariably spent time alone in his company. The ingredients of gossip were ready at hand.

"I spoke to Sister many hours ... but without much success in finding out from her the cause of her trouble," Amadeus wrote later to Mother Stanislaus. "Her replies were, 'I cannot tell you now but I will tell you later. ... The trouble comes from within myself. ... Mother, you have trusted me too much.'"[2]

They did not speak again. That night, Amadeus went early to bed but was awakened about 2:00 A.M. One of the sisters, rising early to fix the fire, had found Sister Sacred Heart's religious clothing—habit, veil, white linens—neatly folded on a trunk. On the piano, she had left a note for Amadeus:

> I can no longer endure my present condition, so have decided
> to sever myself from all connections with the past. I leave a
> check to replace the money I have taken and have charged

---

*Richard Toner's brother, who had also helped at St. Labre's.

the amount to the account of [my father] Mr. B. Meilink, and
will arrange with him. I am fully aware of the baseness and
cowardice of my act, but I ask one favor of you: leave my
name unconnected with any other.[3]

It is hard to imagine the emotions of the three stupefied nuns
who stood around the trunk, looking down at all the symbols of religious life from which Sacred Heart had so ruthlessly divorced herself.

Their first question: where had she gone? Miles City could
provide no refuge, and beyond Miles City lay nothing but prairie.
Suicide must have come to their minds, but the fact that she had
taken $100 and a small valise with some clothes and personal items
suggested that she had some plan in mind. There were two trains on
the Northern Pacific line that stopped at Miles City during the night
hours: the eastbound train would take her to St. Paul, where she
could then get a train for Ohio; the westbound would take her across
the Rockies and into the distant territory of Washington. Although
they had no evidence for either option, it seemed more sensible to
presume that she had gone east and would probably return to her
family in Toledo.

At once, Amadeus wrote to the superior at Toledo. Her prose, often
more dramatic than the situation warranted, was this time justified:

I know not how to tell you the bitterly sad news which I must
impart to you now. You are not prepared for the heart-rending
shock which leaves us prostrate in an abyss of sorrow which
has no name. Our best and dearest Sister Sacred Heart secretly
left us last night at about one o'clock. She laid aside her
religious habit and returned to the world. Where she went I
do not know. I think that she took the eastbound train. She
had been—unknown to any of us—preparing for this departure for weeks. ... No disaffection towards any of us has
produced these terrible results. The truth proceeds from
something entirely different. I am not able to enter into the

agonizing details now. My spirit is broken. Today the death-
blow has been given to our Mission.[4]

For ten days, they waited for news, but no further word came
from Sacred Heart. She had not returned to the Toledo convent nor
to her family.

Meanwhile, in the midst of their anxiety and turmoil, four new
sisters from Ohio, one more than the promised three, arrived in
Miles City: St. Bernard Cotter and Thomas Stoeckel from Cleveland,
Magdalen Cox from Toledo, and Stanislas Miller from Tiffin, a
branch house of Toledo.

Mother Amadeus, who had pleaded so desperately for more
helpers, now dreaded their coming. How could she break the news to
them? What would they think of mission life? Would they, perhaps,
take the next eastbound train back to a life that was reliable and secure?

Her anxiety was not without foundation, and on March 18, she
wrote again to Mother Stanislaus: "The new sisters are shocked more
than I can express; they already regret that they came out to us. I do
not think they will remain. Fear and trembling have seized them."[5]
But her fear that they would return to the East was unfounded. The
sisters remained—some for life, some for the few months during
which they were most needed.

On March 21, in the midst of all their turmoil, they awaited a
visit from Bishop Brondel, who was as yet unaware of their tragedy.
So far, they had been able to keep the "shocking scandal" secret. At
that time, Sister Gertrude was returning to her community at Brown
County, and Amadeus let it be understood that Sister Sacred Heart
had accompanied her. The ruse was successful, and the true story was
hidden for years from the gossip-prone town of Miles City.

There was no doubt, of course, that it was judged a scandal
among the few who knew the truth. Even 100 years later, so unprece-
dented a departure would have raised eyebrows. The process of
terminating religious vows is a formal and lengthy procedure, but
in the case of Sister Sacred Heart, none of the procedures had been

followed. She made the decision alone, without advice and with little preparation beyond those hours of isolated reflection when, as she wrote, she had come to that moment when she could do nothing else. Even had she followed the normal procedures, there would have been little understanding or acceptance of her decision. In those days—and well into the twentieth century—"spoiled nun" was the usual designation for someone who left religious life. At a time when divorce was socially unacceptable, no matter what the circumstances, when it carried a stigma that could not be obliterated, it is not surprising that a nun who left her convent would carry a lasting burden of shame.

"You must bear in your heart the burden of sorrow which I have laid on it," Amadeus wrote to Mother Stanislaus on March 18. "You must not yet speak the terrible truth—silence is our only security."[6] Even Bishop Gilmour was left uninformed until much later.

Finally, on April 17, Stanislaus felt in conscience that she must inform him:

> Were it not for the earnest entreaty of Mother Amadeus to
> keep the lamentable affair a secret to April 16th at least, Your
> Lordship would have known it long ere this ... I know
> absolutely nothing of this, save what I have gathered from
> these letters of Mother Amadeus. I am at a loss what to think
> of it. It is utterly impossible to express our grief and astonish-
> ment on receiving the painful news.[7]

How profoundly moved and humiliated Amadeus was by Sacred Heart's departure is apparent in a letter written to Gilmour more than a year later. "Grief and shame withheld me from approaching you," she wrote in June 1887. "I pledged myself never to look up into your face until I had found her or until I had some good news to tell you."[8]

The "terrible truth" that Amadeus was so determined to conceal was not fully known to them for weeks. Although when the days passed and it became clear that Sacred Heart had not returned to

Ohio, they must have realized what the final sentence of her last note had meant: "I ask one favor of you; leave my name unconnected with any other." The dreaded name was, of course, that of David Toner, well-known to all of them.

The one person Amadeus felt free to confide in from the beginning was Father Lindesmith. Deeply sympathetic to their way of life but experienced, too, in the difficulties of pioneer existence, Lindesmith had been their mainstay since their arrival in Miles City. They had learned to count on him for advice and support. But now, confronted with such jolting news, he had lost his emotional balance, and his diary, in which he had formerly recorded all the mundane details of his daily life, was now narrowed to passionate prayers and lurid fears for this "lost soul."

That she was a "lost soul" Lindesmith had no doubt. The day following Sacred Heart's disappearance, he wrote: "My worst calamity, or the greatest trouble I ever had, happened on Monday morning at 2 AM, Feast of St. John of God, March 8."[9]

For Lindesmith, the shock was aggravated by a profound sense of betrayal. Not only had Sacred Heart done the unthinkable, but David Toner had betrayed the trust placed in him. Lindesmith was not only saddened, but profoundly humiliated that his expectations had been so misplaced.

From the beginning, he placed the ultimate fault squarely on Toner, whom he now saw as the very incarnation of evil: "The Great Dragon in Human form." Sacred Heart he judged simply as a victim, an innocent woman seduced and betrayed. "She is not master any more of her own mind and heart, but she must obey him," he wrote later to Mother Stanislaus.[10]

But even so, her sin remained. He questioned even her "eternal salvation," unless she returned at once to her convent. As time went by and no word was received, his prose grew more frantic. Prayer and sacrifice, he reiterated, were the only means to bring "the sinner" to her senses. He would fast from "flesh meat," he would make a novena of Masses, he would pray to those great sinners of the flesh: Mary Magdalene, Mary of Egypt, Augustine. "A poor distressed and broken-hearted Priest of God prays for 'Mercy' and pity on the poor fallen creature," he wrote, as they still waited for news.[11]

Throughout March and into April, they waited. It was clear by now that Sacred Heart had taken the westbound train. They hesitated to make inquiries lest "the terrible secret" be revealed. It would not have been difficult to identify her. Few young women would be traveling alone in the sparsely settled territory of the Rockies. She would be noticed wherever she went.

Despite her anxiety, Amadeus could no longer remain away from St. Peter's, and before the end of the month, she departed Miles City, leaving Sister Magdalen, only recently arrived, as superior.

The weeks passed with no news of Sacred Heart. A few rumors reached them in April, but they were too vague to be acted upon and were always received with the greatest secrecy. The fact that David Toner was no longer in Miles City surprised no one, since he had indicated earlier that he intended to go west to find better work.

It was May before definite word reached Amadeus: Sacred Heart was in Spokane Falls, a town in the east of Washington Territory, not far from the Idaho border. She had already applied to Bishop Brondel for a dispensation from her vows, but he had explained to her that she had made her vows under Bishop Gilmour's jurisdiction and only Gilmour could release her.

At this news, Amadeus immediately notified Mr. Meilink, who made the 2,000-mile journey to Helena, where they met and then traveled together to Spokane Falls. Whatever hopes Amadeus had had for this meeting had come to naught. Sacred Heart would not see her, nor would she reverse her determination never to return to the convent.

On May 24, Amadeus wrote a long letter to Father Lindesmith, beginning, "All is wrong and with a broken heart I say it. I have no good news to cheer your sorrowful soul."[12]

The story Sister Sacred Heart told her father ran contrary to all their conjectures. Her departure, she explained, was not premeditated; it was "only the work of an hour." "The storm, the strife, the wreck—all within one short hour!" Amadeus wrote inconsolably to Father Lindesmith. She had taken the Northern Pacific as far as Garrison, she explained, and then changed to the Northern Utah branch to Butte City. At Butte, she changed to a stagecoach that took her to Rock Creek in southern Idaho. There she remained, working as a servant, until on April 8—just a month since her departure—she was joined by David Toner.

It was an extraordinary journey for a nun whose only opportunity to travel in Montana had been the trip to St. Labre's and the return to Miles City. The times of the trains, the necessary connections, the route of the stagecoach all necessitated planning, even for a seasoned traveler. It is difficult to imagine that "the work of an hour" had enabled Sacred Heart to make such elaborate plans, and even more difficult to believe that she had started off with no plan in mind. It seems more likely that she had premeditated such a move for some time, although she may not have intended to carry it out as dramatically as she had. Such explanation may also have been a means of sparing David Toner the responsibility for her actions. What she had done, she had done alone, she affirmed. Contrary to Father Lindesmith's assumption, she was adamant in maintaining that she was her own master.

David Toner, unlike Sacred Heart herself, spoke freely with Amadeus, assuring her that he had done his best to have her contact her father and had encouraged her to move to Spokane Falls, where she would have access to spiritual guidance. Amadeus explained that Toner had avowed that he had never encouraged her to leave the convent and, in fact, would have been happy to see her peacefully reestablished at St. Labre's. It was a confusing affirmation, and one that Amadeus could not believe.

> My opinion is that she is completely under his control. It
> appears from what he maintains that his intentions are
> good. ... I firmly believe that if she were free from his
> influence, she could be persuaded to return with confidence

to us. I have very little or no hope that she will break off her
communication with him. She persists in believing that he is
her true friend. I decidedly think that if it were not for him
we could have got her back.[13]

What no one seemed concerned about was what Sacred Heart
herself was suffering. Whether, as she avowed, her departure had been
a rash and lonely act or whether all had been planned with David
Toner, in either case, it cost her the only life she had known. Sacred
Heart was not a novice. She had made her vows at the age of twenty-
seven and was thirty-six when she took her radical step. David Toner
may have had less to do with her decision (which is what they both
avowed) than her sense of abandonment and futility. She had volunteered joyfully for the Indian missions and worked wholeheartedly at
St. Labre's. Then, suddenly, with Amadeus's decision to accept the
Jesuits' invitation to St. Peter's, she had been moved from St. Labre's
to Miles City, an uprooting that apparently cost her dearly.

At Miles City, she was ordered once again to begin a building
project for which it was clear there were insufficient funds. Even more
frustrating was the expectation that she administer a school that
would equal or surpass the other small schools in Miles City, although
she had no teachers who were adequately prepared for the task.

The one person she could count on, Francis Siebert, was moved
to St. Peter's, again at the dictate of Amadeus. Although she had written at length to Amadeus explaining their difficulties, her letters
generally went unanswered. At the beginning of 1886, recognizing
that she was at a point of crisis, she wrote again, acknowledging her
need for help. The winter passed, but she received no answer. No
wonder she may have confided in David Toner and leaned on his
understanding support.

When Amadeus finally arrived, the time had passed when
words could have healed the wounds. Perhaps what propelled Sacred
Heart into an immediate decision was Amadeus's revelation that she
intended to assist Father Peter Prando in opening a mission on the

Crow reservation in southeast Montana. Although there were three missions already stretched beyond human capacity, Amadeus could not refuse the possibility of a fourth. Where she would find the nuns to staff yet another house, she did not know. God would provide. Amadeus's enthusiasm for the future was boundless; it consumed her energies. Sacred Heart's remonstrances over the conditions at Miles City went unheeded. What once must have elicited Sacred Heart's admiration as a holy passion now seemed akin to an obsession. Miles City, she feared, would never get the help it needed; Amadeus had lost interest. A future of anxiety, frustration, and overwork stretched before her endlessly without alleviation. Perhaps, it may be conjectured, it was such a specter, not simply an attraction to David Toner, that determined her to put into operation the decision that must have been shaping for months.

The meeting at Spokane Falls changed nothing. On May 18, her father left to return east, "overcome with grief at being unable to persuade her to return to any Ursuline Convent."[14] Amadeus returned to St. Peter's a few days later. David Toner moved on to Shoshone country in Idaho, and then to Walla Walla in southern Washington. By mid-July, Sacred Heart had joined him. Some time later, she received a dispensation from her vows from Bishop Alphonse Glorieux of Idaho and she and David Toner were married. For a while, Father Lindesmith continued to write to her and encouraged the nuns to do so. But in time, the waters closed over, and Sister Sacred Heart was never mentioned again in any convent records.

Shortly before Amadeus had left for her cataclysmic visit to Miles City, Bishop Gilmour had written a letter to the community in Toledo that would seriously affect the Montana missions:

> About two years ago a colony of Sisters from your Community
> went to Montana. Since that additional help has gone from
> your house and from Cleveland, and now the third time I
> have permitted help to go to help carry on the work begun.

In consequence of this movement a spirit of restlessness has crept into some of your members and there has arisen a feverish desire to go to the Indians, forgetting that your first duty is to your own home. Montana is well enough when we have help to spare, but hereafter Montana must depend on itself. ... Further discussion about Montana is now out of place and will cease.[15]

It was an extraordinarily stringent letter from a person who had hitherto shown himself to be generous and supportive, but he could not endanger the work in Toledo to satisfy the needs of Montana. Perhaps he was beginning to understand that nothing would ever be enough for the expanding vision of Amadeus. In any case, it was clear that the missions must now be considered independent, staffed by young women whose religious vocations were directed specifically to the native people of Montana.

It was another challenge, and Amadeus accepted it without hesitation. Sometime during that year and the following one, she

St. Peter's Mission, art class. Courtesy of Ursuline archives, Great Falls, Montana

contacted bishops throughout the country, sending letters to diocesan papers, pleading for helpers for their "noble cause." The response was extraordinary. The existing files are filled with letters from young women applying for admittance, from priests recommending girls in their parishes, requisite baptismal certificates, letters of "good conduct," and other documents. Within the next ten years, the novitiate at St. Peter's accepted candidates from Kentucky, Wisconsin, Maine, Connecticut, New Mexico, Missouri, New York, Massachusetts, Michigan, West Virginia, and as far away as Ireland, Alsace, Prussia, and Canada. If Bishop Gilmour had feared that his decision might curtail the work of the missions, his fears were groundless.

St. Peter's was becoming a substantial community. They were receiving increasing numbers of children from the white settlers who often arrived without warning or formality. "They come [with] bags and boxes as they come tumbling in. We never know at what moment a team may drive up and leave us a load of boarders. They have no ceremony here."[16] Indian boarders were also increasing, and the three log cabins that the Jesuits had initially provided were now totally inadequate.

In addition to the 200 acres made over to them by the Jesuits, Amadeus had acquired 160 additional acres through the Homestead Act. With this security, she began building. First came a log house for the Indian boarders, then a washhouse, and finally a chicken coop, where Mary Fields, the indefatigable worker, kept a flock of several hundred chickens.

On October 30, they celebrated their second anniversary at St. Peter's with full festivity. Even some chocolate after dinner, a rare treat, was provided by Father Damiani, the Jesuit superior, which, he explained, he had found in the pocket of Father Imoda, the old missionary of legendary fame. Neither Damiani nor Amadeus mentioned the fact that Father Imoda had died some time earlier.

By mid-November, the weather had turned bitterly cold and the task of keeping the children warm became ever more taxing. "We hear the wolves howling every night and the wind keeps up a continuous storm," Amadeus wrote. A few days later, she added, "Last week two very large wolves (not coyotes) came prowling round the house much to the dismay of the nuns but not the children who are accustomed to such visits."[17]

The nuns were now staffing two boarding schools: one for white children and one for Indians. There seems to have been no thought of combining them. In practical terms, the needs of the pupils were very different: the Indians needed to learn the most rudimentary skills; the white boarders were ready to continue their basic education. Amadeus was determined that both groups be provided with what would be most "appropriate." Thus, for the white pupils, she did her best to provide—in addition to the ordinary curriculum—the more exotic arts of musical training and woodcarving.

The Indian pupils spent the morning with their books; in the afternoon, they were put to learning domestic skills—baking, cleaning, washing, ironing, sewing, and embroidery. The Jesuits had already established such a schedule in their mission schools, and from the beginning, Bishop Brondel had warned the sisters at St. Labre's not to keep the Indian children at their books all day but to see that they were instructed in practical skills.

When St. Peter's was at its prime, Jesuit brothers supervised carpentry shops, care of cattle, wheat growing, metalworking (such as shoeing horses), as well as a successful printing shop, which produced pamphlets, Indian dictionaries, books on Christian doctrine, as well as elegantly printed programs for special school events.

The boys' work was essential to maintaining an increasingly large establishment. As for the nuns, such help as the older girls provided was invaluable in alleviating the domestic work of their growing household. That such "unpaid labor" was exploitative certainly never crossed the nuns' minds. In such an age, all children were expected to help with the care of the family. What the Indian children were required to do, the nuns saw as an important part of the effort to "civilize" them in preparation for insertion into a white world.

In this, the nuns' thinking reflected that of society at large. The earlier theory of "the vanishing American," the idea that the Indian was "like the seasons, meant to pass but not to return again," had proven invalid. The years had passed, but the Indian remained. Even living in isolation on the reservation had not resolved the problem. While some of the more aggressive ranchers who coveted reservation land and saw the Indian solely as an obstacle to their own aggrandizement would have favored a policy of "extinction" (a policy frequently espoused by the U.S. Army), by the last quarter of the nineteenth century, most viewed "assimilation" as the only practical solution to the "Indian question." The Committee on Indian Affairs had proclaimed: "such is their condition, at present, that they must be civilized or exterminated, no other alternative exists. ... All desire their prosperity and wish to see them brought within the pale of civilization."[18]

Such assimilation, of course, took no account of who the Indian was. Ross Toole put it well when he wrote:

> Our policy toward the Indian has been no policy at all. It has run an extraordinary gamut from extermination to impracti-cal Christian humanism, but it has always been a policy which ignored the Indian himself and his peculiar heritage.[19]

While the nuns may be exempted from the charge of "imprac-tical Christian humanism," they assuredly do incur the charge of failing to understand adequately the "peculiar heritage" of the Indian. Their narrow Christianity could not accept any ritual or symbol that fell outside the Roman Catholic dispensation. Even the Protestant missionaries—the "Short Coats," as the Indians called them—were judged as hostile forces to be opposed. No wonder that the strange asceticism of the sweat lodge, the excesses of the sun dance, the bodily laceration of funeral rituals appeared to the nuns as signs of the devil from which the children must be snatched at any cost. Even well beyond the convent ethos, there was little room in nineteenth-century America for the breadth of wisdom necessary to value a way of life that, in the white man's perspective, seemed barbarous and malign.

From Amadeus's point of view, St. Peter's was faithful to its mission, following the ordinary path of mission schools, teaching the rudiments of language, instructing in domestic tasks, Christianizing at every opportunity, and rejoicing in the apparent piety of their charges. Its success, however, was simply a goad to her zeal. Despite her poor health (she had not recovered fully from the pneumonia that had almost claimed her life), she rarely stopped working, even when forced to her bed. Firmly believing that her letters to diocesan papers would soon bear fruit, Amadeus was sure there would be more nuns, and in that faith, she began planning for her next mission.

St. Peter's Mission, botany class. Courtesy of Ursuline archives, Great Falls, Montana

Chapter Six

There are three other missions waiting for us.
—Mother Amadeus Dunne

Long before Amadeus had sent out her pleas for missionaries, she had set her sights on three new missions that the Jesuits were planning to establish. Even as she described at length to Bishop Gilmour her poor health, her "depression of mind," "the passing trials and disturbances of missionary life," and their desperate need for more sisters, she continued to set her sight on distant horizons. In January 1886, she wrote enthusiastically to the bishop:

> There are three other missions waiting for us. First: the Mission
> adjacent to St. Labre and near Fort Custer. This mission is
> among the Crows, a tribe of Indians consisting of four thousand
> souls. Father Prando, s.j., the Cheyenne missionary, pays them
> occasional visits. Soon a Jesuit house is to be built at the Crow
> Agency. Second: Holy Family Mission at Badger Creek, about
> one hundred miles north of St. Peter's and among the Piegan
> and Blood Indians, tribes belonging to the Blackfoot Nation.
> Third: St. Francis Xavier Mission at Fort Belknap.* This mission
> was opened December 8, 1885 by Rev. Father Eberschweiler, s.j.
> for the Assiniboine and Gros Ventre Indians. ... Late in autumn

---

*Although Father Eberschweiler had originally hoped to call his mission after the great Jesuit missionary Francis Xavier, his mission was eventually named St. Paul's. St. Xavier's became the mission to the Crows.

Father Eberschweiler had his rude hut and log chapel built; in spring he will build rough schools and by September he will want missionary nuns. The enclosed letter from Very Rev. Father Cataldo is an invitation for us to accept the schools of [the mission].[1]

Unlike the majority of the Jesuits serving in the Rocky Mountain Missions, Father Eberschweiler was not from the Italian province of Turin, but from Germany. Exiled by the anti-Catholic policies of the Kulturkampf, he had arrived in Buffalo, New York, in 1872. Assigned to various missions, nothing fired his energies until the enterprising Father Cataldo charged him with opening a mission for the Gros Ventres and Assiniboines in the territory near Fort Belknap in northern Montana.

Here, Eberschweiler found his mission and his home. His enthusiasm and ingenuity were at last put to full use, and he lost no time in carrying out his assignment. He was hardly there a month when he wrote back to Cataldo, "Now it seems to me that God's Providence guided my ways to this poor people which is entirely abandoned and gave me a knowledge of their great temporal and spiritual needs with an intense desire to help them."[2]

At once, he negotiated with Washington for suitable land for Indians, sufficiently distant from what he perceived as the corrupt influence of the whites at Fort Belknap. By the summer of 1887, he had four buildings under construction: a main building with a dormitory for Indian children, two smaller buildings, and a log church.

By September of that year, he was ready to receive the Ursuline nuns who had agreed to staff the school.* The two sisters chosen for the work were Martha Gahan, the first postulant from Miles City, and Francis Seibert, a member of the initial group, now an experienced missionary after three years at Miles City and St. Peter's. From her

---

*Father Eberschweiler already knew the Ursulines of Toledo, where he had once been chaplain.

first week in Miles City, she had begun to sign her letters "Montana Francis," now an apt symbol of her identity.

It was the positive results of the letter that Amadeus had sent to various dioceses across the country that made it possible to staff further missions. By 1888, six young women had arrived at St. Peter's to begin their religious training with the avowed purpose of serving in the missions for Native Americans. One was from Ireland, one from Baltimore, one from New York City, and three from Ohio. The idea of novices being trained in a small mission such as St. Peter's rather than in an established monastery was not universally approved, but Amadeus was convinced that special formation was needed for this special work.

Such vocations were an encouraging start, and on September 9, she wrote with satisfaction to Toledo:

> Today our dear missionaries leave us for the Little Rockies. Sr.
> Francis is in charge of the new mission, Ursuline Convent of
> St. Joseph. Sr. Martha goes with her and one of our Indian
> girls, a large, strong, able and willing young woman to help
> them with their work. With Sr. Francis' departure I lose my
> dearest and best companion. I hope earnestly that you will
> send someone to help her.[3]

St. Paul's Mission, sewing and laundering. Courtesy of Ursuline archives, Great Falls, Montana

A week later, Amadeus wrote again, still hoping that Toledo would send them more sisters, despite Bishop Gilmour's restriction. This time, there was a certain barb in her letter: "I enclose you the latest news that I have from Sister Francis and although your interest in the missions is diminishing, still I feel sure that many will like to hear how their poor dear Sr. Francis is facing her wild rocky camp. I hope God will send someone to help her."[4]

"The wild rocky camp" was indeed that. Father Eberschweiler had not exaggerated when he extolled the beauty of the site, but he had neglected to mention its isolation. On September 12, he met Sisters Francis and Martha at Fort Belknap as they descended from the stagecoach after a grueling four-day trip. Here, they had a night to rest, while Eberschweiler wandered through the agency, reminding the Indian parents of their promises and coercing them to let him have their children for the mission school. On the morning of September 13, he bundled children and nuns into a sturdy wagon and they set out for the last portion of their journey—some sixty-five miles from Belknap Agency to the new mission. The final leg of their journey lasted more than sixteen hours and was fraught with difficulties, among them an accident in which the buckboard had overturned on the primitive road. It was after midnight when they arrived—in total blackness. There were no friendly missionaries to welcome them. They were the first inhabitants.

It is hard to imagine how by September 15 school began with twenty bewildered Indian children. Within a month, Eberschweiler was writing concerning the needs of the mission to "Miss Catherine [*sic*] Drexel," whose name was becoming well-known for her philanthropy. Kate Drexel, a wealthy heiress from Philadelphia, had already manifested her interest in the Indian missions. In September 1887, accompanied by her two sisters and guided by Monsignor Stephan of the BCIM, she had traveled through the bleak country of the Dakotas. She was deeply moved by the poverty of the Indians and the hardships under which the missionaries lived. Always generous, she now became determined to alleviate something of the misery she had seen.* Father Eberschweiler could not have written to her at a more propitious moment:

> Today one month ago, I left Belknap with two Ursuline Nuns
> and twenty Indian children early in the morning ... The Indian
> school is established. It is a boarding school. ... The little
> chapel, so dear to you [she had already sent him a donation], is
> indeed little. It is a room 20 x 10 feet, adjoining to the school-
> room which is 25 x 20 feet and separated only by folding doors
> which at the time of the divine service are opened. The
> establishing of the human temples to the Holy Ghost is only at
> the foundation. ... I hope also to have another Father with me
> after a while so that the work for the salvation of these Indians
> will be doubled. Also another Nun will come.[5]

A month later, encouraged by a favorable response, he wrote again, asking for a "Sunday suit" with long pants for the boys. And also some clothing for the girls, ages six to thirteen, "in red and blue." The missionaries would give them to the children for Christmas. There was now a railroad station at Fort Belknap, he explained, so the donations "could be brought on the new railroad track." To give status to his request, he described the visit of one of the Assiniboine chiefs, who was "very pleased with everything in the school."

The establishment of the railroad had simplified the problem of freight and correspondence, but it did nothing to diminish the difficulty of getting a letter from the mission to the post office. At the beginning of 1888, Amadeus had written to the sisters at Youngstown, giving them the address for the new mission: St. Paul's Mission, Little Rockies, Belknap Post Office, Chinook, Montana. Then she continued: "Their nearest Post office is 65 miles distant from the Mission.

---

*Two years later, Katharine Drexel would begin her formation as a religious with the Sisters of Mercy in Pittsburgh. In 1891, she founded the Sisters of the Blessed Sacrament for Indians and Colored People. She was canonized in 2000.

Imagine how you would feel if you had to travel 130 miles to post a letter. In stormy weather, it takes a week to get from St. Paul's Mission to Belknap and there are no human habitations along these 65 miles. None dwell there but mountain lions, wolves and the lynx."[6]

Even so, Francis continued her habit of writing detailed letters to Toledo. In February 1888, just five months after their arrival, she wrote to her good friend Sister Assumption:

> I am writing at one end of the table in the children's refectory
> and a big Indian Chief is taking his breakfast at the other; he
> came from Belknap three days ago. He, Running Fisher, is the
> Chief of Police there and came to bring the good news from
> Washington, through the Agent, that the Indians are to be
> removed from Belknap to the reservation. We have no
> particulars yet. I have his son, Rattle-snake-bush—his name
> before his baptism, now it is Ignatius. He is a very promising
> lad. He never saw a letter before he came and now he reads
> well in the first reader. ... We have Benediction every Sunday
> and First Friday. When I close my eyes and hear Father

St. Paul's Mission, schools and convent, circa 1910. Courtesy of Ursuline archives, Great Falls, Montana

Eberschweiler singing at the altar I am carried back to times
gone by but as soon as I see the poor humble chapel I know
that I am in Montana among the Indians where the walls are
frescoed with mud. Do not worry about me. I have made up
my mind to be contented anywhere. It is very strange, I never
get lonesome—too busy for that.[7]

"Too busy" was certainly an inadequate description of their
days. As in most of the mission schools, classroom subjects (reading,
writing, arithmetic, catechism) were taught in the morning. In the
afternoon, the children were engaged in learning practical skills.
That the one log cabin housed the boarding school and the convent
did not make their lives easier.

The burden of teaching fell upon Francis, while Martha coped
with everything else. To Eberschweiler's credit, he acknowledged the
difficulties of such an arrangement, writing to Katharine Drexel of his
hopes to improve conditions for "the poor sisters" who should have "a
house of their own and a beautiful institution for the girls."
Eberschweiler's background had given him a great love and belief in
the value of a "beautiful environment." "It is of great importance," he
continued, "that the place be improved in every respect, that buildings, church and convent of the nuns be very inspiring and attractive
to the Indians." His ideals were lofty and must sometimes have seemed
unreal to the two sisters immersed in the hard labor of daily living.[8]

The following July, the mission prepared for the first visit of
Bishop Brondel. It could not have come at a more difficult time.
Measles were endemic that summer—one child had already died at
St. Peter's—and Francis wrote to Sister Assumption: "The children
came down with measles before his arrival and had to be put in the
two good rooms which had been reserved for the bishop. He was
much fatigued after a sixty-five mile trip in the prairie with the burning sun and no shade all the way." Even so, it was a joyous event.
They had a pontifical High Mass, the house was blessed, and ten children were confirmed. The moment of glory came when the Indian

children sang the "Laudate" in Latin, surely a triumph to both the missionaries and Indians.[9]

With help from Katharine Drexel, Eberschweiler began that summer to construct additional buildings: "We are having a new schoolroom and refectory for the boys, a larger kitchen and pantry and a clothes and storeroom," Francis wrote.

By October 1, Sister Santa Clara from St. Peter's had joined them to assist with their forty-nine children. By the beginning of 1889, the mission had grown to fifty-two children and five nuns and—most wonderful to Eberschweiler's musical soul—Katharine Drexel had provided them with an organ. "The organ with its showy case and one full series of reeds with a sweet tone is a pleasure to all," he wrote to her gratefully in his somewhat awkward English. "I venture to invite you to come and see St. Paul's mission. Our Ursulines would gladly do their best to receive you as well as we can," he assured her.[10]

Despite its isolation, St. Paul's Mission was remarkably successful. A new road had been built that shortened the distance from the railroad and made access for freight and correspondence less difficult. The Indians had begun to move from Fort Belknap as Eberschweiler had demanded and so the school had expanded dramatically.

In the summer of 1889, Leopold Van Gorp, S.J., visited the missions of St. Peter's and St. Paul's. Van Gorp, an erect, reserved man whom the Indians called "Tall-Man," was a practical administrator, and in a letter to Father Cataldo, he assessed in detail what he found at St. Paul's.

> I was agreeably surprised, to find the school doing so well, as well as regards the number of pupils, viz. 102, of whom there are 62 boys, the balance are girls. … Their ages range mostly from 6 to 12; a few from 12 to 14. This, no doubt, makes it easier to manage them. … The children are very well behaved, docile, and doing very well in their school exercises and also in their manual work. There is less trouble in the management of this school than of any of our schools that I have seen.[11]

While Van Gorp made no mention of the sisters, it was they, of course, who were largely responsible for the success of the school. Both Eberschweiler and the Jesuit brother who worked with him had other concerns, leaving the Ursulines to supervise the lives of the children.

Along with their classroom duties, the nuns were responsible for providing food for 100 children daily, as well as meals for the hired men (eight in number) whom Eberschweiler had engaged to work on the new buildings. But Eberschweiler, although a hard taskmaster, was also a compassionate superior, deeply concerned that the austerities of the nuns' lives be alleviated in whatever way possible. He was determined that they would have a house of their own, which would afford them some privacy from their boisterous charges. In this vein, he petitioned the government to grant the Ursulines 160 acres of adjacent land, which would provide necessary distance from the Indian camps that were being set up in the area. The affirmation of this request was happily received in October 1889.

By the beginning of 1890, Eberschweiler, while far from satisfied, could take satisfaction in all he had accomplished in a little more than two years. Although he had a debt of some $2,000, he could count on the continued financial help of Katharine Drexel and the assistance of Monsignor Stephan at the BCIM. He longed for more sisters and did what he could to gain the sympathetic ear of Mother Amadeus at St. Peter's. His most urgent need, however, was for another Jesuit, so that he would be freed to travel among the Indian camps to evangelize the adults. That, he felt sure, would come. Meanwhile, he would follow Father Cataldo's leadership in making education the primary concern of the missions.

Only two weeks after Sisters Francis and Martha arrived at St. Paul's to begin their school for the Gros Ventres and Assiniboines, three Ursulines arrived at St. Francis Xavier's Mission in southeastern Montana to begin a school for the Crow Indians under the direction of Fathers Peter Prando and Peter Bandini (brother of Joseph, then stationed at St. Peter's). With Gilmour's permission, Amadeus had promised Father Cataldo a year earlier that the Ursulines would assist in the projected mission at St. Xavier's.

Like most tribes, betrayed from the beginning by broken treaties, the Crow had been coerced into ceding much of their dearly loved ancestral land. This, along with the needless slaughter of the buffalo, had destroyed their way of life. Their wise chief Plenty Coups looked at his people and wept: "When the buffalo went away the hearts of my people fell to the ground. They could not lift them up again. After this, nothing happened. There was little singing anywhere."[12]

But the Crow were resilient people and knew the advantage of compromise. Unlike the Sioux and the Northern Cheyenne, their mortal enemies, they learned to adjust to the demands of the whites, and, as a result, were accorded a vast reservation. Father Aloysius Vrebosch, writing after fifteen years of missionary labor, admitted that, initially, he had found their customs barbarous and degrading and the people far from compliant to the new religion that he preached. Yet he praised the men as "a perfect type of manhood, tall and well-proportioned," and acknowledged that they

St. Xavier's Mission school. Courtesy of Montana Historical Society, Helena, Montana

were an intelligent people, deeply devoted to their children and more industrious than many Indian tribes.

The initial hurdles for establishing their mission included gaining approval of the Indians as well as permission of the agent. Unlike his debacle with the agent at St. Peter's, Prando was now pleased and surprised by the welcome of Agent M. L. Blake. Unlike many situations where the agent was in opposition to the missionaries, this time, the missionaries were fortunate in having someone willing to act in their favor. "What I can do for your Order and the Church will be done with the greatest pleasure and I will always be ready to serve you," Blake concluded in a letter to Father Cataldo.[13]

Encouraged by the necessary permissions and the good will of the Crow, in January 1887, Fathers Prando and Bandini began the trek south from St. Ignatius's Mission. It was hardly a favorable time for travel, and at every juncture, they encountered blizzard conditions. By the end of January, they arrived at Custer Station, but it was almost a month later before they were able to start for the site—some sixty miles distant—chosen for St. Xavier's Mission.

For weeks, they lived in two tents, until at the first signs of spring, they began to fence in the 160 acres allotted to them by the government, and by May, construction for a school and a church had begun. By June, Father Bandini was able to write to Mother Amadeus, informing her that things were now in place for the Ursulines to begin their school.

> In a month or so a frame building will be finished and I would be very glad if it will be at your disposition. We need to have a school principally for the girls to stop their market. These poor creatures at an early age of 13 or 14 are sold continually for a little piece of calico or a little sugar, to the white man.[14]

Amadeus responded at once, choosing three sisters to be sent as the "founders" of a school for the Crow. It was the success of the novitiate at St. Peter's that enabled her to do so. "Our novitiate is doing well," she wrote to Gilmour, "and we hope soon to have our missions sustained by Montana [trained] Ursulines. We have many good applicants to the novitiate. Four of our novices were professed May 8th; they made a vow as did the first Ursulines of Québec to devote their lives to the Indian missions."

Later in the same letter, she continued:

The proudest day I have had in Montana was when I saw these young courageous missionaries, the first fruits of St. Peter's mission, bidding adieu to the cradle of their religious life and hastening with joyful hearts to execute the vow of love their lips had so lately sealed. ... It was a glorious sight to see the Jesuit Father and Scholastics, nuns and novices, Indian boys and girls cheering them on as they sped across the mountain path on their way to Helena in our humble team— a lumber wagon drawn by four cayuses.[15]

St. Xavier's Mission, Ursulines on horseback. Courtesy of Ursuline archives, Toledo, Ohio

It is an extraordinary image that could only have been shaped by a combination of nineteenth-century piety, fervor, and rhetoric.

On the last day of September, four Ursulines arrived at the Custer Agency, having traveled the last twenty miles by stagecoach from Custer Station. In charge of the group was, of course, Mother Amadeus. With her was Sister Magdalen Cox, who had arrived in Miles City from Toledo in the spring of 1886; Sister Joseph Steiner, who had come from Cleveland in October 1884; and Sister Rose Miller, who had arrived from Toledo in March 1885. They could hardly have arrived at a more dramatic moment.

Early that spring, a Crow with the extraordinary name of Man-Who-Rides-A-Horse-With-His-Tail-Wrapped-Up had returned from a visit to the Sioux. While there, he had experienced a vision, a powerful dream for the future. Brandishing a "magic" sword, he proclaimed himself to be not only a chief, but the very son of god, endowed not only with the ability to restore his tribesman to their former glory, but to annihilate the white man everywhere.[16]

It was a radical message, unanticipated by the government, which had been led to believe that the Crow were peaceful and happy on their reservation, adjusting better than most nations to the new order. In the summer of 1887, Henry Williamson, the Crow agent, reported that progress was being made and that he anticipated that the Crow would soon be weaned from their savage ways and become successful farmers.

Clearly, Williamson missed the restlessness of the young braves and the anger provoked by the General Allotment Act passed in February 1887, which terminated tribal lands in favor of distribution to individual families. The provisions of the act ran counter to everything in Indian culture and made no sense to the people whom it alleged it was trying to help. The final provision, that "surplus lands" would be open for white occupation, was the final straw.

The radical message of Cheez-tah-paezh, as Sword Bearer was known in his own language, while not universally accepted, was a welcome call to the young men who were restive under the restrictions of reservation life. To the more skeptical Indians, doubtful of the claims of this new messiah, Cheez-tah-paezh provided proof of his powers. While the Indians were camped out at Soap-Creek, they were overtaken by a furious storm. Sword Bearer stood amid the thunder, lightning, and hail and announced that he was master of the universe. He had caused the storm, he asserted, and when he wished, he would stop it. It was an impressive claim, and one easy to corroborate. When the storm abated, he raised his arms and proved his point. Who could gainsay him?

"All the Crow were struck with terror, just like frogs," wrote Father Prando, who watched the drama with anxiety for the future of the mission.[17]

Even with such displays, many of the Crow remained cautious. The wise men, Chief Pretty Eagle and Plenty Coups among them, knew that war was the inevitable outcome of Sword Bearer's claims, and they did not want war. They were experienced enough to realize that they were no match against the army troops, which were already massing at the agency. But their influence was not enough to stem the young braves.

Throughout the summer, the visionary gained power, and by fall, Man-Who-Rides-A-Horse-With-His-Tail-Wrapped-Up was increasingly accepted as the messiah. His "magic" sword, he proclaimed, had made him invincible. The white man's guns could not touch him. He could not be wounded; he could not be killed.

In mid-September, to flaunt his power and his disdain of the white man's regulations, he led a group of young Crow on a horse raid into the Blackfeet reservation in northern Montana. They returned jubilant, and on the evening of September 30, they rode into the agency proclaiming their triumph. Taunting Williamson, who had threatened to arrest them, the young braves in full war paint and feathers circled the agency, shooting their rifles into the air—or, in some cases, into the agency buildings. At this moment, as though planned for maximum drama, the coach with four Ursulines arrived, accompanied by Father Bandini, who had met their train at Custer Station.

The Crow may well have been more startled than the nuns, who had been warned ahead of time of the Indian trouble. Enveloped in an atmosphere of magic, the Crow warriors watched from their horses while four silent figures descended from the stagecoach. Gowned in black from head to foot, except for a circle of white enveloping their faces, the nuns certainly qualified as part of the mysterious world that awed the Indians. For a moment, hostilities stopped as the nuns were escorted into the agency building. But with dark, the shooting began again. "Such," wrote Father Prando later, "was the welcome and serenade the sisters had on their arrival."[18]

The following morning, despite protests for their safety, the sisters left the agency, beginning the twenty-two-mile trip to St. Xavier's Mission. The Indians, watching the preparations for their departure, ceased their hostilities while the Crow chiefs shook hands with the Lady Blackrobes and wished them well, ordering a group of Indians to ride with them and provide safe escort along the way.

It was a temporary cessation, however. Soon after the nuns' departure, Sword Bearer resumed his battle. During October, his influence grew, and fear increased at the agency that both the Gros Ventres and Northern Cheyenne were being drawn into the movement. By this time, army troops had been moved into the agency, while the Indians massed by the hundreds on the surrounding hillsides. At the ensuing battle, Sword Bearer's claim to divinity was proved false when a soldier's bullet struck his arm and blood poured forth as from any human wound.

For those who had believed in him, it was a profound disillusionment. Their messiah had played them false. Their dream of reclaiming their world had betrayed them. For those who had feared him and were threatened by his vision, there was relief. As for Sword Bearer—Man-Who-Rides-A-Horse-With-His-Tail-Wrapped-Up—he may well have come to believe his own rhetoric. Faced with defeat, he tried to flee from the people he had failed, but an angry Indian encountering him by chance shot him to death.

By the time of Sword Bearer's death in the first week of November, the nuns at St. Xavier's had already opened a school. Although aware of the threat of a massive Indian war, they gave little attention to their danger, using their energies to getting the school started. Although at first, fear of the impending battle kept most of the children at home, by Christmas 1887, there were fifty children in attendance.

Amadeus had already left them by the middle of October, not waiting for the outcome of the Sword Bearer affair, but not before she had drawn up a contract with Father Bandini outlining the duties and privileges of the three Ursulines. She had doubtless learned from her experience at St. Peter's that it was essential to agree from the beginning on the organization of the mission before difficulties arose. "The Contract," as she referred to it, was specific and practical, consisting of ten articles:

1. The Reverend Jesuit Fathers will be the Nuns' directors.
2. The Mission School House will belong to the Nuns, for which they will pay (in quarterly payments) $400 per annum until paid for. The House will be given to the Nuns at cost.
3. The Nuns will board the Jesuit household (Fathers and Brothers); do their washing and mending as long as desired free of charge.
4. The Fathers reserve to themselves the right of the free use of the Chapel.
5. The Fathers will as soon as they can free the Nuns from taking charge of the boys.
6. Until the separation of the boys from the girls the Fathers promise to provide a Prefect to take care of the boys in the dormitory and during recreation hours, and the Nuns will board this Prefect and pay him ten dollars per month. If this Prefect be a Jesuit Scholastic the Nuns will not be obliged to pay.

7. The Nuns will board two working men free of charge
   and in compensation these men will furnish all
   necessary fuel and do the Nuns garden work and
   freighting to and from Custer Station when desired.
   The nuns will receive $15.00 per month for each of the
   other men that may be obliged for the present to
   board.
8. The Nuns will do the sacristy work and washing gratis.
9. The Nuns will not be required to do the men's washing
   or mending.
10. Sister Mary Amadeus will get five Ursulines for the
    Crow Mission and one of these will be a music teacher
    (not obliged to be of first class) and until she furnishes
    these five Nuns she will pay the wages of a hired
    laundress.[19]

The priests were too gratified at the presence of the Ursulines
to demur at the terms of the contract. Prando was delighted by the

St. Xavier's Mission, Bishop Brondel and Jesuit fathers and boys. Courtesy of
Ursuline archives, Toledo, Ohio

immediate success of St. Xavier's. In less than three years, he was able to boast of a school, a church, a residence for the priests, a bake house, and an icehouse, along with the registration of well over 100 children.

Despite this glowing report, the sisters continued to shoulder more than their share of hardships. "The sisters have no dining room," the annalist noted. "They eat in the store room." Even more difficult was the fact that when the mission was swept by a wave of "contagious disease," the lack of space made it impossible to isolate the infected children, thus increasing the difficulties of nursing.

Although by 1890 there were five Ursulines at St. Xavier's, only two were free to teach; the other three were fully engaged in sewing, cooking, nursing, and the insatiable demands of the laundry. St. Xavier's was the fourth mission school the Ursulines had agreed to staff. Mission life was undoubtedly far from what Amadeus had in mind when she first enthusiastically accepted the Jesuit proposal to staff a mission school. The work of education, she was discovering, extended far beyond the classroom, into the unremitting drudgery essential in sustaining a mission.

Chapter Seven

I beg of you to hasten to my aid.

—*Mother Amadeus Dunne*

When Mother Amadeus left St. Xavier's Mission in October 1887, she traveled east to visit the St. Labre's Mission. St. Labre's continued to be the "runt of the litter." Even Amadeus, with her visionary optimism, admitted that St. Labre's was a difficult mission. In a letter to the Toledo community that fall, she acknowledged, "St. Labre's has many advantages and many great disadvantages but it holds its head erect although it is almost overwhelmed by gravest difficulties. All the Montana Ursulines have very special sympathies for St. Labre's because it was the loadstone that attracted us hither."[1]

Despite the sisters' relentless work, St. Labre's did not thrive. Most experienced missionaries agreed that no tribe was more difficult to work with than the Cheyenne. The cause was not hard to find: no tribe had

St. Labre's Mission, nuns and children. Courtesy of Ursuline archives, Great Falls, Montana

suffered more betrayal and humiliation. No promise ever made to them had been kept. Even now, although their present reservation had been finalized by executive order, efforts continued to have the Cheyenne moved to less-valuable land. The following year, Father Bandini wrote to Monsignor Stephan in Washington that he had learned that the son of President William Henry Harrison had a vested interest in Montana cattle and was exerting all his influence to alienate some of the reservation land in order to give it to his cattlemen friends.[2]

Such rumors kept the Indians on edge and made them quick to resist the pleas of the missionaries to send their children to school. What could they trust in a white man's school? Those who did come expected to be fed, and the nuns had few resources they could count on. Their efforts at farming were unsuccessful, and consequently, they had to purchase all their supplies—an impossible expense. Although St. Labre's had been accepted as a contract school, the government funds were often late or were categorically denied because of discrepancies in the detailed accounts that the Indian office demanded. With Indian children, attendance was at best random, making it impossible for the nuns to provide the meticulous accounts the Indian office demanded.

In January 1888, Sister Ignatius wrote to Bishop Gilmour, apologizing for not having written more often and explaining that she had little favorable news concerning the mission. Although they now had a Jesuit chaplain, Father Aloysius Van der Velden had many responsibilities, she explained, and could only be at the mission sporadically.

> As a result, our poor Indians have made but little advance in
> the knowledge of God, hence we have been working against
> the current. I must admit we have been discouraged but never
> so far as to give up. No, My Lord, we love the Indians and by
> the grace of God we are resolved to live and to die amongst
> them. We see, as yet, no result to our labors, we are simply
> holding the fort for our successors, and with God's help, will
> die in the struggle if need be rather than surrender.[3]

Van der Velden himself seemed less discouraged, noting that the attendance at the Christmas services was good—despite the fact that the Indians arrived several hours late. They also now had a small log chapel where he offered Mass each Sunday, and ten children were preparing for their First Communion. All were hopeful signs, but even so, Father Van der Velden admitted that, "A trifle is sufficient to overturn all and turn them in the wrong direction."[4]

While Sister Ignatius was also encouraged by the renewed interest of the Indians, the material concerns of the mission filled her with anxiety. In January of that year, she had written desperately to Monsignor Stephan that they still had not received funds for the last quarter and as a result were unable to feed their children properly. As a consequence, many of them had returned to their homes. The fact that their building (used for both school and dormitory) was far from adequate posed another obstacle. Having been advised that Miss Katharine Drexel was often a generous source of help, Ignatius wrote to her, explaining their plight and asking for funds to build a substantial schoolhouse.

The letter she received in return from Monsignor Stephan, who channeled Katharine Drexel's money through the BCIM, began on a discouraging note:

St. Labre's Mission, Indian encampment. Courtesy of Ursuline archives, Great Falls, Montana

The idea you appear to have that Miss Drexel will assist in the
building of large, costly school-houses is an erroneous one,
and those who have thus informed you speak only their own
opinion. She is willing to help, as far as she can, all the Indian
Missions. ... She has, it is true, given to a few Indian Missions
considerable sums for building purposes, but as the money
has not always been judiciously applied and has resulted in a
demand for more money, she has naturally become more
careful. ...

But this bleak paragraph was more than offset by the final sentence: "It affords me much pleasure to announce the good news: a
gift of $5,000."[5]

The gift, however, could not be immediately put to use. The
Indians were increasingly restive. Children came and went sporadically, and the number actually attending school fell to twenty—the
lowest they had ever had.

In April, when Father Cataldo came to make his visitation, he
was openly disappointed by the state of the mission. With Jesuits so
badly needed in other more flourishing missions, it was clear that he
thought St. Labre's should be closed. "These Indians are not yet ripe
to receive the faith and it can take still a long while before they will
be," he announced.[6]

When, soon after, Bishop Brondel visited St. Labre's, he
affirmed Cataldo's judgment. He found the Indians "ill-disposed."
After long and unproductive talks with the chiefs, he advised closing
the school during the months of May and June. While no immediate
action was taken, Van der Velden was recalled in July and the nuns
were left once again without a priest. In October, the school was
"temporarily suspended" for three months, and on October 10,
Ignatius wrote to Stephan: "We dismissed our few children this
morning and I assure you, Reverend Father, it was a most painful
task. We will take our departure to St. Peter's Mission, the
Motherhouse of the Ursulines in Montana."[7]

Some months earlier, the superior of the Toledo community had written to Ignatius: "Everyone here sympathizes with you without knowing the real cause of your sufferings. We think of you daily and the most frequent exclamation is, 'Poor Ignatius, I wish she would come home.' Yes, darling Sister, you have warm friends with loving hearts and open arms to welcome your return. God is here as well as there."[8] Although this avowal of affection must have been a strong enticement, Ignatius held on, working with her two sisters to close the house and starting the long trip to St. Peter's just as winter was setting in.

When Amadeus returned to St. Peter's in November 1887, it was to a mission teeming with activity. Their second mission had fast outgrown its original buildings. Her efforts to attract vocations had met with remarkable success. By the beginning of 1888, the novitiate could boast of seven novices, several postulants—and a waiting list! The school consisted of thirty Indian girls and twenty white girls— housed separately. It was clear that the three small log cabins given by the Jesuits and the shacks they had constructed for the laundry and kitchen were no longer adequate.

Encouraged to contact Miss Katharine Drexel, Amadeus wrote to her at length at the beginning of January. The letter was long, detailed, and cogently argued. "We are seventy in number," she wrote, "crowded into our lowly log cabin convent. ... We have no lodging of our own; the old cabins belong to our Jesuit Fathers who allow us to use them till we can get a school and convent built. ... We want to build a convent for the missionary nuns, a Novitiate, an Indian School and a school for poor white children." Their resources were meager, she explained; they had nothing beyond the government allotment of $9 per month for each Indian child. "And with this we must furnish board, clothing, bedding, books, furniture, medicines, fuel and light." Their white boarders were charged $10 per month, a sum, however small, that they were not always able to pay.

At present, the sisters had on hand $4,000 to start the new building. With this amount, they had already begun to erect the basement walls. They planned a building 116 feet long, 67 feet wide, and two-and-a-half stories high. "We want to recommence building this spring but we have no money to proceed. To get the building under roof and to finish it in the rough ... will cost $10,000 ... to complete the building it will take $5,000 more." Amadeus made no apologies for requesting so large a sum, asserting that there was no group working among the Indians more deserving than the Ursulines.

> When you help us you help many Indian missions because
> what good you do to us soon reaches them. As soon as the
> novices are professed, they are sent out to help our overbur-
> dened Sisters in other Missions or they go forth with elder
> Nuns to open new Mission Schools. ... We are the only nuns
> that make a vow to devote our lives to the care of Indian
> children. We are allowed this privilege as were the first
> Ursulines of Québec in 1639.[9]

Amadeus's claims were impressive, and the following March, she received word through Bishop Brondel that she would receive $5,000 toward their new building and could expect within the next few months a smaller check for their novitiate.

That summer, Father Eberschweiler traveled from St. Paul's to visit the Ursulines at St. Peter's and wrote enthusiastically to Miss Katharine Drexel: "To my greatest joy I heard of your donation of $5,000. ... Although the superioress is strengthened in her generous undertaking for the elevation of the female portion of the Indians out of their awful present misery in this country, she is nevertheless greatly troubled by money difficulties. ... Oh, help her!"[10]

Amadeus, however, waited for no further help, but immediately put to work the money on hand. The following September, the cornerstone was laid for "St. Peter's Boarding School for Girls." The *Great Falls Daily Tribune* sent a reporter to cover the event, which was attended by neighbors and visitors. Ninety children walked in the impressive procession with Father Damiani,

S.J., presiding over the ceremony. "BUILDING A GIRLS SCHOOL AMID THE MOUNTAINS WILD" declaimed the *Tribune*'s headline on September 15.[11]

Following the spring thaw, the work continued, but Amadeus was already in serious financial difficulty. That May, she wrote a ten-page letter to Monsignor Stephan outlining her problems in detail. The building that she had anticipated would cost about $20,000 was now assessed at $40,000. If Monsignor Stephan found this new sum exorbitant, she could point out the quality of the building, its size, and the use to which it would be put—the education of the poorest and neediest—an exaggeration, surely, since the most elaborate part of the building would be used by white children.

In fact, her financial problem was far more serious than she was willing to acknowledge. It was not simply that she needed money to continue the building, but that she had already plunged into debt by ordering all the necessary materials and engaging the workmen without any means of remuneration. In addition, she had used for the Indian school the monies raised by the white settlers for a school specifically for their children. It was the first of a series of financial indiscretions that would continue throughout her life. It would antagonize the tradesmen she dealt with, tarnish her reputation, and infuriate Bishop Brondel, who, in some way, felt responsible for her actions. For Amadeus, however, it was never a question of integrity—she intended nothing deceitful. It was simply that the needs she saw were so immediate, so desperate, that she felt they must be assuaged at any cost. That others did not share her vision was something she never quite accepted.

"My most urgent needs," her letter to Monsignor Stephan concluded, "are to get $15,000 to put a roof on, to get cornice and gutter on so as to have the stone walls protected from the rain and then to have $2,000 more to pay persons that are impatient for their money. I beg of you, dear Reverend Father, to hasten to my aid by getting the present debt paid off and by getting Miss Katharine Drexel to complete the building and pay the entire cost."[12]

Amadeus's aspirations were far beyond her means, however, and when, some time later, Father Van Gorp visited St. Peter's, he was shocked by what seemed to him gross mismanagement. In a letter to Miss Katharine Drexel, he wrote, "The new building has not been carried on very judiciously. Many mistakes in the way of building, too many extras; the inside and also some of the outside finish is too extravagant and expensive a character for an Indian country and the present requirements. The consequence of all this [is] they are buried in debts."[13]

Meanwhile, however, despite her anxieties, Amadeus continued the work, and in July, a reporter from the *Great Falls Daily Tribune* again visited St. Peter's. "A better location for a seat of learning could not be found than this," he wrote. "Surrounded by mountains, the scenery is fine, elevated about 500 feet above the sea; the air is light, pure and bracing and the climate exceptionally healthy ... within easy reach of the railroad at Cascade."[14]

Amadeus could hardly have wished for a more glowing endorsement. Fired with enthusiasm, she described in detail her plans for the finished school: gray sandstone, in plain Gothic style; kitchen, dining rooms, storage, and furnace in the basement; classrooms, music rooms, reception room, fine art, and chapel on the first floor; dormitory, bathrooms, infirmary, and rooms for the sisters on the third floor. It would be heated with six large furnaces, and furnished with hot and cold water.

To the homesteaders in central Montana, the building must have sounded palatial. Small wonder that it would cost $40,000.

With characteristic optimism, Amadeus assured the reporter that the school would be ready the following fall. In fact, the new school did not open its doors until 1891, two years later.* By that time, Amadeus had assumed the responsibility of two additional missions: St. Ignatius's and Holy Family.

---

*There are no conclusive records indicating where or when the necessary monies came from.

Since early fall of 1889, Father Cataldo had been pleading to have the Ursulines come to St. Ignatius's Mission to open a kindergarten for the Indian children. At first, Amadeus had refused unequivocally: she could spare no nuns for another mission. As late as January of the following year, she had written to the community at Toledo that despite the insistent entreaties of the Jesuits, she had been firm in her refusal. Yet ultimately, the lure became too seductive. Although she recognized the risk in spreading her limited resources further, when she assessed what they had already accomplished, it seemed to her that every venture had been blessed a hundredfold.

At St. Xavier, things were moving well under the experienced and zealous leadership of Fathers Prando and Bandini. The affection of the Crow for Father Prando was such that the school was already flourishing and they would soon need a larger building. Shortly after the arrival of the Ursulines, Father Bandini had written at length to Katharine Drexel explaining the nature of their work and begging for assistance to meet their debt. Before the month was out, he learned that he would receive $500. "Scarcely I could believe to my eyes," he wrote to Katharine Drexel in gratitude. "I communicated to the sisters and we went in the chapel to thank God and to pray for you."[15]

Success made Bandini bold, and before long, another letter went to Katharine Drexel, this time requesting an organ. Bandini's letters seemed to have a golden touch—several months later, an organ arrived, having safely made its long and perilous journey. Ecstatic, Bandini wrote at length:

> It is a great instrument for the glory of God and for the
> conversion of the Crows—the Crows want music and with
> music they learn the prayers and with music are attracted to
> us. They have a great passion for it. They make of split wood a
> kind of flute and they blow all the day. ... My intention of
> starting a boys' band it is not only for the Crows generally but
> for the school especially. I would like to attract the attention

of all the country and their children to our school with
something they like above any other thing.[16]

Toward the beginning of 1888, Bandini had written to
Monsignor Stephan giving him an account of the mission. They had
room for seventy-five children, but were expecting eighty to 100 as
soon as the spring weather started. He wanted to begin growing
sheep, since this was good country for that, but so far, he had only
four horses and two cows, for which he was still in debt. Although
there were now five Ursulines working in the school, he still had to
employ several people for teaching. All this was a great expense, and
he was hoping for two Jesuit brothers to come soon.

Although the Ursulines shared Bandini's enthusiasm over the
growth of the mission, the work it engendered made them desperate
for help. In the beginning of 1888, Magdalen Cox wrote to Bishop
Gilmour, giving him details of the mission and confessing that she
did not see how the nuns could continue unless sisters were sent to
help them.

> I do not tell you this to complain of the crosses and sufferings
> of the Indian Mission life; but I feel I am speaking to a kind
> father who would willingly give us help if it were possible ... I
> am writing this at twelve o'clock [midnight] and at four
> o'clock tomorrow morning must find me ready to make the
> fires through the building, then dress the children—the
> youngest of whom is only two years of age—and through the
> day to work and teach these dear little ones. While I am
> writing this Sister St. Rose is busy baking bread, for the day is
> not long enough to do all that is needed for as large a family
> and our work must be prolonged into the night.[17]

It was the response and the development of the children that
gave them the courage to continue. "The Crow children are really
bright," Magdalen wrote in a memoir discovered after her death.

"They show ability and talent in learning to read and write. They succeed in arithmetic, music and anything they are set to study."[18]

To provide proof of how much they had learned in less than two years, she had the girls write a Christmas letter to Monsignor Stephan.

> We are trying to be good and learn all we can. Thirteen of us
> have made our first communion and we have been confirmed;
> soon we shall be children of Mary. We all wish you a Merry
> Christmas and a Happy New Year.[19]

The letter was signed with thirteen signatures, all with Western names—unfortunate evidence that Father Bandini's rule that only English was to be used in the school was rigorously enforced.

To those working at St. Xavier's, all the signs were positive. Debt was accepted as a fact of missionary experience. Government subsidies, though often perilously late in arriving, generally came through. What mattered most was the work that was being done, and for now, the success of that work was sufficient to buoy their spirits.

St. Paul's, the mission that had been started at approximately the same time as St. Xavier's, was enjoying a similar experience. Much to Eberschweiler's musical delight, they, too, had an organ through the inexhaustible generosity of the revered Miss Katharine Drexel.

By the summer of 1889, the mission expanded further. Eberschweiler announced that they might expect as many as 150 children in the fall. With that in view, he had received permission to begin building "big beautiful stone buildings" and also to advertise for a prefect to work with the increased number of boys. His description of what would be expected of such a prefect would have daunted any but the most sacrificial:

> This should be a gentleman, a good practical Catholic, able to
> keep boys in order and teach them the elementary school
> branches. ... Out of school time he has to be day and night
> with the boys, keeping them in order and working with them

or playing with them ... all according to the order of the day. He would have a room, i.e. a cell, in the boys' dormitory, get his board and $40 per month.[20]

The three Ursulines (Francis Seibert, Martha Gahan, and Santa Clara Henry), while admittedly overworked, took pleasure in the success of the mission and were given courage by the admiration of Bishop Brondel and the approval of the Assiniboine chiefs. In addition, the fact that the government had approved their petition for 160 acres of land gave them a feeling of stability.

Of the three missions in which the Ursulines participated, only St. Labre's continued to be a source of concern. How deeply Amadeus was moved by the failure of this first mission is clear in a letter from Bishop Gilmour in reply to her in the winter of 1889:

> You and your work are neither unnoticed nor unvalued. Labre
> has for the moment failed. It will not be always so. Your other
> places grow and hold and in time will be blessed with abundant
> fruit; seed well sown is never lost. ... Your trials are all seen and
> noted and the God that cares for the sparrow will see that his
> workers are not forgotten. So fear not nor be discouraged.[21]

She was further cheered when, after a five-month suspension, the nuns were able to return to St. Labre's in March 1889, with Father Van der Velden firmly in charge. In late February, he wrote confidently to Monsignor Stephan:

> The school will be started again on the first of March and it
> seems with more success. The Indians got a good lesson by
> taking off the sisters. They see all right enough they must not
> fool too much with their children or otherwise all will be lost.
> They promised 40 to 50 children—little ones. I hope they
> keep their word.[22]

By the end of March, they had registered forty-six children and Van der Velden was negotiating to erect a school for the boys that he hoped would be finished by September.

But such planning was always tenuous. Once again, the whites were agitating to have the Indians moved, thus making the land available to white homesteaders. The strongest voice against such injustice came from General Nelson Miles of Fort Keogh, who had worked peaceably with the Cheyenne since 1877. In protest, he wrote to the agent of the Tongue River Agency, decrying this manifest injustice:

> Referring to your letter of May 15 in regard to the proposed
> removal of the Indians, I would say that, in my judgment,
> there is no good reason or justice in doing so. ... There is no
> reason why Indians cannot be well treated and allowed to live
> in peace in the vicinity in which they were born.[23]

His intervention saved the reservation—at least for a time— enabling St. Labre's to continue for another indefinite period.

No doubt it was the successful development of these other missions that led Amadeus to concede to the Jesuits' request to participate in St. Ignatius's. Her spirituality endorsed the theory that God's providence could never be tested too far, and on March 17, two Jesuits, Father Cataldo, and Father Leopold Van Gorp, arrived at St. Peter's to accompany the chosen missionaries to St. Ignatius's. The superior of the new school was to be Sister Perpetua Egan, who had joined the Ursulines in St. Louis in 1882 and come to Montana six years later. Young as she was, she was the senior of the group, since the others (Santa Clara Henry, Martha Gahan, and Marguerite Langeois) had been sisters for less than two years.* One other

---

*Sisters Santa Clara Henry and Martha Gahan had both come as novices to St. Peter's. Sister Marguerite Langeois had entered in Tiffin, Ohio, but made her novitiate at St. Peter's. Throughout Ursuline records, there is confusion about the name "Langeois," which is sometimes listed as "Longways."

Ursuline was in the group, Mary Rose Galvin, a promising young novice who was Amadeus's "secretary" and companion.

On the morning of March 18, they set out in a springboard wagon to travel the fourteen miles to the nearest railroad station, at the town of Cascade. There were fourteen all told: six Ursulines, two Jesuits, two Indian girls who would help on the mission, and a number of men to drive the wagon and help with the luggage. The stretches of prairie around St. Peter's were always windy, but on this morning, the winds were of almost hurricane proportions. The nuns tried to wrap their mantles around their faces to save themselves from the force of the gale, but, despite their efforts, Sister Perpetua's shawl blew away entirely, entangling itself in the wheel of the wagon.

Cascade, with the arrival of the Great Northern, was becoming a thriving little town, and the nuns, shepherded by Father Cataldo, had lunch in the recently established Riverside Hotel while they waited for the train that would take them to Helena. Amadeus pronounced the meal "scanty" and the dessert (a sort of custard pie) "queer," but the others had no trouble with their lunch.

The trip to Helena took only two hours, and it was still daylight when they arrived at Montana's capital city. That night they spent with the Sisters of Providence, and at 7:00 P.M. the following evening, they boarded the Northern Pacific for Ravalli, a little town named after a revered Jesuit missionary, only five miles from St. Ignatius's. It was close to 2:00 A.M. when they reached Ravalli, and, once again under the protection of Father Cataldo, they spent the night in the local hotel.[24]

The next morning, a wagon took them the remaining distance, and before noon, they had reached their destination. No fatigue or anxiety could have dampened their wonder at the scene before them. Situated at the foot of the Mission Range, St. Ignatius's was, without argument, the most beautifully located of the western missions. Now, in mid-March, the mountains rose, snow-covered, against a bleak and cloudy sky. It was a painting—with the mission houses looking small and insignificant huddled beneath those daunting presences.

St. Ignatius's was not only the most beautiful and largest, but also the oldest of the Jesuit missions. Its origin can be traced to Father Peter De Smet, who made his first contact with the Flathead Indians in 1844. Ten years later, St. Ignatius's Mission was established. The following year, the Indian chiefs were gathered at a site called Hell Gate, a few miles south of the present town of Missoula. Here, a treaty was drawn up that would change the lives of the Indians forever. By the terms of the treaty, the boundaries of their reservation were moved northward from their ancestral lands in order to satisfy the demands of white settlers. As compensation, they were promised a mission school that would educate their children in reading, writing, arithmetic, as well as trade schools for blacksmithing, carpentry, and other industrial skills. The treaty, however, failed the Indians on both scores: they lost their ancestral lands in the Bitterroots, and the government failed to provide funds for the promised school.

The Jesuits, however, were determined to keep their part of the bargain, and in 1864, they sent a request to the Sisters of Charity of Providence to send a group of nuns to begin a school for Indian girls.

St. Ignatius's Mission, panorama view, circa 1891. Courtesy of Jesuit Oregon Province archives, Gonzaga University, Spokane, Washington

They could hardly have searched farther abroad, for the mother-house of the Sisters of Charity was located in eastern Québec, in the city of Montréal. Unfazed, however, four sisters began the trip that would take them four months. Since an overland route was impossible, they took a ship from Canada, traveling by boat to Panama, where they crossed the isthmus on horseback. Here, they took a ship once again, for the voyage up the coast to Vancouver, where their sisters had a small community. Although this formidable journey took them six weeks, their travels were far from over. The most perilous and exhausting part of their trip lay ahead of them. From Vancouver, they set out, accompanied by two Jesuits, across mountains and rivers and lakes, traveling by canoe, by horseback, and by foot to the Mission Range, and finally to their home at St. Ignatius's.[25]

At once, they began a boarding school for Indian girls. For the first years, the school was maintained solely by Jesuit funds and by begging trips by the sisters. By 1874, the government had at last agreed to regular allotments for a specified number of children—$100 per year for forty children. Although hardly sufficient to cover basic expenses, the school became so successful that by 1883, the number of children covered by government allotments was raised to 100.

In 1886, Van Gorp received a letter from the Office of Indian Affairs that must have cheered his heart:

> It is gratifying to learn that the pupils are making rapid
> progress in their school studies, and industrial training, as
> well as in acquiring a knowledge of the English language. He
> [the school inspector] also speaks in the highest terms of the
> order, cleanliness and system prevailing in everything
> pertaining to the school.
>
>   The zeal and energy displayed by yourself and assis-
> tants in this noble work is worthy of commendation, and I
> take pleasure in informing you that it is fully appreciated by
> this office.[26]

Two years later, E. D. Bannister, the inspector of schools for the region, wrote to the secretary of the interior with high praise for St. Ignatius's: "I consider it to be the best equipped and the most intelligently conducted school in the Indian service," he wrote, recommending that the government contract be increased.[27]

With such commendation, the mission flourished. By 1889, new buildings had been erected and there were 150 Indian girls and close to the same number of boys in attendance, with fourteen Sisters of Providence and an equal number of Jesuits to supervise their education. Buildings had kept abreast of the increased number of students, and when the Ursulines arrived in 1890, the Sisters of Providence had progressed from a small log cabin to a three-story building with dormitory space for the children, a dining room, an infirmary, as well as a section reserved for the nuns. Next to this was the Girls' Industrial School, with several classrooms and a large sewing room. The boys, too, had their dormitory and industrial school, with shops for saddle making, shoe making, carpentry, black-smithing, and printing. In addition was the bakery, where Indian women, supervised by a sister, provided bread for the entire establishment. The washhouse, too, was run on a heroic scale.

The mission that the Ursulines were about to join was a complex town of well over 300 people. It was soon to be made even more complex by the projected addition of a nursery school, caring for fifty to seventy Indian children between the ages of two and four. It was an original concept—as yet untested.*

---

*An original concept for the missions, but not for American education, which was beginning to develop a strong interest in early education.

Chapter Eight

We were really happy; the children were docile,
good and eager to learn.

—Sister Thomas Stoeckel

There was certainly no scope for fame or glory in the work the Ursulines were undertaking at St. Ignatius's. Even their arrival received meager attention in the daily account kept by the Jesuits (written in laborious Latin): "The Ursuline sisters arrived on March 22; they will take care of children—both boys and girls—between two and five years old. They will inhabit the old mission house."[1]

Clearly, the new arrivals were low on the totem pole. The Sisters of Providence, with twenty-five years of experience behind them, had established their schools and their workshops. They were already well known and accepted by both Indians and whites. The Jesuits had even more to boast of. In addition to their schoolrooms and workshops, they had created a gristmill, a sawmill, and a print shop—remarkable assets in a territory that had none of these. What the Ursulines had come to do was of a far more humble nature: they were to establish a "school" for children between the ages of two and five. To call it a kindergarten would glorify it beyond its scope. At best, it was a prekindergarten or nursery school.

Nothing in the Ursulines' training or experience as teachers prepared them for the task. They could count only on their common sense and their natural maternal instinct—scant resources for dealing with the dozens of small, bewildered children who soon filled the house.

The motive behind this new work seems today to be both wrongheaded and insensitive. But both Jesuits and Ursulines saw it as an enabling factor in their work of "civilizing" Indians. "Save the Papoose," a slogan initiated by Commissioner Thomas Morgan, was widely adopted by those who saw it as a simple and peaceful solution to the "Indian question." "Saving the papoose" meant taking Indian children away from their families as early as possible and educating them entirely in a white culture. Thus, having no access to their own language or the customs of their people, it would be easy for them to adjust to a white civilization. The anguish and rebellion experienced by older children sent to white schools would thus be obviated. Instead, the "kindergarten" would produce a generation of happy little papooses eager for citizenship.

Peter Ronan, the Indian agent usually so sympathetic toward the Indians in his care, expressed high praise for the establishment of a kindergarten as an ideal solution. His reasons are clearly delineated in his 1890 report to the Indian commissioner in Washington:

> The children, if taken into the school at the age of two or
> three or four years, and kept there, only occasionally visited
> by their parents will, when grown up, know nothing of
> Indian ways and habits. They will be thoroughly, though
> imperceptibly, formed to the ways of the whites in their
> habits, their thoughts and their aspirations. They will not
> know, in fact be completely ignorant of the Indian language,
> and will know only English. One generation will accomplish
> what the past system would require generations to effect.[2]

The Ursulines found nothing objectionable in such reasoning. Many years later, Amadeus reflected: It was "believed to be the best way to complete the civilization and Christianization of this tribe." In her view, the experiment had been successful.[3]

The Indians, however, had been slow to accept such reasoning. Not only were the children loath to lose their prized freedom, but their parents were reluctant to have them go. They loved their children passionately and had their own ideas about their education.

While the whites saw the Indian children as totally undisciplined, they were, in fact, disciplined according to their own traditions. They were taught endurance, courage in the presence of pain and danger, patience in difficult situations. They were taught the skills essential to their way of life—hunting, fishing, curing meat, tanning leather, making clothing, and decorating it beautifully with native materials. They learned respect for the tribal legends and rituals, as well as reverence for their elders and loyalty to their tribe.

In short, they were not without education, but it was an education holistic and appropriate to their way of life. White man's learning (reading, writing, arithmetic) might be an acceptable addition to their Indian education, but it could never replace it. In the Indian view, children taken off to white men's schools would be at a disadvantage for the rest of their lives.[4]

Even so, on the opening day, a remarkable number of small Indians arrived to begin the process of civilization. Within the first few

St. Ignatius's Mission, primary school. Courtesy of Marquette University Libraries, Bureau of Catholic Indian Missions Records

weeks, the nuns had some twenty children to care for. Philosophies of education were put aside in favor of soap and water. The children, the oldest of them just four years old, were bathed and scrubbed clean. Their hair was cut short to make it more manageable and painstakingly combed and recombed to free it of lice. The nuns, either unaware of or insensitive to the symbolic value of long hair to the Indians, were ruthless in discarding what they saw as another source of disease. Their ministrations were angrily resisted and avoided whenever possible, as small, greasy bodies slipped out of the nuns' grasp. The concept of modesty, which demanded that bodies be covered and that girls avert their eyes lest they fall upon a naked boy or even a naked girl—or indeed, their own small bodies—was beyond the children's experience. White man's clothes were anathema to them, and the demand that their feet be always encased in shoes was bewildering and irritating.

But to the missionaries, clothing naked bodies was an essential element of civilization. Sewing machine treadles whirred continually as every available scrap of material was transformed into dresses and pants. One unidentified memo records that so urgent was this process, seamstresses were brought in from Helena to expedite the project.

Amadeus stayed at St. Ignatius's only long enough to see the kindergarten established, and then with her companion Sister Rose Galvin, moved on to visit the other missions. Before she left, however, she was careful to witness a contract, "An Article of Agreement

St. Ignatius's Mission, school buildings and residences, circa 1900. Courtesy of Ursuline archives, Great Falls, Montana

between St. Ignatius Mission and the Ursuline Nuns." It was a far more detailed document than the agreement drawn up at St. Xavier's Mission three years earlier. Both fathers and sisters were learning the value of clearly delineated duties and responsibilities.

It is hereby agreed upon between the Fathers of St. Ignatius Mission, the party of the 1st part, and Rev. Mother Amadeus, the party of the 2nd part, to wit:

1. That the Ursuline Nuns shall establish and maintain at said St. Ignatius Mission a community of their Order, in number sufficient to do the work stipulated below.

2. That the Sisters of said community shall furnish the necessary care and services for the successful carrying on of a Kindergarten of Indian and half-breed Indian children of an age suitable for such an Institution and in such numbers as may be obtained and the Fathers deem proper.

3. That, moreover, the Sisters of said community shall see to the washing and mending of the clothes of the Fathers' community and of the boys of the Boarding School of said Mission, as well as to the general cleanliness of the said school, but no further than the Fathers wish them to take care of the same.

4. That the Fathers of said Mission, shall, as a matter of course, supply and furnish the necessary buildings for the Sisters and those under their charge, the same being and remaining the property of the Fathers. They also agree to supply and provide all that is required for the running of said institution, i.e. boarding, clothing, etc., etc., of the Sisters and the children and to pay for whatever outside help may be deemed necessary.

5. It is further agreed that in view of the services thus rendered or to be rendered to the Mission for the good of the Indians and of the School, the Fathers shall

make a yearly allowance to the Mother house of the
Sisters of $200 (two hundred dollars) for each of the
sisters. The Fathers shall also pay the traveling expenses
of the Sisters employed at the Mission, as regards the
going to the same, but shall not be responsible for
traveling expenses of those who leave except as far as
may seem proper to the Fathers.

P.S. The above is intended as a temporary arrangement. But if
the Almighty blesses the work and the Sisters should so prefer,
they may after three or four years build a House of their own
somewhere on the other side of the contemplated new Church,
the Fathers helping them to secure a piece of ground for that
purpose and they will moreover try their best to have the
Indians donate to them a quarter section of land, if possible.
The Fathers will give $3,000 (three thousand dollars) towards
the building of this permanent house, the same to be given only
when the house is under roof. In case the government should
withdraw its allocation then another contract is to be made.[5]

It is questionable that the Ursulines realized the extent of the
manual work required of them by the contract. Since St. Ignatius's
had been chosen as the training center for young Jesuits preparing
for the Rocky Mountain Missions, the mission laundry had to serve
fifty Jesuits in various stages of formation (six priests, ten brothers,
eighteen theologians, fifteen philosophers), along with a considerable number of hired men, and 100 or so Indian boys, in addition to
their own children. The work of the laundry in itself was quite sufficient to employ the three nuns full time, but the Jesuits considered
it only an addendum to the essential work of the kindergarten.

In every way, the Ursulines were dependent on the Jesuit community. Although St. Ignatius's was a contract school, receiving from
the federal government a given allotment for each child, the newly
arrived Ursulines were excluded from the benefits of government
contracts. According to the regulations of the Bureau of Indian

Affairs (BIA), only children five years old and beyond were eligible for government allotments. Thus the kindergarten that the Ursulines had been asked to establish was totally dependent on what the Jesuits could provide, along with subsidies from the BCIM.

Despite the hazards, by early summer, Amadeus felt sufficiently secure in the development of the kindergarten to turn her attention to a possible new venture.

Although for the Ursulines, St. Peter's was a highly successful mission with its schools, its populous novitiate, and its position as motherhouse of the Ursulines of Montana, for the Jesuits, it had never quite accomplished its goal. Established for the children of the Blackfeet tribe, it only partially fulfilled its purpose, since most of the Blackfeet lived in the foothills of the Rocky Mountains in the northwest section of the reservation. By 1886, Father Cataldo had already requested and obtained permission to erect a mission in this area, and the following year, Chief White Calf had granted them a section of land.

Unlike the bleak environment of St. Peter's, Holy Family Mission was beautifully situated. Later, Father Prando wrote of it:

> No more beautiful spot could have been selected out in that
> wild and dreary section of Montana. Hidden away at the edge
> of a cottonwood grove, on the banks of the Two-Medicine
> River, protected on the north and west by the high cliffs
> through which the river has cut its path, with a narrow fertile
> meadow stretching to the northeast for three or four miles,
> the mission buildings stand, enjoying what would almost be
> termed a different climate from the surrounding prairie.[6]

It was not until 1889, however, that construction was able to begin, through the generosity of Miss Katharine Drexel, who contributed $14,000 to begin the school. It must have been one of her last gifts as "Miss Drexel," because in May of that year, she entered the convent of the Sisters of Mercy in Pittsburgh, the first step toward preparing herself to found the Sisters of the Blessed Sacrament for Indians and Colored People.

While the gift was adequate to begin initial construction, the Jesuits were still dependent on government allotments for their pupils. Such allotments were already being questioned, and Monsignor Stephan's persuasion was needed to win their cause. "That there is crying need for additional educational facilities for the Blackfeet children is shown by the statement in the Report of the Commissioner of Indian Affairs for 1889 (page 394), that the school population of the Blackfeet Reservation is 450, while school accommodations are provided for but 50 children, leaving 400 without educational facilities."[7]

The government could hardly argue with its own statistics, and Holy Family, as the mission was to be called, was registered as a contract school.

Meanwhile, Damiani had brought from St. Peter's three Ursulines who would staff the girls' school: Angela Lincoln, Irene Arvin, and a postulant, Monica Martin. No trio could provide clearer evidence of the diversity of vocations that arrived at St. Peter's with the goal of offering themselves to the Indian missions. Monica, the youngest of the three, had arrived at St. Peter's only a few months before. Born in Opelousas, Louisiana, in 1866, there is no record of how she learned of the Montana missions or how she made her way from southern Louisiana almost to the northern border of the United States. She was twenty-four years old when she received the postulant's cap and never wavered in her vocation. "Beloved pioneer" she was designated by the *Anaconda News* at the time of her death in 1919.

Irene Arvin was already a professed religious when she arrived at St. Peter's. She had entered the Ursulines of St. Louis in 1882, where she was professed three years later. It was not long before she heard the call to more radical service and traveled west to offer herself for work with the Indians. After a short period of orientation at the motherhouse, Amadeus appointed her as one of the three who would work with the Jesuits to establish Holy Family Mission. Even this, apparently, did not dampen her zeal for far-off service, and when the Alaska missions were founded some twenty years later, Irene volunteered and remained there until her death in 1934.

It was Angela Lincoln, however, whose name would be longest remembered. Born into a wealthy Cincinnati family in 1857, she was the fourth of seven children—six of whom were girls.* An essay memorializing her after her death comments, "The Lincoln home-life was preeminently Christian, Catholic, intellectual, and well-bred."[8] It was certainly all of that, and a good bit more. Mrs. Lincoln had strong theories about bringing up children. Whatever else they were to be, they were not to be provincial; they were to be citizens of the world. As a first step toward this cosmopolitan goal, she did her best to hire maids who spoke other languages, training her children's ear from their earliest years.

Money provides advantages, and Mrs. Lincoln saw to it that whenever possible, her daughters had the advantage of a European education. Some of them, at least, studied for short periods in France and Germany, improving their language skills and increasing their sense of poise and self-confidence. Florence, bright and ambitious, benefited to the full. When she completed her education with the Ursulines of Brown County, Ohio, she was more than ready to assume a primary place in Cincinnati society.

For a few years, she fulfilled the role expected of her, and then in the spring of 1879, at the age of twenty-two, she asked to be admitted at the convent of the beloved nuns who had educated her.

The Ursulines of Brown County were, of course, delighted. She was one of their own and one of their best. From the beginning, they had high hopes for her. It was undoubtedly a disappointment when, a few years after her profession, she asked permission to leave Brown County for Montana.

---

*Some records indicate that there were eleven children in all, of whom seven lived to adulthood.

Mother Amadeus was as impressed with Angela Lincoln as Brown County had been. Now in her early thirties, she was a remarkably beautiful woman, even within the confines of religious garb. Religious decorum had not constrained her responses—her reactions were quick and passionate. She had a spontaneous quality that matched Amadeus's own. She was volatile and articulate and fearless in the face of obstacles. Amadeus assessed her at once: here was a woman who was not afraid of visions.

The convent they found waiting for them on their arrival at Holy Family in mid-August was a long frame building with one half for the Jesuits and the boys and the other half for the Ursulines and the girls. At the beginning of September, school began in earnest, although, as always with new schools, they found the Indians reticent and suspicious. "In theory all was very fine," Sister Amata Dunne, the niece of Mother Amadeus, wrote many years later, "but when it came to parting with their darling papooses, it was quite another story. Indian Chiefs, old men, young bucks roamed unceremoniously through the boys' school; squaws with scampering toddlers as well as back-cradled babies, looked about curiously in the girls school—messing up the rooms faster than the Ursulines could get them prepared."[9]

Father Philbert Turnell agreed with Amata's assessment. "The greatest drawback seems to be the lack of confidence on the part of the Indians who keep aloof and hearken to every tale that circulates

Holy Family Mission, original building, 1890. Courtesy of Ursuline archives, Great Falls, Montana

against us and do not come to church on Sunday," he wrote to Katharine Drexel.[10] Even so, they soon had seventy children in attendance, despite the fact that they could not yet offer any of the industrial subjects they had agreed to in their contract.

Although the Jesuit house diary reports optimistically that the school was doing well during its first years and that a number of pupils had already been prepared for their First Communion, Father Turnell provided a more realistic account. Even when the children were registered, he observed, it was hard to keep them. Their mothers, seeing little sense in such education, did everything they could to get them home. When lying and excuses did not work, they encouraged the children to run away, then hid them in their tepees. When even that did not work, they took another tack, arguing that since in sending their children to the mission they had relinquished their most cherished possession, they should receive substantial gifts in compensation.

Early in 1891, Turnell wrote frequently to Katharine Drexel, now Sister Drexel, pleading for additional funds to alleviate some of their privations and, even more importantly, to provide educational

Holy Family Mission, new convent, circa 1900. Courtesy of Ursuline archives, Great Falls, Montana

resources. They had nothing on hand for teaching, he explained, except for a few old readers.

His concern, however, was not only for the lack of resources, but for the incompetence of the teachers. In February of that year, he wrote to Monsignor Stephan, "I much regret to be compelled to say that the training of the girls at this school is not what it should be, specially on account of lack of discipline and sisters competent or willing to reinforce it. You would oblige me by advising me what to do under the circumstances." He had, he explained, already written "often" to Mother Amadeus, "asking her to send an efficient and competent teacher for the girls, but in vain. ... "[11]

It was a complaint that dogged Amadeus to the end of her life. Perhaps she was one of those who agreed with the dictum often ascribed to G. K. Chesterton that "anything worth doing is worth

St. Peter's Mission, mandolin class. Courtesy of Ursuline archives, Great Falls, Montana

doing badly." She was not indifferent to the situation at Holy Family. Had she sisters who were better prepared for their tasks, she would have sent them. Meanwhile, she pointed out, there was a Christian presence at work among the Blackfeet children. Surely, that was better than nothing.

Shortly after Amadeus's return to St. Peter's, she wrote at length to Monsignor Stephan, describing in detail the work of St. Peter's Mission. The purpose of the letter was to encourage the Indian bureau to provide for additional children. The Indian parents were eager to send their children, because St. Peter's provided every advantage, she explained. The boys' industrial school trained them in every craft as well as gardening and stock management. The girls were equally provided with excellent teachers. "The girls have been taught dress-making, cooking, washing, house-cleaning, bread and butter making and out of school hours, receive instruction in music, drawing, embroidery and flower-making."[12]

While, in her usual style, Amadeus promised a bit more than she could produce, she did succeed in getting a young woman from Cincinnati, Lavinia Whitfield, to teach wood carving to the sisters, who were then to instruct their pupils.

Conditions at St. Peter's tested Miss Whitfield's mettle. The cold, the loneliness, the primitive conditions were more than she had anticipated. She later described her Christmas experience.

> Picture to yourself a deep valley or basin dotted over at irregular intervals by numerous cabins, surrounded on every side by snow-wrapped mountains. ... A more unpleasant day never dawned even in the Rockies. The sky was overcast with a peculiar yellow haze, a wind blew down from the mountains, colder than any that ever blew before, surely. At night-fall the wind has increased to a blizzard. ... Crowds of half-breeds and ranch people are said to come down on every Christmas eve night to attend midnight Mass. Only a comparative few were here, however, owning to the awful weather. ...

We all bundle up and we go shivering across the yard
to the poor little log chapel, amid such a crowd and knelt on
the dirty floor. Again our thoughts rush backward to the
beautiful church of last year—the glory of the sanctuary, the
perfume of flowers, white roses drooping in snowy profusion
everywhere ... the swinging censors and that heavenly
fragrance, the incense. ... But this Christmas it was different
certainly. The poor lights, the dirt, the bare logs, the stifling
heated atmosphere, the rough men and the equally rough
women—mostly half-breeds. The whiskey-laden breath of
some rancher or miner floated gently but firmly into one's
helpless nostrils. ... So passed my first Christmas Eve in a
Montana Mission.[13]

Despite her initial reactions, however, Whitfield stayed on
after she had finished her teaching contract. She met and fell in love
with a rancher; they married, and she ended her life on the plains
that at first she had found so grim.

That year, St. Peter's was afflicted not only with bad weather, but
with mortal sickness. In the spring, an Indian child died of diphtheria.

St. Peter's Mission, new convent and school, circa 1890. Courtesy of Ursuline
archives, Great Falls, Montana

Contagion was inevitable in such crowded conditions, and by the end of May, four children had died at the mission. By mid-June, the epidemic was at last contained, just in time to welcome Bishop Brondel, who arrived to confirm thirty-five of their children and fifty adults from the surrounding area. Brondel raised their spirits by staying with them for a few days and praising the work they were accomplishing. "[He said] he could never express in words his love and appreciation for our Order and his wonder at what God had wrought by our feeble instrumentality," the annalist wrote. "He said we were his first-born, that none could pluck this honor from us."[14]

It was encouragement they sorely needed, for despite their efforts, they were constantly in debt. The new building, in planning since 1887, was still not completed. They were so desperate for money, wrote one of the sisters, that they were planning a "Sewing bee—making 700 aprons." To whom they would be sold and at what price remains a mystery. Such meager efforts did little to diminish their debts, which had reached staggering proportions.

Yet despite these debts, despite their overwhelming burden of work and Amadeus's constant ill health, St. Peter's Mission flourished. In the fall of 1891, the annalist noted triumphantly that they now had nuns from Toledo, Cleveland, Youngstown, St. Martin, and Tiffin, Ohio; St. Louis, Missouri; York, Nebraska; San Antonio, Texas; and Grand Forks, North Dakota. On October 5, they received their fiftieth postulant, and by the end of that month, seven more young women had arrived to begin their religious life.

There was more than enough work for all. By December, their new house was completed at last, and two days after Christmas, Bishop Brondel arrived for the ceremonial blessing. On the last day of 1892, Brondel said Mass in the chapel of their new home, and on January 1, the solemn blessing took place. "He ate breakfast in one of the school rooms," the annalist noted. "At 2 P.M. the procession met at the door of the Fathers' house—boys, then girls, white and Indian—winding past the corral, we crossed the bridge followed by six altar boys, Father Bandini and scholastics and his Lordship."[15]

But the "glorious event" concealed a life of grueling poverty. They owed money and they had none to give. "No coal or oil in the house—or sugar. We trust lovingly and cheerfully the Providence of God. ... No help from St. Joseph. Not one cent! ... This year was filled with trials, poverty, sickness, cold, misunderstanding and difficulties with the Fathers all piled up to make life here at St. Peter's."[16] Thus the annalist's last notation for 1892.

Amadeus, however, exhilarated by the success of completing their new house at last, transcended the difficulties of daily living, and when the Jesuits encouraged her to join them in establishing a mission in Pryor, some fifty miles west of St. Xavier's, she agreed.

The decision to erect a mission in Pryor had been initiated by Father Prando. His friendship with Chief Plenty Coups, who had made the land around Pryor Creek a rallying point for the Crow, was undoubtedly an influence in his determination to provide a Catholic presence there.[17] After weeks of exploring the territory, Prando was successful in obtaining government permission to build a church and a school. Chief Plenty Coups was delighted, since this would take care of those Indians living too far from St. Xavier's to profit from its advantages.

By this time, Chief Plenty Coups, now in his prime, was venerated by his people as a chief of great importance. His skill in diplomacy, they acknowledged, had won for them far more advantages than a more aggressive behavior would have done. For a decade, he had parlayed adroitly, holding firm against the encroachments of white ranchers. Now, with the reservation boundaries firmly established, he graciously offered Prando part of the land with the proviso that not only a church, but also a school, be established for the Crow children.

The winter of 1892 was a particularly severe one, and prudence would dictate waiting until spring before attempting to open the new mission, but in midwinter, there were rumors that a Protestant group was planning to move into the area. This was sufficient for immediate Jesuit action. The Ursulines were notified at once, and in late January,

three sisters left St. Peter's to begin the trip to Billings, then on to
Custer Station, and eventually to St. Xavier's. Sister Thomas Stoeckel,
who had arrived in Miles City from the Ursuline convent in Cleveland
in the winter of 1886, was in charge of the group. Her companions
were Sister Agnes Dunn, not yet twenty years old, who had made her
vows at St. Peter's only four month earlier. The third member was Sister
Patrick Brown, still a postulant. It was a journey they would never
forget, initiating them into the dangers of mission travel.

At St. Xavier's, they were welcomed joyfully by the five
Ursulines in charge of the Indian girls' school. Their stay, however,
was far longer than they had anticipated. For three anxious weeks,
blizzards raged about them. Finally, on February 22, the weather
cleared, becoming almost springlike. Exhilarated by their good fortune, they set out for Pryor, unprepared for the hazards resulting
from a sudden thaw. They knew they could expect no provisions at
the newly established mission, and so they loaded trunks, bedding,
school equipment, and provisions into a large sleigh. The three
nuns traveled in a smaller sleigh, "well wrapped in fur coats and
blankets," Sister Thomas wrote, remembering all the details of that
perilous journey.

They lumbered successfully across the frozen Big Horn Creek
only to watch with horror the ice cracking behind them. It was the
beginning of disaster. In the afternoon of that first day, they found
the snow had melted, leaving them with a road so deep in mud that
it was almost impossible for a sleigh to negotiate. Sister Thomas
remembered graphically the hazards that awaited them:

> Reaching the foot-hills by five o'clock we were obliged to
> camp there for the night, although we were yet fifteen miles
> from the Cowboy Ranch where we had hoped to stop. Now
> the real trouble began. In turning from the roadway, the
> tongue of each sleigh broke, leaving us with our sleighs in a
> mud puddle! Unable to leave our places because of the mud
> beneath us, we could only rest as we were, and without

supper. The driver of the big sleigh took one of our horses and rode to the Cowboy Ranch for help.

When the mud became frozen, the other driver prepared bunks on the ground for the priest and the men.* To keep warm, two of us sisters lay down on the floor of the sleigh. There was not room for three so I tried to sleep on the seat of the sleigh. Towards midnight the cold became intense. I climbed into the baggage sleigh and lay down on the bundles with a dead pig for my pillow. Cold and stiff, I stood this till four o'clock. When dawn appeared, I made up my mind to walk. As fast as my stiffness would permit, I walked along the crusted road, reciting the while my morning office, prayer and rosary.

Strange cries of animals came to me from every direction, but singular to relate, I felt no fear. Returning to the sleighs by 6 o'clock, I found I had been missed and the place was being scanned for me. A fire was made, we had our much-needed breakfast, and were ready to start when, to our joy, we saw a wagon and team coming from the Cowboy Ranch.

Our freight and provisions were transferred to the wagon. When all was packed, and the wagon sheet roped over the bundles, we were cordially invited to get on top. Climbing up by means of the muddy wheels, we held our positions on the wagon by supporting our feet against the ropes. One of the Sisters was obliged to sit next to the driver. On reaching a dip in the road she slipped from the seat and fell in the mud just back of the horses' feet. That our dear Lord protected us seems certain, for the horses never moved and Sister escaped unhurt but besmeared with mud. After this, we were asked down from the sleigh when crossing bad places in the road.

Muddy, wet and tired, we reached the Cowboy Ranch by dusk. Supper was eaten with a relish. The cowboys showed

---

*This priest is never identified.

us every courtesy. They seemed to feel honored by the
presence of Sisters and told us we were the first ladies to cross
that road. The one bedroom of two beds was placed at our
disposal. To our horror we found pistols under each pillow.
We were afraid to move, but tried to sleep. All the men,
including the priest, and those of our party, slept on the floor
in the kitchen.[18]

The next morning, they continued their journey, leaving their
heavy freight at the ranch until such time as the roads would be
more navigable. They were soon to discover that the most difficult
part of their journey was far from over. Their horses were not equal
to the hills, Sister Thomas observed, "and we had to walk up muddy
hills and slide down the side of snowy mountains."

That evening, they rested under a small tent and tried to partially
dry their frozen habits by the fire. "A fierce wind made sleep impossible
in wagon or tent, so we sat up till dawn when we had breakfast, packed
our belongings and started on another day's travel." A large part of the
journey was across prairie, where there was no source of water except
the melted snow and ice in the hoof holes made by the cattle.

Late that afternoon, they came in sight of Pryor Mountains and
saw in the distance the figure of Father Prando waving and ringing a
bell to call the Indians to welcome the missionaries. It had taken them
three days of travel to cover the fifty miles, with two sleepless nights
spent out of doors in the freezing February weather. "[So I welcomed]
the choir of sisters who came to spend their lives in this new apostolic
vineyard," Father Prando wrote exultantly. The accommodations that
he offered them could scarcely have been more minimal. The Pryor
Mission was still a dream, consisting only of a small church, empty of
everything but altar and stove. "But in that little structure dedicated
to the worship of God, we felt safe at last," wrote Sister Thomas.

Here, for the next few months, the nuns were to live and conduct a school. The empty church was all they had. On March 19,
their first pupils arrived: seven boys, clearly dragged against their

will. Fortunately, Sister Katharine Drexel continued her help, and as soon as weather permitted, work was begun on a proper school. By September, they had a two-story frame house with capacity for both a convent and a school building. The church was restored to its original function, and the number of children increased. "Those were sweet, peaceful days," Sister Thomas reminisced. "We were really happy and the children were docile, good and eager to learn."

While Sister Thomas and her companions were trying to make ends meet in their makeshift school, Amadeus had agreed to participate in yet another mission. St. John Berchmans's Mission at Arlee, some thirty miles south of St. Ignatius's, was to be the last of the Ursuline missions. While the nuns would be engaged in other schools (Roundup, Anaconda, Great Falls), none of these was established to take care of Native American children. Arlee was the last and, as it turned out, the shortest lived.

Chief Charlo, the Salish chief who had fought long and bitterly to save his people's homelands in the Bitterroot Valley, had by 1889 conceded defeat. It was not, however, until the fall of 1891 that Charlo—now old and almost blind—came with the remnant of his people to the Flathead Agency. "I will go," he wrote, "I and my children. My young men are becoming bad; they have no place to hunt. My women are hungry. For their sake I will go."[19]

Mary Ronan, wife of the agent Major Peter Ronan, watched that final procession, recording it in all its colorful detail in her memoir:

> It was a unique and, to some minds, a pathetic spectacle when
> Charlo and his band of Indians marched to their future home.
> Their coming had been heralded and many of the Reservation
> Indians had gathered at the Agency to give them welcome.
> Then within a mile of the Agency church the advancing
> Indians spread out in a broad column. The young men kept
> constantly discharging their firearms, while a few of the
> number, mounted on fleet ponies, arrayed in fantastic Indians
> paraphernalia, with long blankets partially draping the forms

of warrior and steeds, rode back and forth in front of the advancing caravan, shouting and firing their guns until they neared the church, where a large banner of the Sacred Heart of Mary and Jesus was erected on a tall pole. Near the Sacred emblem stood a valiant soldier of Jesus Christ, the Reverend Philip Canestrelli, S.J. With outstretched hands the good priest blessed and welcomed the forlorn-looking pilgrims.[20]

It was undoubtedly compassion for Charlo and his band that led to the development of the mission at Arlee. From the beginning, the Jesuits had fought against the voracious greed and broken promises that had forced the Indians out of their homeland. Now, at least, they could offer to the remnant at Arlee a church and a school. Amadeus at once agreed to help, and in September, Angela Lincoln, as superior, accompanied by Laurentia Walsh, originally from New York, and Barbara McDonald, a postulant, opened a school at Arlee.

With the opening of St. John Berchmans's Mission at Arlee, the Ursulines were engaged in eight missions to Native Americans—a giant achievement in a period of eight years. In the winter of 1891, Bishop Brondel wrote to Bishop Gilmour in Cleveland indicating how deeply he valued the work of the Ursulines: "It is seven years since your Lordship sent me the Toledo Ursulines, six in number. The community has increased to about forty. They have seven schools with over 700 boarders. No wonder then that whilst mentioning this, I thank again your Lordship."[21]

It was Brondel's last letter to Gilmour. Two months later, the bishop of Cleveland was dead.

That same year, the Ursulines lost another patron. In July 1891, Lindesmith, having reached retirement age, left Montana to return to his home state of Ohio. Before he left, however, he visited the convent at Miles City, where he had first met the Ursulines, seven years earlier. While Lindesmith's friendship with Amadeus was to be lifelong, she would never again be able to lean on his support and counsel as she had in those first years. It was a loss that moved her deeply.

Chapter Nine

Soon St. Peter's would be another Québec.

—Sister Pélagie Gosselin

In early spring of 1893, with their new home established and their novitiate full, Amadeus began plans for a trip east, a "begging tour" to solicit volunteers and funds for the Montana missions. Toledo, her original convent, was to be her first stop. Accompanying her were Sister Angela Lincoln and a fifteen-year-old Gros Ventre girl, Watzinitha (White Plume Woman), who had been at the mission since she was eight. No one was surprised that Angela was the chosen companion. It was obvious that Amadeus found in her a perfect assistant: generous, docile, efficient—and totally dedicated to Amadeus. Watzinitha, too, had from the beginning been singled out as a favored child.

On April 19, just at the supper hour, the annalist recorded, Amadeus arrived with her two companions. It was nine years since she had said farewell to her community, years filled with heroic deeds and marvelous events that she and Angela Lincoln now recounted in glowing detail. They were irresistible tales garnished by two preeminent storytellers. The community was intrigued by the stories of poverty and sacrifice, of desolate countryside, and impoverished Indians lying outside the pale of salvation. Of course, they insisted, they would contribute whatever they could to assist the heroines of the Montana missions. To celebrate Amadeus's presence, a concert was given in her honor, attended by pupils and their families as well as by the nuns.

The following weeks were spent visiting Ursuline schools, describing in vivid detail their work with the Native Americans and soliciting funds for the missions. By mid-June, they were on their way north to visit the Ursuline Monastery in Québec City, a visit that was to affect the missions dramatically.*

When in 1639 Marie de l'Incarnation Guyart and her two Ursuline companions, at the request of Jesuit missionaries, had arrived in Québec to start a school for Indian children, they had found a rugged little settlement of a few hundred pioneers. They had the honor—and the attendant hardships—of being the first women religious in America. In time, their cramped little house on the banks of the St. Lawrence had grown into an impressive institution, faithful to its monastic tradition and with schools for white children as well as Indians.

Everything about the Québec monastery stirred Amadeus's spirit. The great stone building, the silent narrow corridors, the long black processions, the choir with its high carved stalls, the grillwork protecting the nuns from "the world"—all of this appealed to her romantic strain.

It was a matter of mutual admiration. Amadeus was a well-known figure, renowned for her work on the Montana missions, for her boundless energy and charismatic spirit. Like the Pied Piper, she had drawn young women from the four corners of America to a life of heroic sacrifice. The Ursulines of Québec saw in her a second Marie de l'Incarnation: a spirit passionate, single-minded, sacrificial; a woman who embraced the cross and lived with the spirit of Jesus Christ for the salvation of souls. Amadeus, they felt, was living out the dream of their foundress.

When she asked if they would offer to help the Montana missions, the answer was a foregone conclusion. They saw in the western missions a way of sustaining their original goal, while Amadeus rejoiced that their presence would not only assist in their work with the Indians, but would renew their monastic tradition.

---

*Mother Amadeus had visited the Québec monastery in 1877 while superior of Toledo to discuss with them the Ursuline tradition of cloister, to which they were scrupulously faithful.

By the time the missionaries left on July 3, three sisters had been selected from those who had volunteered: Sister Pélagie Gosselin, Sister Félix Talbot, and Sister Elisabeth Sirois. Arrangements were made for the sisters to meet Amadeus in St. Paul, Minnesota, on August 14, to travel with her to Montana.[1]

Encouraged by their reception in Québec, they traveled west to the monastery at Trois Rivières, founded from Québec in 1697. Their initial success had emboldened them to hope that Trois Rivières might also provide Montana missionaries. Shortly after their arrival, Angela Lincoln spoke to the assembled community of their work in Montana. History is fortunate in having had an annalist who lost no detail of that colorful meeting.[2]

They were an impressive threesome. No one had ever questioned the remarkable charism of Amadeus, now just one year short of her fiftieth year. Angela Lincoln, just thirty-six, was tall, graceful, and imposing. Watzinitha—generally called by her baptismal name, Immaculata—was their centerpiece. Dressed in her neat, dark school uniform, her long hair braided, and her opaque dark eyes shyly cast down, she was the very exemplar of what devout Indian maidens could become—with help.

Angela addressed the community in French that was "fluent and elegant" and with a Parisian accent acquired during her school years in Paris. Angela was nothing if not articulate, and the occasion spurred her on to a grandiose description of their work. The annalist who later transcribed her notes explained apologetically that what she provided was only "a poor pale summary" of Angela's "burning words." She did not minimize the hardships or the perils (the cold, the dirt, the unremitting work, the dangers of blizzards, of wolves, of losing one's way on the limitless prairie), but transformed them into something wonderfully desirable. "What animates the Ursuline missionary," she avowed, "is the glory of God, the salvation of souls, and forgetfulness of self. Our mission has been founded in suffering, we are very poor but our consolations are in proportion to our sacrifices. We are gay. Our joy is contagious; it is an epidemic."

As for their life of prayer, she continued, they followed the regulations established by monastic observance: they rose at 5:00 A.M., they had Mass, office in choir, examination of conscience, recreation, spiritual reading in common, Vespers, Matins, and Lauds, points for meditation, a second examen, and retired to bed by 10:00 P.M. The daily order, she described, would be hardly recognizable to those working in the missions; nor might they be able to agree with her description of their life as a "contagion of joy."

But those who listened to Angela in that steady and measured atmosphere of the monastery of Trois Rivières responded like the disciples of Emmaus: they felt their hearts burn within them. From the number who volunteered, three were chosen. Marie de l'Espérance Tessier, twenty-five years old and three months professed; St. Bernard Trudeau, thirty-one years old and three years professed; St. Scholastique Lajoie, a coadjutrix sister, forty-nine years old and twenty-nine years professed.

Next, to the surprise of all, Amadeus suggested an arrangement very different from that which had been made at Québec: Why wait? she asked. Why not have the volunteers accompany them at once, sharing their travels in the United States and then returning with them to Montana? Amadeus left no room for demur. They would all leave the next afternoon for Montréal. The volunteers, given less than twenty-four hours to prepare for their new life, experienced for the first time the imperious decisions of their new superior.

Twenty-four hours later, shortly after noon on July 4, they were on their way. In that short time, they had received the bishop's permission and blessing, packed for the unknown, said farewell to their community, and boarded the train for Montréal.

That night they spent with the Grey Nuns in Montréal. Everyone was lovely to them, reported Marie de l'Espérance, who kept a diary of their trip.[3]

The next morning, they began the daylong train ride that would bring them to New York City. It was all too rapid for them to experience homesickness. After their years in a cloistered monastery, the color, the bustle, the noise around them usurped their concentration. The meals in the dining car, the mesmerizing scenery along the wide Hudson River, the anticipation of New York City itself staved off their weariness. It was ten o'clock when they arrived in New York Central Terminal and another hour before they reached Bedford Park, the Ursuline convent situated in the northern section of the Bronx.

The Ursuline convent had been completed only a year before. It was large, imposing, and still bore the stamp of newness. Everything there was a source of curiosity to the Canadian sisters. "This is a convent which enjoys every convenience," Marie de l'Espérance noted, alluding especially to the many sinks with bases of white marble and with both hot and cold running water. With a careful eye, she noted that the sisters were provided with white soap—a luxury in Canada. The hardwood floors, the reception parlors adorned with beautiful statues, a huge crucifix, and religious paintings, the large laundry with its modern equipment—all evoked her admiration. The convent was, she admitted, far more elegant than Trois Rivières, but, she proclaimed loyally, it was not kept nearly so clean.

They had more than enough time to acquaint themselves with the community, for the day after their arrival, Amadeus and Angela Lincoln departed for an unknown destination "on business." Although the nuns were kind and helpful, few of them spoke French, and the visitors were, for the most part, left to their own devices. The days wore on with little for the new missionaries to do, and the homesickness that they had resisted rushed on them with a vengeance.

By July 10, St. Bernard admitted that she was ready to take the road back to Trois Rivières. Two days later, however, Amadeus and Angela returned, and the following afternoon, they set off for Pennsylvania.

It was the beginning of four weeks of bewildering travel as they accompanied Amadeus from Philadelphia to Pittsburgh, to Toledo, to

Chicago. Once again, they were left alone for days with no explanation while they waited for Amadeus to return from her mysterious "business journeys." At last, in the second week of August, the group was reunited at St. Paul, Minnesota, and began the final lap of their journey to Montana.*

On August 10, they arrived in Helena, with a long trip still ahead of them.

Here, Amadeus left them once again, explaining that she must continue on to visit the other missions, taking with her Sister Scholastique, who was to begin work at once at St. Labre's. The others, a party of eight in all, were helped up on the waiting wagon, where they did their best to make themselves comfortable, sitting on sacks of flour and sugar and boxes of nails. "Imagine! Seeing us seated in a wagon drawn by four horses ... and thus forty long miles crossing the mountains along very difficult roads," wrote St. Bernard later that month.[4]

At their arrival at St. Peter's, they found the nuns expectantly waiting for them. Their first view of their surroundings impressed them deeply. The situation of the house was very beautiful, St. Bernard observed, adding, "if you can say that about a country where there are no trees at all." The mountains protected them like a grill, she continued, "like a true Chartreuse." The climate, too, was ideal, with little rainfall and a constant wind that kept the air pure and dry. But it was the poverty that moved her. "I don't know how to describe the extreme poverty here. The chapel above all is very poor with just a little altar, a small box for the tabernacle, no choir stalls but just simple benches for the nuns to kneel on." Far from discouraging them, the bleakness of their surroundings made their hearts more ardent than ever.[5]

---

*The group that left St. Paul for Montana had grown to nine; three missionary volunteers had joined them from New York and Pittsburgh. It is hard to imagine what prompted Mother Amadeus to bring the three Canadians with her as she crisscrossed the United States. It was a long, expensive trip that seemed to have no practical goal. Perhaps she felt it would be easier on the new missionaries to travel with experienced sisters, but they could have joined the Québec sisters with far less difficulty.

A week later, on August 19, the three nuns from Québec arrived. The plan to meet Amadeus in St. Paul had somehow gone awry and they had made their own way to Cascade, where they had found a young Canadian who took care of the remainder of their trip. Their welcome could not have been warmer. "There couldn't have been more joy had three angels descended from heaven," wrote Sister Félix, the youngest of the three, adding that they had a grave responsibility, because everyone expected so much of them. "They think here that we are all like Marie de l'Incarnation."[6]

Like the sisters from Trois Rivières, the Québec sisters were also moved at the beauty of the scenery. Looking down from one of the buttes, Félix wrote, "The spectacle is so beautiful, so impressive that there were tears in our eyes. Our dream has become a reality."[7]

For another week, they waited, hoping daily for Mother Amadeus's return. Finally, on August 29, at eight o'clock in the evening, she arrived, greeted by embraces, tears, clapping, and laughter. There was no doubt how dearly she was loved and reverenced.

With the arrival of Amadeus, the tempo of the convent changed. On September 8, Bishop Brondel arrived and the feast of the Nativity of the Virgin Mary was celebrated by singing Vespers "according to the Québec ceremonial."

Amadeus, enamored by the spirit of Québec, had begun her campaign to elevate the religious tone of the Montana missions. The Québec nuns were willing enablers. It had taken them but a short time to observe that there were many things that should be changed for the better. Pélagie had already written home asking for material from Québec that they could use to improve religious life on the mission.

The arrival of Brondel—whose native language was French—gave them a golden opportunity to confer with him concerning some of their observations. Unwilling to discuss these matters publicly, they asked for a private audience. "We gave his Eminence a list of different changes that we thought would be for the good of the Community," Pélagie recorded later.

Their first suggestion was that a community council be formed, an effort, no doubt, to moderate Amadeus's unquestioned power. Amadeus, of course, was named superior, with Pélagie as her assistant and treasurer; Elisabeth was named zelatrix—a kind of community overseer. Angela Lincoln was to be mistress of novices; and Sister Félix was to be sent north as superior of Holy Family Mission. This complete reorganization was more than the Québec nuns could have hoped for. "The Bishop said that he hoped that soon St. Peter's would be another Québec," Pélagie noted with satisfaction.[8] Less than a month after their arrival, the Québec sisters had begun to transform a mission into a monastery.

What no one seemed to consider in this dramatic restructuring was the response of the original members of the community. That sisters who had only just arrived, who had not yet visited the missions, who did not even speak English should suddenly be in charge of the motherhouse seemed to some bewildering and to others outrageous. While they readily admitted that life on the missions was far from perfect, they were not ready to admit that it needed such reformation. What had seemed an ideal to Amadeus was quickly showing its thorny side. St. Bernard, in writing to Trois Rivières, gave a sympathetic voice to what the Montana nuns were undoubtedly feeling: "They [the Québec sisters] have what they wanted but they should have had to work to get those titles."[9]

Pélagie, the oldest and most experienced, was the moving spirit. Félix accepted her new role with apprehension, well aware that she was ill equipped to govern a mission she had never seen. Elisabeth, fatigued and lonely, saw nothing but insurmountable difficulties in the role she was assigned. But Pélagie was entranced with the opportunity to reform the missions according to a manner of life she understood and endorsed. She had no doubt that she was doing what Amadeus had intended in inviting them to Montana. If there was initial turmoil, she was sure that, ultimately, their objectives would be accepted.

The most reasoned account of these events came in a letter from St. Bernard written "in confidence" to the superior of Trois Rivières several months later:

> She [Pélagie] wanted the authority to redress whatever was
> contrary to our Holy Rule. Poor Mother had a big task. She
> did her utmost with the power she had but it seems that she
> went too quickly. She wanted perfection where she should
> have been satisfied to find good will. This sort of conduct
> didn't win the affection of the community. The Montana
> sisters had not been trained this way and they found it very
> painful to be subjected to all the fine points of our Holy Rule.
> They asserted without qualification that they did not want
> her as assistant, that her election had not been legal, that they
> had had no opportunity to give their vote.*[10]

There is no doubt that St. Peter's was based on a model far different from the well-established monastery of Québec. The "model" came from the spirit of Amadeus and, like her spirit, was spontaneous and capricious. The needs she saw around her directed her; they were immediate and imperative and took precedence over Rule—and frequently over prudence. Pélagie was shocked at the lack of training given to the novices, to the poor preparation of the young teachers, and appalled by the financial confusion she discovered in her role as treasurer. As assistant to Amadeus, she felt a responsibility to make substantive changes but lacked the power to do so.

Neither of her companions seemed able to respond to her goal. Elisabeth was growing daily more listless, more fearful, less confident in her ability to carry out her position. Félix, too, in the

---

*Since Bernard Trudeau and Marie de l'Espérance Tessier had left St. Peter's in late September, it is interesting to conjecture what was the source of her information. Certainly, it did not come from Pélagie Gosselin or Elisabeth Sirois, or from the Montana sisters, none of whom spoke French—with the exception of Angela Lincoln. The only contact they had with St. Peter's was a visit from Amadeus Dunne in early March.

harsh climate of the Blackfeet reservation, was lonely and overburdened. She felt no impulse to reform their life; simply living from
day to day was all she could manage. Late in December, she wrote to
Québec describing their poor, simple celebration of Christmas: "I was
listening to the harmonious sounds of the harps, the violins, the gui-
tars, and the mandolins in Québec and our poor singing made the
tears run down my cheeks."[11]

Letters from Pélagie indicated that things were not improving
at St. Peter's. Amadeus was almost always sick, remaining in her
room for days at a time. Pélagie was overwhelmed by the financial
situation of the house, which was becoming more and more critical,
with creditors constantly demanding to be paid. "I don't know how
they will get through the winter if help does not arrive," Félix wrote
to Québec, adding, "I do not believe, dear Mother, that God can bless
the work of the Ursulines in conditions like this." Both she and
Elisabeth were seriously considering returning to Québec. They did
not want to abandon their missionary life, but they wished to remain
Ursulines according to the manner of Québec.[12]

Despite the difficulties, however, Pélagie remained firm, convinced of the value of what she was trying to accomplish, especially
determined to establish a more monastic spirit at St. Peter's. In some
of this, she was successful, as the annalist noted at Christmas: "This
night, the solemn office of Nativity was sung at St. Peter's Mission for
the first time in the Indian Missions of the Rocky Mountains with
remarkable beauty and solemnity. Ten professed nuns and eight
novices sang the sublime chant of the church with devotion and
pathos and faultless precision."[13] The celebration undoubtedly owed
much to Elisabeth and Pélagie.

The beauty of such a ceremony, however, was hardly enough
to convert the Montana nuns to Canadian customs. The sisters at
St. Peter's hardly knew what had happened to them since the
arrival of the Canadian sisters. The three from Trois Rivières had
gone at once to their mission assignments, but the others had
clearly brought a foreign spirit to the community. At first humbly

grateful for their presence, the sisters soon began to resent their overriding influence. Even more bewildering was Amadeus's deference. Did she expect them to be transformed into a French monastery? For a while, it seemed that she did. This was something they could not accept.

At the beginning of January 1894, three chillingly hostile entries appeared in St. Peter's annals. January 5: "[We are] grieved to see the havoc wrought in our home by Québec notions." January 13: "Nothing but sorrow from the interference of the Québec nuns." January 14: "May God ... restore Mother's health and sweet authority and grant us perfect restoration of our former peace, union, and charity."[14]

The annalist's narration of how this disunion had come about diverges dramatically from other sources, casting a dark shadow over the motivation of the Québec nuns. "They hatched a plan," read the annals, so that they would be given various charges of importance. They treated Amadeus coldly, refusing to accept their assignments to the various missions. They deceived the bishop in order to get what they wanted, telling him that unless he agreed, they would return to Québec. It was a litany of the most dubious accusations, indicating the rancor of at least part of the community.

There is no evidence to support the annalist's interpretation. Pélagie, imprudent perhaps in her zeal, was doing only what Amadeus had indicated. The problem stemmed, in part, from unreal expectations. Amadeus had glorified the Québec sisters as the very ideal of religious life, while they had imagined her as the incarnation of their foundress. In the struggle of daily mission life, the reality, far less heavenly, began to emerge. There was, however, a more deep-rooted issue: a conflict between a monastic tradition and the missionary needs of the New World. Amadeus, always the visionary, had dreamed of having them both. The sisters of Montana were more realistic: one or the other would suffer. There was no place for cloister on the prairies; there was no time for the intricacies of monastic life. Their life was not perfect, they admitted it, but it fit their mission, and they would not sacrifice it.

The conflict came to a head when, on January 22, Bishop
Brondel arrived to celebrate a religious profession. Alerted to the friction in the community, he sent for Amadeus. No doubt he saw Pélagie
and Elisabeth as well. What actually took place is lost to posterity;
there are only the community annals to direct us, and the account in
the annals continues the same self-righteous and accusatory tone:

> Mother conversed with the Lordship and obtained from him
> the abolition of the changes and innovations introduced by
> Sisters Ignatius and the Québec Sisters. His Lordship was
> moved to think of our sufferings and indignant wished at
> once to send Sisters Pélagie, Elisabeth and Félix back to
> Québec but our gentle mother obtained for them a respite and
> concluded with His Lordship to send them first on trial to a
> mission. We were unspeakably grateful to God for lifting this
> heavy cross off our bruised shoulders.[15]

By the beginning of February, Elisabeth had been freed from
her office of zelatrix and traveled to Holy Family to join Félix. But
Félix was not to remain much longer at Holy Family. Her inexperi-
ence and outspoken spirit bewildered Father Peter Bougis, who
wrote to Amadeus asking that another sister be sent to replace her.
Within weeks of Elisabeth's arrival, they were both transferred to St.
Paul's. Félix, having found Father Bougis as difficult as he had found
her, was delighted, "Like a bird when the cage is opened," she wrote
to Québec. Despite the horrors of the trip (they had been delayed for
hours because the train had been stuck in five feet of snow), they
were delighted to be at St. Paul's, where the superior, Mother Francis
Seibert, "has won our hearts."[16] Relieved of the duties for which
they had never felt adequate, they settled in for the work they had
come to do.

Pélagie, however, did not share their reactions. She could not
accept the haphazard government of the house, in particular the
adulation surrounding Amadeus. "I tell you in confidence that they

will canonize her while she is still alive," she wrote to the superior in Québec. She had done her best to explain the problems to the bishop but had little success. "Everything is explained on the grounds that it is 'missionary life,'" she continued. While she often felt that their presence had accomplished little, she took credit for "putting some order into this business."[17]

Her presence at the motherhouse was coming to an end, however. Even though she had been divested of all authority, the community was not comfortable in her presence. She left St. Peter's at the end of March, abandoning whatever dreams she had for reshaping the missions, and traveled 300 difficult miles southeast to Pryor, where she was to be superior at the newest and poorest of the Montana missions: "a little mission with one professed, one novice and one postulant. The same room serves as their refectory, their dormitory and their classroom."[18]

In February, shortly before Pélagie's departure, the community at St. Peter's endured their most anguishing experience: the first death on the missions. Sister Veronica had been born Sarah Ferris in Philadelphia, Pennsylvania, July 1872. There is no record of how she came to know of the Montana missions—perhaps through a priest, perhaps through an announcement written by Amadeus for the diocesan paper. She arrived at St. Peter's on September 9, 1890, just eighteen years old. Three years later, on September 8, she made her religious profession. Already frail, the cold, the inadequate food, and the burden of work overwhelmed her. She lived for only five months after her profession, dying during the first week of February. The ground was frozen fast, but neighboring men came to help the sisters dig the grave, situated on a little rise overlooking the mission. "As we looked down we saw the mission wing," the annalist recorded, "the snow, the pine, the straight lines of smoke ascending from the house of the Fathers and our home."[19]

That summer, they sustained another loss, very different in kind, but also very painful for them. Mary Fields, their faithful servant and friend who had come from Toledo to nurse Amadeus during her illness in 1885 and who had insisted on remaining at St. Peter's, was forced to leave them. Black Mary, as she was called, had always been unique. Her black skin would have been sufficient to mark her off, but there was more. Striding along in her mannish clothes, her girth distinguishing her from all the women and most of the men, Black Mary obeyed no conventions. She drank, she smoked, she cursed, she carried a gun, and she had a reputation for using her fists when angered.

But with the nuns, she was a devoted and generous helper. Work was her métier, and she never shirked it. She planted a vegetable garden; she raised enough hens to provide them all with chickens and eggs. She worked tirelessly on the construction of their new house. She was solely responsible for picking up their freight from the railroad at Cascade. Winter and summer, she drove the convent wagon across muddy roads or snowdrifts, hauled the freight, and then started back to the mission. The trip was not without hazards, and more than once, Black Mary spent the night on the prairie in freezing temperatures, the howling of wolves not too far off. She neither complained nor dramatized her adventures. It was all part of her work. Her passionate devotion to Amadeus knew no bounds, and her devotion was reciprocated. Grateful for all she had done for them, Amadeus promised that they would always care for her, that St. Peter's would always be her home.

Not everyone recognized Mary's devotion, however, seeing only a rough and quarrelsome black woman who would take none of their offensive comments. She had often been known to pull her gun, but when rumor reached Bishop Brondel that she had actually killed a man, Brondel had had enough. He was tired of the constant complaints and the refusal of the nuns to curb their "black woman." This time, he took firm action, writing to Amadeus "to get that black woman out of there." Their protestations were unavailing, and Amadeus had to break the news to Mary.

The annals for July 27 recorded:

The bishop has ordered that she be dismissed from the
Mission but the community has determined to support her
wherever she goes. It is hard for Mother to dismiss this
faithful servant in her old age and one trembles to think of
Mother's sorrow and trouble in so doing but the bishop's
orders are peremptory. He has heard aspersions of the poor
woman's character which no one has ever yet been able to
prove. She was overbearing and troublesome and yet it was
our firm intention to keep her till death.[20]

While Amadeus was unable to keep her promise that Mary
would always live at St. Peter's, she was able to help her financially,
establishing her in a small restaurant in Cascade. But Mary Fields was
no businesswoman, and twice the restaurant failed. Again, through
the influence of Amadeus, she was given a job of responsibility, with
the U.S. Postal Service, meeting the trains at Cascade and driving a
two-horse team to deliver mail. After ten years of service, she
resigned, at the age of seventy-two. Her beloved Amadeus was no
longer in Montana, and there were few nuns she knew still left at St.
Peter's. But by this time, she had won the admiration and affection
of the townspeople, who did what they could to take care of her in
her last years. She died in the hospital in Great Falls in December of
1914, her exact age unrecorded, and was buried in Cascade, a great
granite stone marking the grave of this legendary figure.[21]

With Mary's departure, the nuns began to realize how different life would be without her. She would never accept any money
for her work, and now they found that a hired man came at a great
price. Some of those they hired could not be trusted to do the work;
others wanted to have their families with them, expecting to receive
food from the mission kitchen. Fortunately, the number of vocations continued to increase, and every new arrival found herself
immediately inundated with work. As the Canadian Ursulines had
discovered, the glorious panegyric delivered by Angela Lincoln on
their life of prayer and the joys of community had little to do with

mission life as they found it. Even so, the young missionaries who came to St. Peter's persevered, adjusting their dreams, honing their motivations, and finding joy in the small advances in Christianity made by their pupils.

Earlier that year, on January 18, the nuns had celebrated a tenth-year anniversary. Just ten years before, the original six sisters had arrived in Miles City with the single goal of establishing a mission for the forsaken Cheyenne. Now they had nine missions, including the school at Miles City. The original six sisters had grown to more than sixty. It was an extraordinary accomplishment. Some would say it was the fulfillment of a dream, but for Amadeus, the dream was only beginning. "We have nine missions," she had explained proudly to one of the Canadian sisters, "but we will have fifteen."

Chapter Ten

As long as there is an Indian in Montana,
we will stay.

—*Sister St. Bernard Trudeau*

Only Scholastique, in her distant mission of St. Labre's, had been spared the imbroglio at St. Peter's. Perhaps because she was older and had fewer romantic illusions, she had adjusted surprisingly well to the hardships of mission life. Once she had recovered from the fatigue of six weeks of travel, she accepted the rigors of St. Labre's without complaint and with practical ardor.

She had arrived at a relatively favorable time. The mission, which Father Cataldo had closed the preceding July because of an upsurge of the ghost dance, had reopened in March 1893, to the satisfaction of the Indians, most of whom had come to recognize the advantage of education for their children but did not want them removed to the far-off government school at Fort Shaw. The indefatigable Father Van der Velden, with the help of Sister Katharine Drexel, had succeeded in putting up a new school building, assuring the skeptical agent that they would soon have eighty-five children.

But every success was balanced by a failure. The effort to cultivate a tract of land had been "a complete failure." Not only had they lost all the resources they had put into the venture, but they were now left with no winter provisions. Desperate, Van der Velden wrote to Stephan:

> We are obliged to build without delay as a severe winter is
> expected for this section of the country. Moreover the
> miserable log huts in which we live are beyond repair and in

such condition that we had to prop one of them lately for the sake of preventing it from coming down on our heads. ... We must provide ourselves with a dwelling however simple it be.[1]

Scholastique's letters home gave few details of these hardships but focused on their efforts to Christianize the Indians. Luke Van Ree, a young Jesuit who was helping at the mission, gave her comfort as he spoke of how difficult the Cheyenne were to convert, especially the adults, whose hearts were hard to reach, needing years of patient encouragement before they would listen. But Van Ree, young and optimistic, was unfazed by the difficulties, and in a letter to Katharine Drexel, expressed his hope for the future:

It is true from a spiritual and religious standpoint this mission
is better at present than we ever dared hope. The feeling of
the Indians toward us is excellent. In great numbers they
come daily to the prayers, to the sacrifice of the mass and to
other religious services; they begin to approach the
Sacraments regularly ... all must acknowledge that the time
for grace for these poor Cheyennes has finally arrived.[2]

His fervor, his optimism (and the fact that he understood a little French), made him Scholastique's lifeline. Like Van Ree, she saw hope in the devoted young girls who helped the sisters with the housework and in the children who longed to make their First Communion.

The following year, Van der Velden was at last able to begin building a church, a project for which he had been soliciting—unsuccessfully—since his arrival at St. Labre's. At first, he had used an old shack (fifteen feet by twenty-two feet) with a single window, but, wrote the annalist, "the air was unbearable when the Indians and children were gathered together." The only recourse was to use part of the school. But this, too, was far from satisfactory. "It was a very bad accommodation. It did not make any other impression upon the

Indians ... but that of a room in which they were used to talk and laugh when on Sunday they visited their children."[3]

All of Van der Velden's pleas for money had fallen on deaf ears. When neither Bishop Brondel nor the Jesuit superior was able to offer him anything, Van der Velden took things into his own hands. During the months when St. Labre's was closed, he used his "spare time" to solicit funds. "This last month I have labored considerably," he wrote in a letter to Holland. "Letters were mailed by the hundreds in all possible directions. My patience as a Hollander, which tells me 'it must be and it shall be,' is the only thing which gives me strength to stick to it. So to work then and to find persons to help me beg ... Heaps of letters are lying around. Three times a week the mail leaves and each time it receives a good load."[4]

By the summer of 1895, his unremitting labors had succeeded and he had sufficient funds to begin his church. "When finished," wrote the Jesuit annalist, "it promises to be of a great help in giving the Indians a better idea of religion, and especially a better idea of the reverence due to God."[5]

By the spring of 1897, the church was completed, and on April 27, Bishop Brondel arrived to officiate at the consecration.

Such triumphs were small, however, compared to the vastness of their task, and Scholastique, in her letters to Trois Rivières, acknowledged that mission life was not smooth—not "covered in velvet," as she expressed it. She loved working with the Cheyenne, loved trying to improve their lot and teach them about God, but community life was often difficult. Her superior knew no French, making even simple communication difficult. The other missions were so far away that they felt isolated and unsupported. She had written to Bernard and Marie de l'Espérance, now stationed at St. Ignatius's, but rarely heard from them, although they had given her news of the unfortunate affair with the sisters of Québec. "They are far from being appreciated," she wrote of the latter, conjecturing that this was undoubtedly because they had tried too hard to be reformers. With her clear, practical wisdom, Scholastique concluded that the underlying problem in the

Montana missions was that they were trying to do too much. "When you try to grasp too much you hold on to nothing."[6]

Meanwhile, Bernard and l'Espérance were experiencing a very different sense of mission. St. Ignatius's was large and well-established, and while there was more than enough work to do, they were not so overwhelmed as in the smaller missions. Despite her homesickness, Marie de l'Espérance's first letter home was full of the wonders of St. Ignatius's. "St. Ignatius is much richer than St. Peter's. Our convent is lovely—good beds, excellent food. The Sisters of Providence have a beautiful convent and then there is the church, the Father's house and fifteen cabins for the Indians. The view is wonderful. Our eyes are always on the wonders of the Creator."[7]

Even Christmas did not disappoint them. Their midnight Mass was deeply moving, Bernard wrote: the carillon ringing clear in the winter air; the canons thundering in the dark; the Indian women wrapped in colorful shawls, with babies on their backs and toddlers at their sides; a solemn liturgy with good singing under the direction of the Sisters of Providence. There were more than 800 Holy Communions, all told. The work the mission was doing with the Indians—both children and adults—was gratifying and inspiring.

But like Scholastique, Bernard found difficulties in their community life. In a long letter to her superior at Trois Rivières, she listed her grievances at length. There seemed little effort to obey the Rule. She wondered, sometimes, if the superior really knew the Rule. The communal penances were never observed; everything seemed to be at the discretion of the individual. As for prayers, there were endless litanies that left no time for prayers of Rule. The novices received very little training and seemed to be professed according to Amadeus's whim—some within a year, while others were kept waiting three years. Although she acknowledged that Amadeus was a remarkable leader, she was concerned by the rumor that when her term ended, a group of sisters was planning to have her reelected for life. Such a process was clearly contrary to Ursuline rule.

Although Bernard had an opportunity to discuss the situation when Amadeus visited St. Ignatius's that March, she felt her observations regarding their community life were not well received. While Bernard's concern was the quality of their religious life, for Amadeus, this was secondary. Her primary concern was, as always, the work of the missions. Bernard's criticism, however, made Amadeus anxious. Aware that Félix and Elisabeth were still restless and dissatisfied, she began to question if the Trois Rivières sisters could be counted on. On this point, Bernard replied positively. "We assured her," she wrote, "that as long as there is an Indian in Montana, we will stay with her."[8]

Amadeus's concern about the Québec sisters was not without foundation. Although Elisabeth and Félix found St. Paul's Mission more congenial than Holy Family, they remained unsettled. While for the first few months the kindness of Mother Francis Seibert and their mutual companionship encouraged them, by June, Elisabeth was writing home that everything they were trying to do was useless. The work on the mission was overwhelming. Although they had recently acquired a washing machine—a wonderful help—they desperately needed a bread kneader. Providing bread for more than 150 children was an insupportable task. Only the older and stronger girls had the strength to knead the massive amounts of dough—and many of them were suffering from tuberculosis.[9] The house was badly in need of repair, yet no improvements could be made, since they were already heavily in debt. Their situation seemed so hopeless that they had not the courage to continue. Sister Elisabeth had, therefore, written to Bishop Brondel, and also to the bishop of Québec, asking for money to return to Québec.

When Amadeus arrived in August, they affirmed that their minds were made up, that they were only waiting for a letter from Québec. Then, just seven days later, everything changed. In mid-July, Father Charles Mackin arrived to replace Father Balthasar Feusi, a kind and innocent Jesuit who had let the mission be swindled by unscrupulous men. Mackin, with a sound and experienced business sense, had been sent to do what he could to save the mission.

While Mackin was known to his Jesuit colleagues as a practical manager rather than a spiritual counselor, the sisters at St. Paul's discovered in him a vein of spirituality that touched their hearts. His counsel affirmed them in their vocation. While not minimizing their sufferings, he convinced them that God wanted them where they were. Through him, wrote Elisabeth, they saw the will of God. "Finally, after a year of struggle and suffering, we have won the victory; our perseverance in the missionary life is assured—but at what a price."[10]

That fall, for the first time, their letters home were about their work rather than their own suffering. Félix was the teacher; Elisabeth the jack-of-all-trades. The former spoke with affection of her "28 little savage flowers. ... I sleep with them, take my meals at the same table, recreate with them, pray with them; in a word, the only time they leave me is when they go to Mother Francis for their instruction." Elisabeth helped in everything "with patience and devotion." "All our hope is in these children whom we raise and who give us a wonderful hope for the future."[11]

Although Elisabeth had despaired of ever learning English, she found that there was plenty for her to do. While Félix was with the children, she took care of the sacristy and the multitude of small jobs always calling to be done. "I always have something in my hand: a knife, an ax, a needle ... " If they didn't become saints, Elisabeth concluded, it won't have been for lack of opportunity.[12]

While Félix was clearly the dominant figure, Elisabeth was indispensable. She helped with the singing and created costumes for the elaborate program for the closing of the school year.

The boys' school was responsible for a drama entitled *Major Andrée*, a Revolutionary War tale including George Washington, Lafayette, and "fifteen or sixteen other personages." It was a play chosen, no doubt, to increase the spirit of patriotism. The military costumes, imaginative rather than authentic, were created out of whatever remnants Elisabeth could discover. As for the girls, they were portrayed as Bohemians, singing and dancing in multicolored dresses, "fantastic bonnets and decorated shoes." It was a very successful program, loudly applauded by delighted parents for whom ritual and spectacle were of prime importance.[13]

Even with such success as this, the parents' support of the school remained limited. Although impressed by what the mission was able to do for their children, they remained suspicious of the Blackrobes and their religion.

Nor did they trust their medicines. When their children were seriously ill, they wanted them at home, in their tepees, where their medicine men could practice their own tribal cures. Most discouraging of all for the missionaries was the fact that even the children who had been at the mission for several years often returned to their "pagan state" as soon as they left school. "They become as savage as their parents who do not have the advantage of knowing any better," Félix recorded sadly.[14]

More sad news had reached them at the beginning of 1895. Pélagie had been transferred from Pryor to Miles City because of a serious problem with her eyes. Bernard's prediction that a woman who had such a strong will to dominate would not remain long in the little insignificant mission at Pryor had proved wrong. Although Pélagie's last act before leaving St. Peter's had been to give Amadeus a list of salient points of rule that she felt should be enforced, she did not bring her need to dominate to Pryor. She came with her full energy to serve. Pélagie was not afraid of poverty or tribulation. She was wholehearted and enduring, free from that habit of looking back to assess the choices one has made. Of the three sisters from Québec, she was the one who had never considered returning home.

In a strange way, Pryor suited her energies. "It is so poor," she wrote. "We haven't even a statue of the Blessed Virgin. How poor Jesus is here. He is despoiled of everything."[15] They were all overworked with no time for prayer, not even private space, since they had to be with their fifteen pupils constantly in order to train them properly. These are "pure" Indians, she explained in a letter to Québec, who follow all the customs of the Crow. On Sundays, the

nuns had to shake hands with them at the door of the church as they
came "all covered with feathers and necklaces and bracelets."
Afterward, they'd have a feast, sitting around on the ground, eating
everything with their fingers.

> As for attendance at Mass and Benediction of the Blessed
> Sacrament: the adults come more to see their children and
> listen to them sing than for any spirit of devotion. The
> women keep yelling, the babies keep crying and the dogs
> barking. This along with the music and the chant makes quite
> an uproar. Here, dear Mother, there is nothing to please
> nature—only the cross with fatigue and suffering. But I am
> really happy in spite of everything for I have the honor to do
> something for these poor souls. I love the children very much;
> they are docile and affectionate. ... I am ready to remain here
> as long as God wishes.[16]

By the end of 1894, however, Pélagie's cross had taken another
form. She had contracted what she called *granulation des yeux*, which,
no doubt, was the dreaded disease of trachoma. Living so close to
their Indian children, the sisters needed the utmost caution to avoid
this virulently contagious disease. Pélagie may not have recognized it
for what it was until it had progressed dangerously.

In early December, in the company of Amadeus and two other
sisters from Pryor, she traveled to Billings to see a doctor. The trip
almost ended in disaster, for in the failing light, the driver lost his
way and they plunged down an embankment and into a six-foot-
deep river. Pélagie's account is succinct and factual compared to the
vivid elaboration provided by St. Peter's annals, an account in which
Amadeus, in true nineteenth-century hagiographical style, becomes
a saintly heroine.

> The party consisting of Mother, Sisters Pélagie, Clara and Mary
> drove off from Pryor Creek at one pm ... they were in a new

surrey with two splendid horses. ... At 6:30 the driver entered Blue Creek, an arm of the Yellowstone, at the old crossing. He was making for the new bridge which that day was just completed. Mother's eyes were closed—suddenly Mother was awakened by a shrill cry from Sister Mary. "Mother, look, we are drowned!" The water had reached Sister Mary's neck; Mother was plunged in to her shoulders. Large blocks of ice floated down the rapid current. The horses with ears cocked, necks stretched to the utmost, barely kept their lips out of water. They snorted and moaned like animals in the presence of death. At this ghastly scene the driver fainted.[17]

It was, of course, Amadeus who brought him to consciousness, helped him out of the water, and gave him instructions to take another horse and ride to a nearby cowboy camp to get help. Here, the poor man fainted again, "falling mute and senseless at the threshold." When he was brought to, he could only murmur, "Nuns in the river."

It was enough, however, to set the cowboys in motion. "These brave men rode at once to the rescue and with all gallantry and deep respect of honest American hearts lifted the nuns out of their watery grave. ... The silent stars had crept out apace to witness the ghastly scene of mercy and of peril." A fire was made, and the nuns spent the night in a little cabin, sheltered from the wind, but frozen in their icy clothes.[18]

The perilous trip was little help to Pélagie. The medication given her by the Billings doctor did her no good, and by the end of the year, Amadeus had transferred her to Miles City, where she would be closer to medical help. Miles City was everything Pélagie deplored. At Miles, the Indian children for whom she had been willing to give her life were replaced by the ordinary children of white settlers. Her sickness made it impossible for her to teach, or even to participate in the work of the house.

Most painful of all was the quality of religious life. "There is no regular life here," she wrote. There was talking in the refectory, no instruction for the novice, flagrant violations of the Rule. In addition, the house was like an icebox. Since she had only sandals, her feet were always freezing.

At last, in February, after months of ineffective treatment, she had an operation for her eyes—a long, painful experience, since no anesthetic could be used because of the nature of the surgery. It would be months, the doctor warned, before her eyes would completely recover.

She was now entirely useless, dependent upon others for everything. She had to be taken care of in the most humiliating ways. She could not see to light a lamp, to negotiate the steep, narrow stairs, or to get to the privy without help. The worst of her humiliations was that because of the highly infectious nature of her disease, all of her clothes had to be washed separately, and the cloths used for her eyes had to be burned. For a woman of Pélagie's dominance, it could not have been a more crucifying trial. "Those who are yearning for sacrifice," she wrote, "have only to come to Montana where they will surely be satisfied."[19]

For the first time, she thought of returning to Québec, but now her sight was too seriously impaired to permit her to travel alone, and Sisters Félix and Elisabeth, after so much uncertainty, seemed happily settled at St. Paul's. All that was soon to change, however.

In early summer of 1896, Amadeus visited the missions with a disturbing and unanticipated pronouncement. All sisters who had been professed in other Ursuline communities would now be required to become lifelong subjects of the Montana missions, severing all affiliation to their communities of origin.[20]

For those who had come generously to assist for a period of time, it was an outrageous demand. In fact, it countermanded Bishop Gilmour's original document, drawn up when the original six had set out from Toledo. That document had stated unambiguously, "The sisters going from Toledo will be free to return to their convent in case of failure or dissatisfaction." Although there had been substantial changes since then, there was nothing that indicated that volunteers must make a lifetime commitment.

What had impelled Amadeus to take this step was, no doubt, her fear that she was losing her most mature and seasoned missionaries. The preceding year, three of the original six—Sisters Holy Angels Carabin, Angela Abair, and Ignatius McFarland—had returned to Toledo. A short time later, Sisters Rose Miller and Magdalen Cox, foundresses of St. Xavier's Mission, also returned to Toledo. That same year, Sister Joseph Steiner, who had first arrived at Miles City in 1885, returned to Cleveland, and another sister, John Berchmans Rogers, to Lake City, Minnesota. While postulants in considerable numbers continued to arrive at St. Peter's, Amadeus, with her constant dreams of mission expansion, felt she could ill afford to lose anyone, least of all those who were mature and experienced.

Once again, it was Bernard, in a letter to her superior at Trois Rivières, who provided the fullest account of what transpired when Amadeus arrived at St. Ignatius's the first week of June 1896:

> She had a clear goal in mind ... this year she wants all the outsiders [*religieuses étrangères*] to join her community. She is requiring us to sign a document by which we will renounce the right to return—and you, on your part, will lose the right to recall us—to our monastery. You understand, dear Mother, that it is very difficult for us to accept these conditions. We are prepared to continue working here for some years but the thought of committing ourselves for life, this, I repeat, is very difficult. The main reason is that here we do not lead anything like a religious life. ... Mother Amadeus wants to keep us with her but if you knew, Mother, how irregular and imperfect the life lived by the Ursulines in Montana! After all, what good will it do to save souls if we don't save our own and if we neglect our own perfection.[21]

Supported by their superior in Trois Rivières, Bernard and Marie de l'Espérance stood firm, refusing to sign the document despite Amadeus's continued coercion.

Finally, seeing that she was losing the battle, Amadeus made some concessions. Those unwilling to sign the document giving themselves entirely to the Montana mission could continue to work on the missions but would be considered "outsiders." It was a strange and injudicious solution. The so-called outsiders were, in fact, zealous volunteers willing to devote years of their lives to mission work. If anything, Amadeus had every reason to be grateful to them, yet she was treating them like inferior religious, unwilling to make the sacrifices demanded by missionary life. In a letter received at St. Ignatius's toward the end of October, she confirmed her decision to permit the "outsiders" to remain, but stipulated that they would no longer be considered "missionaries."

For Bernard, usually of a temperate disposition, it was too much. Her letter to Trois Rivières was eloquent with wrath:

> I assure you that if we are no longer missionaries in name we are certainly so in our work. Yes, Missionaries! Your two daughters flatter themselves as being so. One of us takes care of all the Fathers' washing while the other one is scrubbing and cleaning up these poor little savages. I am beginning my second year of being deprived of recreation with the community—I have not been with them a single time in a whole year! [I am] always with the children from morning to evening and evening to morning. Is this not to be a missionary? I have to put up with their habits, I have to get up seven or eight times a night and to breathe their stench, etc., etc., Is this not to be a missionary ... and further to be deprived of my beloved mothers and sisters of Trois Rivières, the religious family that I love so much. Now tell me, Mother, if your children of Montana are not true missionaries? Everything for the greater glory of God![22]

For the Canadians, it was the final humiliation. No sacrifice they had made was acknowledged or valued. The ardent religious life, the fervent prayerful community, the joys they would find in a life of sacrifice—all the aspects of life in Montana promised them so eloquently in Angela Lincoln's romantic rhetoric during her visit to Canada now seemed only an illusion. What they had found and what they cherished was the service they rendered to the poor Indians. But ultimately, this did not satisfy their vision of religious life. They had been trained in another model. They did not want to choose, but they were being forced to do so. "Please believe me, dear Mother," Bernard wrote to Trois Rivières, "had Mother Amadeus not issued such a proposition we would never have asked to be recalled, even though it would have been sweet to return to our dear cloister, but we would love to have continued our work here as long as there were schools for these dear savage children."[23]

Scholastique, now at Pryor, agreed, writing home that she had tried to make Amadeus understand that they could not belong completely to Montana; that as religious with a vow of obedience, they were not free to abandon the monastery of their profession. "Thus our mission to the Indians has come to an end," Scholastique wrote sadly.[24]

At St. Paul's, the Québec nuns had reached the same conclusion. Sisters Félix and Elisabeth had been joined that summer by Pélagie, and by early fall they had received a letter recalling them to Québec.

By December 1896, despite generous effort on all sides, the experiment had ended. It was a sad commentary on the vagaries of human weakness.

Once letters from Canada arrived confirming the decision for all six sisters to return to their monasteries, plans for their travel went into operation at once. Scholastique had written to Amadeus asking that her ticket be arranged so that she could travel to Billings, where she would join Bernard and Marie de l'Espérance. To Scholastique's dismay, Amadeus showed no inclination to pay her expenses. Scholastique had been at Pryor only six months and was loath to ask this "poor little mission" to underwrite the money she would need for her trip home. She was equally loath to ask Trois Rivières, since for the last four years she had been absent, contributing nothing to her home monastery.

All six sisters faced the same humiliation. Amadeus was intransigent, reminding the superiors in Canada that she had paid the initial expenses to Montana and that "the thought of the return expense never crossed my mind." A further letter to an anonymous "Reverend Father" is even more intractable:

> I paid all the traveling expense of the Three Rivers Ursulines to Montana. ... I thought you would surely pay the homeward trip. I know it is very hard to ask your Reverence to incur this but when you consider how hard it must have been for me, three years ago, when I was overwhelmed in debt to defray the traveling expenses of seven nuns from the East to help in the work in the Indian Missions and how utterly impossible it is for me now ... I think and trust the goodness of your heart will make you relent and change your purpose.[25]

There is no record indicating how all these travel expenses were defrayed, but by the beginning of January 1897, all six sisters had returned to their monasteries.

The union of Canada and Montana had not succeeded. The Montana missionaries found the exactions of monasticism overwhelming and irrelevant to the stark life of the plains; the Canadian Ursulines found those very exactions a source of life and peace.

Perhaps no one suffered more from this failure than Amadeus. This union was her dream, and Amadeus had a disconcerting way of taking dream for reality. Ministry and monasticism—she had envisioned an enriching union. Both sides had tried, but they had failed. Three and a half years of unrelenting work, of sickness, loneliness, and—worst of all—misunderstanding, were over.

Chapter Eleven

*Last night I kept lifting up my hands
and heart to God for help.*
                    —*Mother Amadeus Dunne*

In the year following the departure of the Canadian sisters, Amadeus was forced to reconsider her dream of fifteen missions. She was about to enter a period that would test her optimism to the measure. The next eighteen months might well have been called her *Annus Terribilis*.

The golden age of missionary activity, as it was later termed, was coming to an end. Contract schools, which the government had used as a means of "civilizing" and controlling the Native American population, were considered no longer necessary. Government schools, now becoming more numerous, were easier to manage. Under government control, a uniform curriculum could be established with identical textbooks used for all schools. As an added advantage, federal administration would put an end to the endless friction between various religious denominations as well as friction between agents and religious supervisors. Equally important: the Indians would be more firmly under government control. The tendency of the missionaries to align themselves with the native population rather than with the encroaching white settlers was an increasing source of unrest.

In 1895, with the passage of the Indian Appropriation Act, conditions for mission schools changed dramatically. This act, which was to take effect in June 1896, forbade the use of government funds for the education of Indian children in sectarian schools. St. Peter's, as well as other missions, had been feeling the sting of reduced assistance for several years and now had to face the fact that they would receive no further payments. The Jesuits, who for some time had been questioning their usefulness at St. Peter's, were better prepared for the blow than were the Ursulines. Now that Holy Family Mission was satisfying their objective of working with the Blackfeet, the fathers no longer considered St. Peter's essential.

Although Father Damiani had always been enthusiastic about St. Peter's, the superiors who succeeded him had been less keen. Father Francis Andreis, assigned as superior in 1893, gave the lie to Mother Amadeus's eloquent testimony of the beauty of St. Peter's. "This is a dreadful place in every regard," he wrote to a friend that winter. "Debts have accumulated to a frightful amount, winds blowing constantly with an intense fury, no neighborhood. ... I suppose the intention of Father Van Gorp was to give me an easier position but surely I came, as the saying has it, from the frying pan into the fire."[1]

For Amadeus, however, St. Peter's was always to be the capstone of her enterprise. Well aware that it was unrealistic, and even undesirable, to assume that her missions could continue with a staff of temporary volunteers, Amadeus had been determined to establish a novitiate as soon as possible. Such a novitiate would provide their own staff of sisters trained specifically for mission work and committed for life. She envisioned St. Peter's as the ideal site for a novitiate and motherhouse.*

Until now, her goal had worked well. Not only had the school flourished, but the novitiate was always full. In 1893 alone, eighteen religious were added to the community, coming from as far away as New York. Now, however, with the news that all government subsidies were to cease, St. Peter's was in crisis.

Amadeus lost no time in sending letters of appeal throughout the United States. Unfortunately, her action was not approved by

---

*Unfortunately, the novitiate was established without ecclesiastical sanction or Jesuit approval. "The Jesuits had objected to the Ursulines' proposal of building a huge novitiate at St. Peter's far from other churches and schools. Despite this the novitiate was built and the Jesuits were expected to provide chaplains for the sisters there." Wilfred P. Schoenberg, S.J., *Paths to the Northwest* (Chicago: Loyola University Press, 1982), 204.

the BCIM. In September 1896, the director wrote to Bishop Brondel, warning him that such individual appeals would injure the annual collection for the Indians and asking that he cooperate in this regard. "Any other course will result in much confusion and little or no benefit to the schools. The course I recommend is the regular and proper one, and, if followed, will subserve the best interests of those engaged in Indian missionary work."[2]

Although the restriction limited Amadeus's general appeals, it still left her free to write to Katharine Drexel:

> We have no contract whatever from the government. I do not
> know from day to day how I can possibly feed the many that
> look to me for their support. ... Sometimes I have one
> hundred girls in our Indian School, at present writing I have
> only seventy-five. ... I have been obliged to go in debt rather
> than send the girls away. Our bishop has given me during the
> past year only three hundred dollars, three-fourths of all he
> received from the Annual Collections! He would give us more
> if he could. I felt all along, dear Mother Katharine, that you
> would not abandon us.[3]

But Katharine Drexel, now Mother Katharine, foundress of her own congregation, could not provide all that was needed. By this time, St. Peter's had four boarding schools: two for Indian and white boys run by the Jesuits and two for girls run by the Ursulines. In the twelve years they had been at St. Peter's, the Ursulines had not only constructed a beautiful and substantial building, they had refined the curriculum to a high polish. Reading, writing, and arithmetic had been transformed into calisthenics, penmanship, oratory, Latin, and astronomy for the pupils of the white school, and practical arithmetic, reading, spelling, singing, mental arithmetic, geography, and proficiency in English for the Indians. All the girls were taught knitting, embroidery, crocheting, dressmaking, and some of the arts.

Recognizing the importance of a well-educated faculty, Amadeus imported teachers from the East whenever she could and saw that her own sisters were sufficiently trained. Sister Annunciata Dunne was sent to Helena to study banjo and mandolin in order to begin a girls' orchestra. Two novices, Sisters Amata and De Merici Sheble, were sent to Philadelphia to study music, art, oratory, and carving.

Superintendent William Moss, in his 1895 report, had nothing but the highest praise for what he found. "Most all the sisters here are from the east and are above average in education and intelligence. All the girls in the advanced school room are given lessons in instrumental music and oil and crayon painting, wood carving, etc. All are given vocal music. ... If I were to make any criticism at all, it would be that everything here is so very fine and nice that when they go home the contrast will be too great for them to bear."[4]

With such an investment, it is easy to see why Amadeus could not agree to abandoning St. Peter's. Father Van Gorp, however, always the pragmatist and now superior of the Jesuit Rocky Mountain Region, had no such vested interest. Rather, he saw St. Peter's as squandering men who could be used more profitably elsewhere. His was a realistic assessment, and by 1896, the decision was made to close both boys' schools within the next year or two and withdraw the Jesuit community.

Unfortunately, there is no extant correspondence between the Ursulines and Jesuits during this fractious period of decision, but in May 1898, the Jesuit community withdrew, leaving the Ursulines the priests' abandoned buildings and a long, anxious summer without either spiritual or material resources.

Amadeus was left with scant time to worry about the future of St. Peter's, because that spring, a dangerous crisis had developed at St. Labre's. Although still dogged by poverty—the $8 per month per child allotted by the government hardly covered their needs—with the reopening of the mission in March of 1893, St. Labre's seemed to have entered a more stable period. "The year '93–'94 was more successful than any heretofore," wrote the Jesuit annalist. "The children stayed at school with a very few exceptions. The old Indians also improved in matters of religion. They came to prayers more regularly ... In the church they began to behave themselves a little better."[5]

The more compliant response of the Indians was partly the result of an improved mission school. Two Ursulines, along with a number of Jesuit scholastics, had been added to the staff, thus enabling the nuns to devote themselves entirely to the education of the girls and the domestic work of the mission.

These small successes, however, were soon overshadowed by an ominous conflict between Indians and whites. John Hoover, a poor, simple-witted shepherd, had been found shot several miles from his camp. At once, accusations were leveled against the Cheyenne. This time, the accusations were substantiated—there was sufficient evidence found at the site to identify the culprits.

Immediately, the agent, Captain George Stouch, ordered all the Indians from the mission section of the reservation—near where the body had been found—to report to the agency. Fearful of what would happen when the sheriff, with his vigilante troops, arrived, the Indian women and children flocked to the safety of the nuns' building while the men streamed into Van der Velden's room, asking for protection and advice. Within days, newspapers—as far away as New York—carried lurid and unsubstantiated articles declaring that the Cheyenne were on the warpath, roaming without restraint throughout the country, and that all white women and children had been evacuated.

In fact, it was the whites who were on the warpath, with the sheriff arriving at the agency fully armed, with a mob bent on the Indians' destruction. Stouch, however, was a man of wisdom and restraint. Despite the pressure of the ranchers, he refused to hand over the three culprits—who had peaceably surrendered—without observing proper legal formalities. The state of siege continued, with both sides alert to the possibility of an overt clash.

Although the crisis ended without violence, the Hoover episode was but an additional illustration that the initial enmity between the ranchers and the Cheyenne remained unresolved, with the Indians living under the continual threat of being moved from their reservation to Dakota or some sterile land, leaving Montana's good grazing land for the white ranchers.

Although, as things quieted, some of the children returned to school, mission life had been disastrously interrupted. It was clear that St. Labre's future was again in the balance. Father Van Gorp, never willing to waste either men or money, was already considering withdrawing the Jesuits. In fact, St. Labre's had never been a Jesuit mission; it had been initiated by Bishop Brondel and was under his custody. Although Brondel acknowledged this responsibility, he was angered by what he considered high-handed decisions on the part of the Jesuits, both at St. Peter's and now at St. Labre's. Without the Jesuits, it was problematic whether the nuns could continue their work.

On August 3, Amadeus arrived from St. Peter's. She spent little time discussing the issues. Her decision, no doubt, had been made before she arrived. "She declared at once her intention of holding the mission," the annalist wrote. It was a typical Amadean decision: quixotic, visionary, and—in this instance—successful.

Five days later, on August 8, the Cheyenne chief White Bull, whose daughter Margaret had been a pupil at the school, came to ask the Lady Blackrobes what would now happen to the school. "He

St. Labre's Indian School, circa 1890. Courtesy of Ursuline archives, Great Falls, Montana

asked how long Mother would keep his children," the Ursuline annalist noted. "An instant Mother paused. Then looking up to heaven with the sublime confidence and trust of the saints, Mother answered, 'As long as you will send them, White Bull.'"[6] It was clearly a glorious moment for the annalist: the courage of the Lady Blackrobes triumphing over the faint hearts of their masculine counterparts.

Perhaps, for a moment, it might have seemed that Amadeus's decision might influence the Jesuits, but that was not to be. On August 10, acting under the command of obedience, Father Van der Velden and his compatriot John Van der Pol left St. Labre's.

> At eight o'clock Fathers van der Velden and van der Pol came over to bid us goodbye. As we knelt for their blessing the former said, with a voice choked with emotion, "Sisters, God bless you for your devotion and the many examples of virtue you have given. I leave our Lord with you. Let that be your consolation. Pray sometimes for me and I will pray for you: "Benediction," etc.
>
> We followed the Fathers to their house. Father van der Pol begged Mother to have it cleaned and to keep for herself whatever she would find in it. They told Mother also to take the statue of St. Benedict Joseph Labre over to the convent. The last wagon-load of freight rolled off, driven by Mr. Ed. Yaeger and then Fathers van der Velden and van der Pol drove off in the buggy.
>
> Father van den Velden has labored here 12 years and rode off broken in heart and health, begging God to call him soon to Himself.*[7]

Amadeus stayed on at St. Labre's while they cleaned the fathers' house and discussed the future of the mission. Once again, St. Labre's

---

*In fact, Father Van der Velden lived on as a missionary until 1925.

was being left without a resident chaplain. Father John Victor Van den Broeck, then stationed at Miles City, had offered to come to St. Labre's occasionally, but, despite the development of the railroad, it was still a long and arduous trip with no way to cover the considerable distance from the station at Forsyth, except by horse and wagon. Bishop Brondel grieved for their circumstances but could promise nothing. In fact, it would be five months before a priest arrived at St. Labre's.

Less than a month before, Amadeus had accepted the decision to close the mission of St. John Berchmans's at Arlee, which had been founded just five years earlier. It had been opened in a spirit of compassion for the Flathead chief Charlo, who had suffered so long, unable to surrender the way of life that, to him, was the Indians' rightful inheritance. With most of the tribe now in the area of St. Ignatius's, the mission at Arlee had never thrived, and with the death of Charlo, the decision was made to close it entirely.

While the closure of Arlee was not a major loss, it brought the Ursulines up short. Within a year, the Jesuits had withdrawn—or would soon withdraw—from three missions where the Ursulines staffed schools. For Amadeus, who was still dreaming of expansion, it was, at best, disconcerting.

Bishop Brondel used harsher words. While he had to acknowledge that the decision to close Arlee was probably justified, he could find no justification for the withdrawal from St. Peter's or St. Labre's. The Jesuits, however, were not under Brondel's ecclesiastical jurisdiction, and he was powerless to influence their decisions.

Toward the end of August, Amadeus returned to St. Peter's, promising the nuns that she would return as soon as she could to share the difficult winter months with them. But before her return, she was to endure a major tragedy. On November 26, 1897, the convent at Miles City burned to the ground. The fire had been discovered about 8:00 P.M., and three hours later, the vulnerable frame house was in ashes. There is little to explain the cause of the fire beyond a memoir written by Amadeus some nine years later. "It was during Mother Angela's term of office," she wrote, "that the little frame convent was burned November 26, 1897. The fire was caused by a defective flue—the kitchen flue—for after the fire all the other flues remained standing but the kitchen flue alone was completely demolished."[8]

The report given on December 2 in the *Yellowstone Journal* added little to Amadeus's spare account, except to note that the outcome might not have been so dire had the performance of the fire department been more efficient. Everything, it seemed, had been against them: the freezing cold, the location of the convent, the wrenches that failed to open the fireplugs. The firefighters could do little but watch the flames devour the convent.[9]

In a Christmas letter to her faithful friend Father Lindesmith, Amadeus expressed how deeply she was touched by the loss:

> This joyous day will be a sad one to me. Beside our many
> needs in the Indian Mission, I have now to provide for our
> nuns at Miles City. On Nov. 26 from a defective flue, the
> convent there took fire and burned to the ground. ... Our
> poor nuns were turned out onto the snow when it was 30
> degrees below zero with nothing but the clothing they had on
> their backs. My dear nuns called the pastor in time to save the
> Blessed Sacrament, and they themselves saved the children
> and the papers. But the insurance is not sufficient. Miles City
> convent is a heap of smoldering ashes! Can you believe it,
> Father? The nuns were to leave but the people and the pastor
> protested so with the Bishop that His Lordship has decided to
> let them remain. We shall rebuild.[10]

The decision to rebuild was not easily made. While Amadeus grieved for the loss of the convent at Miles City, honoring it as their first step in their mission to the Indians, it had never been as close to her heart as the missions themselves. The school at Miles City, exclusively for white children, was, in her eyes, simply a necessary adjunct to their real work. Miles City was often used as a refuge for sisters in poor health or for those who had not, as she considered, measured up to the exactions of mission life. Their needs, the requirements of the school, were frequently ignored, and the nuns themselves often felt that their work went unacknowledged. But if Amadeus had at first hesitated in rebuilding the convent—as some documents indicate—in the end, the pleas of the people and the strong recommendation of Brondel shaped her decision.

A month after the fire, the devoted Lindesmith sent her a check for $500 to help in rebuilding. On February 7, 1898, she wrote in gratitude, "Your generous donation reached me here (St. Labre) ...

St. Labre's Mission, First Communion. Courtesy of Ursuline archives, Great Falls, Montana

It seems fifty times itself such a great help it is to me. Last night I could not sleep from anxiety and kept lifting up my hands and heart to God for help."[11]

By the end of December, Amadeus had returned from Miles City to St. Labre's, in time for Christmas, as she had promised. Anxiety and the hazards of travel at such a season had worn her down, and the next six weeks she spent mostly in bed, nursed by Sister Angela Lincoln, who had come from Miles City to take care of her.

At the end of the year, the new chaplain at St. Labre's, Father Joseph Vermaat, a Dutch priest appointed by Bishop Brondel, arrived. He had arrived unexpectedly and nothing was ready for him. The nuns collected bedclothes from their own store and did what they could to make him comfortable. But Vermaat was neither experienced in the work of the mission nor affable with the sisters. "The very unfriendly pastor," wrote a sister from St. Peter's in describing him. They all missed the devoted Van der Velden and the compassionate Prando, who had understood the problems of the school and the needs of the sisters as well as those of the Indians. Vermaat spent most of his time traveling to the Indian encampments, and his duties as chaplain to the mission school played second fiddle.

Holy Family Mission, girls' school. Courtesy of Marquette University Libraries, Bureau of Catholic Indian Missions Records

Amadeus had still not fully recovered from her exhaustion and anxiety over Miles City when a telegram reached her of another fire. On a Sunday afternoon in early January, while all were attending Benediction in Holy Family Mission church, the nuns' buildings had burned to the ground. While Holy Family had suffered the usual hardships and losses since the arrival of the Ursulines in 1890, it had never been a serious source of concern. In 1892, Father Van Gorp had written to Mother Drexel of the state of the mission: "Their present debt is owing to the starting of the mission, when furniture of every kind had to be bought and freighted a long distance. At the beginning as is usual in an Indian school it proved difficult to get the requisite number. ... Now the school is full, has a good name and everything is satisfactory."[12]

Father Bougis, while not contradicting his superior's evaluation, acknowledged the daily difficulties of the mission: "My position here is not easy, and I feel I will be soon worn out. Moreover because of the surroundings, the dispersion of the savages, their character, the climate and so forth, this mission will always be a very trying post. In closing, I can say I have suffered much."[13]

In addition to the intense cold and the sudden blizzards, an occasional cyclone roared down from the mountains, tearing off roofs and scattering them across the plains. No wonder that Father Bougis could aver that he had "suffered much" or that Sister Félix, who had been appointed superior in the summer of 1894, after a few winter months had to admit defeat. Although the mission was beautifully situated from an aesthetic point of view, practically speaking, it was a hard land. Long winters, dry summers, and strong winds made agriculture close to impossible, with the result that most foodstuffs had to be shipped in, at exorbitant cost.

Despite the difficulties, Holy Family Mission prospered. Within two years, the school had outgrown its quarters and, with the support of Mother Drexel, a three-story building was erected for the boys, constructed from local sandstone from the nearby cliffs. The Ursulines were then able to expand the girls' school, moving into the other half of the original frame building. Holy Family was not an easy mission, but its work was stable, and evangelization proceeded at a slow but steady pace.

By 1898, the mission had developed sufficiently to justify it being called "Holy Family Industrial School." A few years earlier, Mother Drexel had given them a small herd of horses. Now there were horse barns and cowsheds, machine shops and toolsheds, a windmill and a storehouse for grains. The boys' school, in addition to classrooms and dormitories, a chapel, and a recreation room, also housed the priests and brothers. The girls' school, while older and less spacious, was sufficient for the students' needs. Here, in addition to the girls' quarters, were the dining rooms for the Jesuits and the workmen as well as the students and the nuns, all of whom—according to regulation—ate separately. The laundry and bakery, considerable enterprises, were housed in separate buildings.

The fire that roared through the nuns' buildings on that cold January afternoon was succinctly described in a single sentence by the Jesuit annalist: "Toward the end of January the nuns' convent and the girls' school was completely consumed by fire."[14] It was Father Prando's later history that added the details that the bakery

Holy Family Mission, drums, nuns, and Indians. Courtesy of Ursuline archives, Great Falls, Montana

and the laundry, essential buildings, had, by the heroic efforts of the mission personnel, been saved from the flames. Even so, there were some fifty children, bereft of all their possessions, to house and feed.

At once, the Jesuits moved the boys from the third floor of the dormitory and did what they could to make it accessible to both nuns and girls; but even with this help, they were inhumanly crowded with disastrous results. The cramped conditions made even basic hygiene close to impossible, and within weeks, the first case of measles had multiplied, with the disease spreading through both schools. "One may readily imagine," wrote the compassionate Prando, "the weariness of those days for the devoted Ursuline Nuns, for then, as now, the drudgery of the kitchen and dining room, wash-house and sick-room fell upon them."[15]

Again, it was Mother Drexel who came to their aid, promising sufficient funds to build a stone building for the girls, equivalent to the one built earlier for the boys. By the succeeding fall, a three-story building, forty feet by sixty feet, had been erected, and when school began that September, the nuns reveled in their "spacious" quarters.

Yet the future of Holy Family remained tenuous. By 1898, government funds were, as one Jesuit wrote, "reduced to a trickle," and by 1900, they had stopped altogether.

All the missions were suffering the same fate. Even St. Ignatius's, the largest and most successful, was faced with dramatic changes. Although the 1899 report of R. C. Bauer, the local supervisor, had nothing but high praise, describing the plant as "elegant," commending the well-ventilated boys' dormitory, the large playground, the successful industrial school, and the "fine cornet band," his praise was not sufficient to stem the tide.[16]

Thomas Morgan, commissioner for Indian affairs, who had already shown himself hostile to the missions, continued his carping criticism: boys and girls should not be kept in separate classrooms and separate dining rooms; they did not receive enough methodical work in arithmetic; they read too loud and without sufficient expression.[17]

A more serious threat was the Browning Ruling—later revoked—which denied Indian parents the right to decide where their children would be schooled; this decision would be the prerogative of the agent, who, of course, would always decide in favor of government schools.[18]

For a while, it seemed that everyone was against them. White ranchers were irritated by the Jesuits' successful effort to have the Northern Pacific pay the Indians for the right of way across the reservation as well as reimbursement for the timber that had been cut.[19] The persistent demand of the whites to open reservation land continued, and in the spring of 1895, Sister Bernard wrote to Trois Rivières that there was serious talk that "the reservation is going to be opened, thus enabling the whites to buy land and put up their buildings."[20]

Despite all the missionaries' efforts to win the Indians' confidence, it took little to arouse their suspicions. When one of the instructors tried to explain to a parent that their son was "dumb"— unable to speak properly—and could not be adequately educated in the mission school, the word was misinterpreted. Understanding that their son was being humiliated by being called "stupid," their indignation arose. No Indian could accept such an insult, and there was a movement to withdraw other children from the school. A more serious episode occurred when a small child from the kindergarten slipped away from the nuns' care and was drowned in a nearby stream. It was a terrible accident that the Indians could not forgive. "There is a strong animus against the Ursulines," the Jesuit annalist wrote.[21]

Eight months later, November 16, 1896, such hostility took visible form when two "half-breed" boys burned their school to the ground. The Jesuit annalist provided a graphic account of the fire:

> November 16: Towards 2:00 P.M. an alarm of fire was given by
> one of the Philosophers who saw large volumes of smoke
> issuing from the top of the Boys School building.

Immediately, the engine was fired, the hose brought out and coupled but it was too late. The fire which must have been going on for some time on the top floor, then uninhabited, had already gained too much way to be so easily checked. After a half hour of futile attempts at checking the fire, the house had to be abandoned to its doom. Orders were given to save what could be as yet got at. All the scholastics and the boys, the employees at the mission and the Fathers with Father Superior as a leader did their utmost efforts to save what was valuable.

A quarter of an hour later the fire was raging with such violence that all further attempts had to be abandoned and all united their efforts towards protecting the other buildings. ... For a moment it seemed as though all efforts were to be to no purpose. The draught provided by the burning building began already to dart terrible flames, now toward the Tower, then toward the Fathers' building. The scholastics holding the hose covered with wet blankets already shrink from keeping their post. The Tower and the north-western wing of the building are steaming fearfully and awfully scorched. Fire is going in a few moments to attack them. The Blessed Sacrament has been removed meanwhile from the chapel and the books of the library transferred by willing hands to the basement of the Church.

The Sisters are praying and our little innocent boys and girls of the kindergarten are praying with extended hands ... suddenly the burnt building collapses and the heat diminishes. The fire evidently will soon be subdued and the danger is over.

Had it not been for the pouring rain and the fact of there being no high winds—and for the courage of our scholastics who with true devotedness exposed themselves to the scorching heat of the fire in order to keep the hose playing at the smoking walls of the threatened buildings—had it not

been also for the effective work of the carpenters and scholastics who were constantly keeping pouring water on the top
roof of our building and spreading over it wet blankets, the
mission would undoubtedly have been a complete wreck.[22]

The following morning, when they were able to explore the
buildings, they found their losses more considerable than they had
anticipated. All the school furnishings, all the beds and bedding, had
been devoured by the flames. Fortunately, the sisters' buildings were
sufficiently distant so that neither the Sisters of Providence nor the
Ursulines suffered any loss.

At once, space was rearranged so that the boys—some seventy
in number—could continue their school. Telegrams were sent to the
superior and to the insurance company, which ultimately reimbursed
them $5,000 for the building and $300 for the furniture. Hardly
enough to rebuild, but at least enough to make a beginning.

While the courage and endurance of the missionaries is
remarkable, their sangfroid in maintaining their ordinary schedule is
overwhelming. At 5:30 P.M. on the day of the fire, they assembled in
the chapel—which had not been injured—for their devotions as
planned: Solemn Benediction with music provided by the children
under the direction of the Sisters of Providence. After supper, they
reassembled for prayers of gratitude that the other buildings had
been preserved. The next morning, despite their exhaustion, they
rose for Mass and spent the day putting things in order. The process
of reorganization was made more difficult by the fact that heavy
rains had damaged the railroad tracks, so that the Canadian Pacific
was not running.

It was not until the beginning of December that the culprits
were found and arrested. "On December 3 Major Carter came from
the Agency bringing along the boy ... who was accused of having set
fire to our building. He confessed to everything before witnesses here
and also before his family. It was found that he had an accomplice.
... Both of them will probably be sent to the reformatory."[23]

The fire could hardly have occurred at a more perilous time. By 1896, St. Ignatius's, like all the missions, was experiencing an era of diminishment. Government funds, already cut dramatically, had now stopped entirely. Within the next two years, many of the industrial shops had to be closed and the number of pupils seriously reduced. Both Jesuits and Sisters of Providence, dependent on federal assistance, were on the cusp of closing entirely. The Ursulines, who had never received government aid, were, in a sense, less affected, although they felt indirectly the poverty of the Jesuits.

By 1898, the decision was made to enforce the terms of the original contract between Jesuits and Ursulines by which the Ursulines would no longer be supported by the Jesuits but would become independent. The contract stated that the Jesuits would obtain for them a suitable piece of land and a sum of money sufficient to begin their new school. Faithful to their promises, the Jesuits provided the Ursulines with forty acres of land, reasonably close to the other mission buildings, a team of horses, and a small herd of twelve cows. The nuns' original building was moved to their new property, and, again with Jesuit help, another wing was added. On June 27, 1898, the Ursulines moved into their new establishment.

The Jesuit annalist, after describing the exact location of this land, added that the Ursulines would also be given "the wash house with boiler and its apparatus until such time as they would refuse to do our washing in which case the wash house would revert to us." It was a harsh statement, suggestive of employer and hired help rather than that of religious colleagues. Even bleaker was the initial sentence: "Until now they had been supported—children and nuns—by ours, but henceforward they will have to support themselves."[24]

It was not long before the nuns began to feel the practical consequences of the move. In January 1900, as a new century began, they wrote desperately to Monsignor Stephan at the BCIM:

> From 1890 to 1898 we were engaged in the charge of the St.
> Joseph kindergarten here for the Jesuit Fathers. We then

opened an independent school and thereafter received one
third of the government contract for the mission. ... This was
a very great undertaking as we had nothing with which to
start, save the house in which we lived. ... The reason for this
change was that the Fathers, on account of the lessening of
the contract, were about to give up the kindergarten. Loath to
abandon it, we resolved to continue it as our own school—
had the house moved to a better location, a new wing added,
water tower erected, etc. ... also the purchasing of a ranch,
cattle, farm implements, etc. ... Each day brings us letters
from our creditors, clamoring for settlement of heavy bills,
due for the past fifteen months. ... Reverend Father, we are in
real distress.[25]

It seemed, in fact, that the *Annus Terribilis* would never end.

Chapter Twelve

Here at the motherhouse
we are all in favor of this union.

—*Mother Amadeus Dunne*

In January 1899, Amadeus received a letter from Mother St. Julien Aubry, the former superior of the French convent of Blois, presently living in Rome. It was a long document, a circular sent to all Ursuline houses in Europe and abroad, announcing a projected worldwide union of Ursulines.[1]

Such a proposal was a major step in Ursuline history. According to Ursuline monastic tradition, each foundation was autonomous, connected to its "mother" house only by its shared history and traditions. Thus the first Ursuline missionaries to Québec, unlike the Jesuit missionaries, became at once an independent house. In the same way, Cleveland, born from Boulogne-sur-Mer, established its independence, as did Toledo in its own time.

The Montana missions, like all Ursuline houses, had been canonically independent from their beginning. Although at first the ties with Toledo had been very close, as the years passed and the original foundresses were replaced by other religious, the ties became less firm. By 1890, Montana had its own identity. It was an independent Ursuline congregation with a superior general and a motherhouse at St. Peter's. The congregation consisted of nine houses and a novitiate. It was a unique model, but one that seemed admirably suited to its missionary vocation.

It is not surprising that Amadeus showed little interest in Mother St. Julien's letter. The proposal of an Ursuline union was of peculiarly European concern, as the nuns searched for a bulwark against the growing spirit of anticlericalism sweeping across the continent. The fate of the European houses, while a matter for sympathy, had little impact on the houses of Montana. Rome was very distant, and the anxieties that troubled Amadeus were very near.

The following month, a second letter arrived, seconding the information of the first and including a letter from Cardinal Francesco Satolli, the cardinal protector in Rome, urging the movement toward unification. Toward the end of that month, a third letter arrived, affirming that there was a growing number of Ursuline houses in favor of such universal union.

Finally, on May 20, Amadeus responded at length to Mother St. Julien. The letter was in French, in the hyperbolic style of Angela Lincoln. "I have received, as though coming from heaven, your three circulars," the letter began. Throughout the four pages, written in an elegant script, Amadeus—through her scribe—avowed her total commitment to the suggested union. "For years I have asked God for this union," the letter affirmed, a union that was worth every sacrifice. "Here at the Motherhouse we are all in favor of this union, a perfect and complete union, under a superior general and with a Motherhouse at Rome. ... We are ready to make every sacrifice—government, finances, dress, customs ... everything."[2]

Angela's rhetoric, consistently extravagant, was sometimes dangerously misleading, sheering from truth to fantasy. "We do not have a penny of debt," she averred, emphasizing their "smiling future." Yet, when she wrote, their debts had reached such heights as to bring down the wrath of even their tolerant bishop. And their "smiling future" was beclouded by the uncertainties of missions that had no longer any secure source of income. "Yet even our bright future, our beloved bishop, our dear converts, this wonderful field that Our Lord has entrusted to us—we are ready to abandon it all, ready to sacrifice everything for the good of the Order."[3]

What impelled Amadeus to jump so precipitously to the movement toward unity? Undoubtedly, she was influenced by her *Annus*

Terribilis. The year 1900 was far from a time of "sunny future" for missions in general, and for Ursulines in particular. Neither Toledo nor Cleveland, nor even the beneficent Mother Drexel, could save the missions from the ruinous debts that Amadeus had incurred. Nor could Amadeus's inveterate optimism shield her indefinitely from the specter of failure. Within a short period, two missions had been closed, two houses burned, two missions left without priestly assistance. Perhaps a place in a worldwide Ursuline union could provide the security they desperately needed.

Toward the end of August 1899, Amadeus received a lengthy and formal letter from Bishop Brondel explaining the next step in the process toward unity. "Therefore, Reverend Mother Amadeus," Brondel wrote, "please bring to the knowledge of the professed Ursulines in Montana this matter and, after collecting the secret votes of all, please send them to us, that we may correspond to the desires of His Eminence."[4]

The report that Brondel returned to ecclesiastical authorities in Rome in October of that year indicated that fifty-seven members of the Montana congregation were in favor of union—a sizable majority. Only a small group objected to the suppression of the fourth vow, which bound them to the work of education.* Brondel's careful statistics seemed to provide evidence against the accusation leveled later against Amadeus—that she had never provided opportunity for the nuns to express their opinion, but had propelled them, at her own whim, into what was to be called the Roman Union.

Although St. Julien was encountering substantial opposition from many quarters, there was sufficient enthusiasm to move forward and plan for a meeting of those in favor during the jubilee year 1900. Amadeus's enthusiastic response had established her as one of the capitulants, and she received an invitation to be in Rome by

---

*The fourth vow was taken by all houses following the Congregation of Paris, to which the Ohio houses adhered. The deletion of this fourth vow was a serious stumbling block for many Ursuline groups.

November 1900. On September 25, the convent annalist recorded: "Mother told us before supper last night that she received word to be in Rome by November 15 to attend the general meeting of Ursulines there to discuss the pros and cons of the Union."[5]

The innocent phrase "to discuss the pros and cons" was later wielded like a cudgel to belabor Amadeus. It was argued by those who opposed the decision that Amadeus had had no mandate from the community to incorporate Montana into such a union. The stated purpose of her attendance at the Roman meeting had been only to discuss the issues, not to make decisions. But all of that was in the future. When, on October 26, Amadeus left St. Peter's to begin her Roman journey, the atmosphere was one of sad parting and wishes for safe travel.

Amadeus's two companions on her journey were Angela Lincoln and Marie Kolinzuten, a young Flathead girl who had been at St. Peter's since childhood. Talented and spiritually inclined, she had been kept on at St. Peter's after her school years to help with the younger children. The hope was, undoubtedly, that she would wish to join the small group of native sisters Amadeus had begun to form. They would be called Virgins of the Sacred Heart and would be trained to work with their own people. Although they would take the three vows of religion, they would not be Ursulines but would have their own rules and customs.

"Our Rt. Rev. Bishop has permitted us to begin a little community in which Indian girls may consecrate themselves to God," Amadeus wrote to Katharine Drexel. "I am very happy to have the promise of your prayers for the success of this undertaking. We have only three candidates so far but I am sure more will apply in the near future. As soon as the work is better developed I shall take great pleasure in telling you of it."[6]

It was an ambitious and progressive undertaking and might, had it succeeded, have changed the history of the Montana missions. Between 1898 and 1900, five Gros Ventre girls began their religious training, first at St. Labre's and then at St. Ignatius's. Three of them left while still novices. One died shortly after becoming a postulant. Only one stayed to make her vows. This was Watzinitha—White Plume Woman—who had accompanied Amadeus on her trip to the East in 1893. But Watzinitha, like so many young Indian women, became ill shortly after entering the novitiate and made her vows on her deathbed in 1901, at the age of twenty-three.*

The record of failure was discouraging. Perhaps Amadeus was coming to agree with those who maintained that Native Americans lacked the inherent qualities to sustain religious life. What no one seemed to consider was that it was not the core of religious life that was being rejected, but the veneer of Western culture. The possibility of adjusting religious life to native culture was an idea not yet on the horizon.

The problems involved in native vocations were still unsolved at the end of the nineteenth century. Accepting Native Americans or African Americans into existing congregations was generally unacceptable. In some sections of the country, segregation laws made it impossible, and everywhere convention deemed it imprudent. Katharine Drexel's response to African Americans was to direct them toward existing black sisterhoods. She, apparently, made no effort to establish a congregation of Native Americans. Undoubtedly, she may have been influenced by Monsignor Stephan, who, despite his zealous efforts to better the conditions of the Indians, approved neither of accepting them into existing congregations nor forming a congregation exclusively for them.

The decision to bring Kolinzuten to Rome, however, lay outside the problem of religious vocation. Although Kolinzuten had shown no inclination to embrace religious life, she was clearly recognized as an unusual young woman. What clearer evidence could Amadeus provide of the importance of the work being done in the

---

*Following the death of Watzinitha, there seemed to be no further effort toward establishing a native sisterhood.

Montana missions than the presence of this "child of the forest"—intelligent, poised and—most of all—a fervent Christian. Like Watzinitha before her, Kolinzuten was to be their centerpiece.

When the Roman meeting opened on November 15, 1900, Amadeus, with the title of Mother General and representing a group of eight houses, found herself in a position of preeminence among the forty-eight delegates. With the charming and articulate Angela, who participated with ease in the French discussions, and with Kolinzuten as an exotic symbol of all that was being accomplished, the Montana missions held a unique position in the assembly. Except for the Ursulines of Canada, the Montana sisters were the only

Kolinzuten (Maria Stuart) on her way to Rome with Amadeus Dunne, 1900. Courtesy of Montana Historical Society, Helena, Montana

Ursulines ministering to native people.* "I have not seen any congregation like ours," Amadeus wrote home with satisfaction. When, the following week, the delegates cast their votes to determine the future of the proposed union, Amadeus again manifested her dominance by confidently casting eight votes, one for each of the missions. The tally was overwhelmingly in favor of the union, and that night, Amadeus wrote to St. Peter's, "The Union of the Ursulines is consummated."

While there were those who doubted that such divergent and distant elements could be shaped into a union, Amadeus was not among them. From the beginning, she had expressed a passionate adherence to the idea of union. While part of her response was undoubtedly her hope for support at a difficult time, there was something more fundamental. The idea of such a union allured her, as had the monastery of Québec seven years before. The image of something so stable, so rooted in the glories of a monastic past, exercised a strong attraction. Europe—Italy, particularly—with its vast basilicas, its medieval monasteries, its ornate treasures and soaring music entranced her.

That romantic quality, which even the hardships of Montana could never deaden, swept over her. She saw the union as part of a wonderful vision: Montana would be lifted up beyond its own hardscrabble existence and become part of a glorious whole. It was a romanticism encouraged by Angela Lincoln, whose early years in Europe had given her a sense of elitism. The union would free them from provincialism and bond them with the Ursulines of Europe, whose educational tradition was regarded as the best on the continent. While another companion might have suggested caution, might have questioned some of the consequences of this Roman Union, Sister Angela did quite the opposite—affirming and encouraging Amadeus's enthusiasm.

---

*The Ursuline missions in China, Thailand, and India had not yet been established. The Dutch Ursulines, however, had begun work in the Dutch East Indies.

Amadeus's first letter about the results of the chapter seconded her initial optimism. Mother St. Julien, who had initiated the concept, had been elected its superior general, and Angela Lincoln had been chosen as one of her assistants. While this was a loss for Montana, they could rejoice that "one of their own" had been chosen for this high place. "I feel sure you will like the Union, and that you will not find the things too hard. Everything is much as it was before, only that we all depend upon the Mother House in Rome and we are canonically united," Amadeus continued. While she acknowledged that there had been some points of controversy, she minimized their importance. "We fought many hard battles and gained many points. ... They tried to make us ask a dowry for each novice but we [the American delegates] refused. We demanded an American delegate in the seat of Government [at] Rome, on the principle of American Independence: no taxation without representation."[7]

In a letter written two weeks later, she again assured the sisters back home that the union would demand no great changes. "The Union is projected on a very broad basis; there is no cause for alarm—you will all be satisfied, I hope," she wrote on December 21. "Cloister for those who have it but none for the United States—at least for some years—many years, I hope. Nothing must interfere with the school work in the U.S." As for their religious habit, there would be some small changes in an effort to syncretize the various groups, but nothing that they could object to. She would provide more details when she returned home.[8]

The months following the chapter she spent in the company of Sister Angela, visiting the Ursuline convents in Italy, France, and Holland. It was Amadeus's first European trip and, despite the hardships of travel, she absorbed it all with a youthful enthusiasm. "Here we grate cheese into our soup, salt the butter, grind the pepper at table; shake hands across the streets, jump over the river, walk in the middle of the streets, while horses tramp the sidewalks," she wrote in amusement. "[You] pay 15 centimes each time you need to be excused, and generally it is a man who runs before you, brandishing a cloth with which he wipes and polishes the seat, flings it open, and bows to the ground as we pass by."[9]

Yet, despite the excitement of travel, she yearned to be home, brushing aside the warnings that winter was a dangerous time for an Atlantic crossing and boarding the _Wilhelm der Grosse_ on a cold February day. The crossing could scarcely have been more turbulent, and Kolinzuten, always of a delicate constitution, was deathly seasick throughout the voyage. Even so, Amadeus did not change her plan to visit Ursuline houses across the United States, giving them details of the Roman Union and encouraging them to join.

It was April 24—six months after her departure—when she returned to St. Peter's. "Pealing of bells," wrote the annalist, "waving of handkerchiefs. Then mother's favorite hymn: 'Heart of Jesus we do thank you' with accompaniment of violin and mandolin."[10]

It was immediately clear to the Montana nuns—no matter how much Amadeus emphasized the contrary—that this new union would change their lives. Amadeus's title and authority as Mother General was already gone. Decisions would now be made by a person they had never met in a city they had never seen. In addition, Sister Angela—always a commanding presence—was no longer with them. While not universally revered, she was recognized as a person who had carried many of Amadeus's burdens. Amadeus would miss her keenly. Present at hand to take her place was Sister Rose Galvin, who had fulfilled the role of superior during Amadeus's absence. She was competent, generous, and fearless—but she was not Sister Angela. It was Angela on whom Amadeus had counted to supervise the construction of the new convent in Miles City and to iron out the difficulties in their recently opened parish school in Anaconda.

There were, in addition, some immediate changes to adjust to. Some adjustments had to be made in the style of their clothing and the design of their crucifix. They had to forfeit the fourth vow, to educate girls, despite their arguments for keeping it as part of the traditional formula of the vows.

But beneath these incidental changes ran a general sense of the unknown. What did it mean that they would be divided into provinces, and how would their provincial superior be chosen? With the vast distances between Montana and other Ursuline houses, it was difficult to imagine how a province would be formed.

On the other hand came a sense of completeness, a security in knowing that they were not alone, that their problems and their privations would find support. There was a certain pride in what had been accomplished, in the fact that Mother Amadeus had played such an important part, and that one of their own had been chosen to participate in the central government. So much, they recognized. What they could not yet see was how American initiative would be refashioned by the shape of monastic tradition.

Mother Amadeus's immediate concern, however, was to assess the state of the missions. Sometime that spring, she wrote at length to Father Lindesmith, who was then serving in a parish in Ohio, informing him that, by and large, things were going well. She wrote with satisfaction of the successful work at St. Labre's. "The mission seems to have taken a new development," she wrote. "We have more of the dear Cheyenne children than our narrow quarters ... will allow ... They are eager to learn ... They flock about us ... and think that the White House—our convent which is white with green shutters—is the hub of the solar system."[11]

The success at St. Labre's was due, at least partially, to the efforts of Angela Lincoln, who while superior wrote almost daily to Mother Katharine, cajoling and flattering in her effort to receive more help. "We could easily have one hundred full-blood Cheyenne children in school had we the means," she wrote in May 1898. "You would be so happy here, dear Mother Katharine! With your means, you could give employment to the tribe, fertilize the soil, make the Cheyenne self-supporting and shelter all the children."[12] While Sister Angela's scheme was more grandiose than Mother Katharine could undertake, she did contribute sufficient funds to improve conditions at the mission.

The other missions, too, continued well, Amadeus affirmed, despite the reduction of government help. They still maintained a "flourishing" boarding school for white children at St. Peter's, along with their Indian school. At St. Paul's, Sister Francis Seibert remained the superior, the only one of the original group "who has remained at my side. The others have wearied of Indian work," Amadeus wrote bitterly. Although St. Paul's was suffering financially, as were all the missions, its successful sheep ranch was providing necessary funds. The new convent at Miles City was another triumph. Considerably larger than their original convent and situated in a "very desirable locality" with sufficient grounds for a garden, it would be a new source of good works when it opened the following fall, she felt.[13]

Her letter was resoundingly optimistic, far more optimistic than the situation warranted. Government retrenchment continued, and while some missions were still under government contract, the allotments were diminishing with each year. Although Monsignor Stephan fought vigorously to maintain federal assistance, he received only limited assurance. Meanwhile, the Browning Ruling—negating the parents' right to choose their children's school—continued, with the result that the agent was able to steer children away from mission schools and toward those of the government.

The problem of registration was further compounded by the inroads made by representatives from the Carlisle project. Carlisle, a small town in southeastern Pennsylvania, was the site of a school for Indian children that had been established in November 1879 by Lieutenant Richard H. Pratt, a Civil War veteran and a cavalry officer.

Several years earlier, he had been responsible for transporting a large group of Indians from Indian Territory, Oklahoma, to Florida for incarceration. Once in St. Augustine, he continued to be in charge of the prisoners. A sensitive man, Pratt became sympathetic to his charges, recognizing in them qualities that, if fostered, would develop them into worthwhile citizens. During the next few years, he succeeded in mitigating their imprisonment, found generous women willing to teach them English, and located work that earned them a small income and helped to restore their sense of dignity. His efforts, from his point of view, were eminently successful. In place of the sullen and despairing savages he had brought to St. Augustine, he now had a group of men patently conformed to the white man's standard. They were, he wrote proudly, clean, orderly, and industrious.

Such success gave rise to wider visions. If Indian children were taken while young away from their homes, their languages, and their customs and provided with the advantage of a white man's education, the "Indian problem" would undoubtedly be mitigated, if not immediately solved. Thus began the Carlisle project. The abandoned cavalry barracks in Carlisle were a perfect site, consisting of some twenty-seven acres. The buildings were in place, the town was small, it was free of Indian bias, and was filled with industrious citizens who would be excellent role models for the children. Best of all, Carlisle was far from the West and all its memories. Here, the children would speak only English, be clothed in white man's dress, and taught according to white man's standards. By means of promises and cajolery, Pratt convinced a number of tribes to send their children east. Late on the night of October 6, 1879, the people of Carlisle welcomed 100 Indian boys and girls.[14]

From the beginning, the hostility between Carlisle and the mission schools was rampant. Partially, it was a question of religion. For those working in the mission schools, evangelization was at the very core of their education; they could hardly countenance an education that would take the children away from what they believed was the only true faith and the one source of salvation.

There were, however, other issues. The Jesuits objected to the cunning ways in which parents were induced to give up their children. They objected to the children being taken so far from home and for such a long period. While the missionaries also operated on the grounds that the children's education would be more successful if they were kept in the mission atmosphere, away from the culture of their families, they also recognized the importance of keeping children in their native environment. Although the prohibition against

native languages was enforced on the missions, its severity was mitigated by the surroundings. Even the rigorous standards of the Jesuits
found something unwholesome in transporting children to what
could only have seemed to them a foreign and frightening land.

The altercation between the redoubtable Father Eberschweiler
and the Carlisle agent was a parable of mutual distrust and hostility.
In June 1890, Mr. W. P. Campbell of Carlisle wrote to the assistant
superintendent of schools complaining of the "aggressive opposition" he had received from "the Reverend Father Eberschweiler" at
St. Paul's Mission. Following Campbell's visit to the Indian camps,
Father Eberschweiler had assembled the Indians and warned them
that "all the children that came to Carlisle would die and go to hell."
He then loaded a wagon with Indian children and, without any
authority, spirited them off to the mission school. To terrify them
even more, Campbell complained, "he exacted a promise from Mary
Brown, a half-breed girl, that she would not go to Carlisle. This in
confession under a threat of being excommunicated, dying, and
going to hell."

Eberschweiler, of course, vehemently denied the accusation,
maintaining that it was all a "hideous lie." The wrangling continued
for some months until Mary Brown—rightly or wrongly—was
induced to sign a letter affirming that Father Eberschweiler had never
threatened her.[15]

But none of these problems clouded Amadeus's optimistic
letter to Father Lindesmith, nor did she mention her personal anxieties. Although Sister Rose Galvin had managed St. Peter's capably
during Amadeus's absence, the community had suffered from a
series of erratic chaplains, one of whom often drank the altar wine,
leaving the community without Mass for days at a time. Even the
parish school at Anaconda, begun at the request of Bishop Brondel,
was beginning to experience conflicts that would dog it for the next
ten years.

Amadeus herself was an increasing source of anxiety to the
nuns at St. Peter's. Never robust, she seemed unable to regain her

energy after returning from Europe. There were long periods when she was confined to her room. Although she diagnosed her illness as a kidney infection, those who were privy to community affairs felt that it was more than physical. She was clearly suffering from severe anxiety as she faced her mounting debts. In her efforts to keep her individual bills to a minimum, she had spread her indebtedness far and wide. As a consequence, she was barraged from every side with daily threats that her credit would be curtailed and that in the event that payment was not received, she could expect to find bill collectors at St. Peter's. If Amadeus had expected that financial help might come to them through the Roman Union, she was now faced with the reality that, so far, the Roman Union was hardly more than an idea. There were years to go before it would be shaped into a reality, and even then, there was no guarantee of financial support.

On top of her financial anxiety came grief at the sudden illness of Kolinzuten. Never strong, the long months in a foreign atmosphere and the fatigue of travel had dissipated her resistance. Toward the end of May, she was stricken with a high fever. As the fever mounted, she was seized with violent seizures. By the time the doctor finally arrived by train from Great Falls, her condition was irreversible. He immediately diagnosed meningitis and gave no hope for recovery. On June 5, just a week after she had been taken ill, Kolinzuten died. With her death, Amadeus's dream of a native sisterhood became more illusory. Despite her natural optimism, it was becoming difficult for Amadeus to sustain her visions. The bleak stretches of the Montana missions were beginning to obscure the high dreams of her months in Rome.

Chapter Thirteen

*I am not going
to give in to these bishops. ...*

—Mother Amadeus Dunne

In October 1902, the new convent at Miles City was ready for occupancy. It was five years since the former convent had been destroyed by fire and Amadeus's initial reluctance to rebuild had been overcome by the insistence of the townspeople. As a warrant of their goodwill, they had contributed property consisting of five acres of appropriate land near the outskirts of the thriving town.

Miles City had changed in the eight years since the Ursulines had arrived. The raunchy Cosmopolitan Theater, replete with poker and roulette as well as a makeshift stage, was superceded by the Miles City Opera House, which provided such superior dramas as *The Mad Lover*, *The Maid and the Mummy*, and *Belle of Japan*. In 1900, the Hotel Leighton was opened, surpassing in service all the existing lodgings. That year, the *Yellowstone Journal* announced proudly: "The Hotel Leighton enjoys the distinction of being one of the most modern and best conducted hotels along the Northern Pacific railroad and its reputation is such that Miles City has become a sort of 'Sunday Town' with the traveling men who make this place in their rounds," Transient rates were fixed at $2 to $3 per day, "according to the size and location of rooms."[1]

As the population grew, the need for education grew apace, and the Ursulines' new convent and school provided for an expanding student population. Three nuns from St. Peter's were selected to open the new school: Sister Cecilia Wiegand, Sister Amata Dunne, Sister

Lutegarde Jones. There is no clearer evidence of how widely the call of the Montana missions had been answered than the origins of these three sisters: Cecilia Wiegand from New York, Amata Dunne from Santa Fe, New Mexico, and Lutegarde Jones from St. Louis, Missouri. The three were to be accompanied by Amadeus and two young Cheyenne girls, Sarah and Amelia, who were to help with the housework.

The party left St. Peter's shortly after noon, traveling by wagon to Cascade, where they caught the evening train for Helena. At Helena, they were joined by Sister Agatha Dolan from St. Xavier's and their first two boarders for the new school at Miles City, Margaret McHale and Loretto Wicke. Here they transferred to the Northern Pacific's Eastbound Number Four, which would take them to their destination. Most passengers were comfortably asleep when, just before sunrise, they were awakened by a terrible crash. The eastbound train had plunged headlong into the Burlington Westbound Number Five. The impact was terrible, immediately setting off a dense fire. The bewildered passengers, dazed by sleep, staggered to their feet, trying to find their way to the nearest door. The following day, the *Billings Daily Times* carried the headline "Two Dead, Four Injured in a Collision of Two Passenger Trains West of Park City." It was Amata Dunne, however, who, in her memoir, captured the scene most graphically.

> We were dozing in our seats when suddenly there was a crash. Our train, the Eastbound No. 4 and the Burlington westbound No. 5, met in a head-on collision. The engines telescoped, the cars slid from their tracks and shot to one side of the locomotives. Fire immediately started in the westbound train, and burning rapidly consumed the Burlington smoker, baggage and mail cars. The mail and baggage of the eastbound also were likewise consumed. The eastbound mail car stood aloft at an angle of some thirty degrees, one mass of flames.[2]

Sister Lutegarde immediately gathered the terrified children while the others, led by Amadeus, started up the aisle to see if they could be of help. They had advanced only a few feet, however, when there was a sudden violent jolt and Amadeus, losing her balance, was thrown to the ground. The trainmen, in an effort to save the other cars from the advancing fire, had tried to reverse them. The train shuddered and the passengers grabbed what they could to save themselves from falling.

For most people, it was a momentary accident from which they were able to right themselves, but Amadeus, having fallen heavily against the seat behind her, was unable to move. Any effort to lift her resulted in agonizing pain, and she was left lying on the floor until some way of carrying her to safety could be found. Finally, she was lifted onto a stretcher, but no point of exit could be found to accommodate a stretcher. In the midst of the chaos and the plumes of smoke, two men were able to lift the stretcher through a window and, at a dangerous vertical angle, lower it to the ground. It was a perilous and painful endeavor that left Amadeus barely conscious. Around her was pandemonium. Flames were still shooting upward and the early morning air was thick with the fumes of burning metal.

Finally, the caboose was yoked to two sleeping cars, and here the injured were carried to be brought to the hospital at Billings. Meanwhile, the nuns had made quick decisions. Sister Cecilia would accompany Amadeus, while Amata and Lutegarde would stay with the children. But when they went to find the children, they discovered that in the confusion, the car they were in had been moved to Park City and would not return until evening. Finally, by 6:00 P.M., after a day of turmoil, the nuns were reunited with the frightened and exhausted children. It was close to 8:00 P.M. when the eastbound train arrived, and after midnight when they reached their destination.

None of them except Sister Lutegarde had ever been in Miles City before, and she knew little of the city, except the way to the old convent—which was little help as they tried to find their new location. In the darkened city, no one knew which direction to take as they trudged along the unfamiliar streets, dragging their suitcases and trying to encourage the frightened and tired children. When, helped by a passing driver, they found their way at last to their new home, they found little to welcome them, as Sister Amata later recorded:

> We entered the Convent by the kitchen door of which Mother had given us the key. It was dark. We struck matches and walked around searching for a lamp. At last we found one down in the boiler room. Having lighted the lamp we went all through the house. Several rooms were locked and we had no keys. We found two bedsteads and two blankets. These we gave to the four children whom we put to bed in the north west basement school room. ... Then we found four large ingrain rugs, and spreading these on the floor in the south west basement school room, we called them our beds. Our shawls were our bedding; and Sister Agatha, having no shawl, lay down between two rugs.[3]

The next morning, Sunday, they set off early for Mass, guided by a clipping from the Miles City newspaper that gave the address of the Catholic church, "a little frame structure, painted white and bearing a bright gilt cross." After Mass, the parishioners greeted them, deeply concerned at the news of the train crash.

That afternoon, they had a dispatch from the hospital at Billings, which did little to allay their anxiety. Amadeus was still in great pain and the doctor had not yet determined the extent of her injuries. They had to wait until a further diagnosis was made.

Despite their continued worry, the nuns at Miles City had little time to indulge their anxiety. School was set to open by mid-October. In a few days, their trunks, which had been fortunately delayed at Helena, arrived. By the feast of St. Ursula, October 21, a stove had been installed in the kitchen, bedsteads for the boarders were in place, electric lights were in working order—and there was an added elegance: an electric bell had been installed on the front door. On October 23, they were ready to put an announcement in the local paper: "The Ursuline nuns announce that they will be ready to receive boarders at the convent on November 1. They would be pleased to have the parents come the end of this week to make arrangements." The curriculum would cover grades one through ten, offering, in addition, a commercial course, a music club, painting, elocution, and physical education. School was opened ten days later, with six boarders and ten day pupils.

Meanwhile, news from Billings was bleak. As soon as St. Peter's had received news of the wreck, Rose Galvin left for Billings, freeing Cecilia to return to Miles City, where she was desperately needed. Throughout October, the medical reports were confusing and often contradictory: Amadeus may have sustained a broken hip, but the doctor was not sure; perhaps it was simply a question of badly bruised tendons and ligaments. Injections of morphine ordered to lessen the pain had left her weakened. Further injury was caused by tight bandages, which had impaired her circulation. It was a litany of incompetence. Clearly, St. Vincent's Hospital was not equipped to deal with Amadeus's serious injuries. By the end of the month, the doctor, frightened perhaps by the deteriorating condition of his patient, advised Rose Galvin that Amadeus should be moved to Helena, where the hospital was better prepared for such injuries. It was not until February, after months of traction in an effort to slip her hip into place, that Amadeus was finally able to take a few steps with the help of a walker.

That spring, at the recommendation of the doctor, she was taken to San Diego, California, where there was a convalescent home run by a group of sisters. Here, it was hoped, the warm climate would help her regain her strength.

Toward the end of April, Sister Angela Lincoln arrived from Rome to assist in her care. Amadeus had looked forward to the pleasure of having her with her, but during the months they spent together, Amadeus found Angela perceptibly changed. Her position in Rome had brought to the fore qualities that surprised and saddened Amadeus. That fall, shortly after Angela had returned to Europe, Mother Amadeus wrote to Mother St. Julien: "I hasten to assure you that Mother Angela during her stay with me was lovely in every way. ... I am sorry to say that such is not the case with all the other nuns. They gave her that precedence which her rank now demands but I fear she was not satisfied with the respect they accorded her."[4]

In fact, Angela seemed dissatisfied with everything. Although restless while in the United States and apparently anxious to return to Rome, Rome itself was a further source of discontent for her. The charming, talented American who had won everyone's admiration was manifesting a critical and arbitrary spirit that made it very difficult for other members of the government. Her relations with St. Julien were particularly thorny. In March, before leaving for America, she had written at some length to Cardinal Ferrata at the Sacred Congregation complaining that despite the recommendation that the power of the Prioress General be moderated by members of her council, in fact, absolute authority was exercised by St. Julien, so that "the French spirit, especially that of Blois" was dominant in the community.[5]

While St. Julien was probably unaware of this formal complaint that had been sent in "strict confidence," she was painfully aware of the chasm that had opened between herself and her American councilor. Although Angela seemed more conciliatory on her return to Rome, it was not long before St. Julien was once again expressing her frustration in dealing with this person who was so independent in her judgments that it was impossible to work with her. "I am much distressed at what has been said about Mother Angela Lincoln," Amadeus wrote in reply to St. Julien. "She is very dear to me. She has, I think, a mistaken idea of her powers. ... She has hitherto always been such a good religious, so dependent on her superiors, so united in heart and mind ... that I am much pained and troubled when I hear of any disaffection on her part."[6]

What St. Julien was wisely able to observe was that it was Angela's passionate devotion to Amadeus that kept her steady; without it, a willful and capricious spirit dominated her. "She needs your wise spiritual counsel," she replied to Amadeus. Meanwhile, she would hope for the best until Angela had completed her term in 1906.

By the spring of 1904, Amadeus was well enough to begin her return to Montana, although she was very thin and still limped badly—a disability that would remain with her throughout her life. It was almost two years since her debilitating accident and there had been dramatic changes at St. Peter's since then.

From the time she had left for Rome, in the fall of 1900, Amadeus had spent only one year back in the Montana missions. She had missed the twists and turns of almost four years of mission life. In Miles City, the new school had been in operation for close to two years. At St. Peter's, they had suffered floods and sickness and the continual specter of poverty. The novices who had entered during that time had not yet met the legendary foundress. During the years of Amadeus's absence, Rose Galvin had been in charge. While Amadeus had retained the office of superior, it was Rose who had, in practical terms, assumed the role of leadership. Amadeus was now sixty years old, worn from twenty years of mission life, and further debilitated by her crippling accident. Rose Galvin had not yet had her fortieth birthday. She was energetic, devoted—and confident. From the beginning, Amadeus had singled her out for leadership; in the absence of Angela, Sister Rose had become Amadeus's right hand. It would soon become clear, however, that such a position was not sufficient to satisfy Rose's ambition.

With the sudden death of Bishop Brondel in November 1903, the Ursulines experienced a painful loss. For twenty years, Brondel had been for them a faithful advocate. They could not be sure that his replacement would be so benevolent. By the summer of 1904, it was announced that Montana was to be divided into two dioceses: Helena in the west, presided over by John Patrick Carroll, and Great Falls in the east, under the authority of Mathias Lenihan. (Except for St. Ignatius's, at the foot of the Rockies, all the missions fell under the jurisdiction of Bishop Lenihan.)

Lenihan was a stranger to Montana. Most of his priestly life had been spent in Marshalltown in central Iowa until on June 27, 1904—after twenty-five years of priesthood—he was appointed bishop of the newly erected diocese of Great Falls. On September 21, he was consecrated at St. Raphael's Cathedral in Dubuque, and ten days later left for his new post in Montana.

He came to Great Falls with a solid reputation as a devoted and zealous pastor: intelligent, articulate, a man "who could get things done." His bad temper was easily forgiven in the light of his other qualities. Unlike his predecessor, who had slipped quietly into his role as bishop, Lenihan enjoyed making the most of his new position. On October 4, he arrived in Great Falls by private railroad car, accompanied by a sizable entourage of priest friends and members of his jubilant family.

The episcopal installation took place on October 9. Great Falls had never seen the like. Although St. Anne's Church could accommodate no more than 200 people, the organizers of the installation had invited some 2,000, with the result that the church was largely occupied by Lenihan's friends (four bishops and forty priests), while the majority of Great Falls' Catholic population knelt on the sidewalk. The *Great Falls Daily Tribune* reported enthusiastically that the new bishop was "handsome," "winning in his ways," and an "outstanding orator." It was an excellent beginning, although there may well have been those who took exception to his reference to the Indians as "savages" and to the land of Montana as "arid."[7]

It was not until November 3, however, that the Ursulines at St. Peter's greeted their new bishop. That morning, they received a phone call from Father Van den Broeck, their chaplain and assistant to the bishop, that His Excellency would come to visit them that evening. It was not an auspicious occasion, as the annalist recorded:

> They arrived about 5:30, came over to the chapel—choir sang
> *Ecce Sacerdos.* He gave benediction, took supper, and then
> went to the parlor to see the nuns. After a visit of about 15
> minutes during which time Bishop made many sarcastic remarks
> by way of wit, he stood up and said he would like to make a
> canonical visitation and see each nun alone, beginning with

the oldest. We all withdrew and he saw Mother Mary Rose
first and then the next three; then stopped very abruptly and
went home. He seems intensely hurt that no Ursulines were
present at the installation. ... I do not think his visit very
favorable.[8]

In fact, it was the beginning of a disastrous relationship
between the Ursulines and their bishop. Unlike some members of the
hierarchy, Lenihan had shown himself cordial and appreciative of
religious sisters. He had invited the Sisters of the Humility of Mary to
Marshalltown, helped them establish a successful school, and even
made it possible for a group of them to attend his installation in
Great Falls. It is not hard to determine what initiated the friction
with the Ursulines. Father Van den Broeck, Lenihan's "listening ear,"
had already formed his opinion about the way religious life was lived
at St. Peter's.

Father Van den Broeck had been appointed chaplain of St.
Peter's by Bishop Brondel just a month before the latter's death in
November 1903. From the beginning, he seemed ill-suited for his
position. He had been in residence only a month when the annalist
wrote: "Father Van den Broeck left very abruptly at noon ... no
dinner and no word whatever of when he will return ... He was very
angry that the indian boys kept him awake all night ... Their mistress
says they were very good. The wind upsets him, too. I do not think
he will be able to stand it long."[9] He did stand it, however, his irrita-
tion solaced by unexplained absences, which left the nuns without
daily Mass.

Whatever impression of the Ursulines the bishop had received
from his assistant, it was aggravated by the absence of the Ursulines
at Lenihan's inauguration. He was accustomed to adulation, especially from religious women, whom he had hitherto treated with
paternal benevolence. The response of the Ursulines was beyond his
experience. While St. Peter's was a four-hours' journey by wagon or
stagecoach, Lenihan did not consider this a sufficient excuse. Why

the Ursulines did not attend remains something of a mystery. Perhaps they felt they needed permission from Amadeus for such a singular occasion, and Amadeus was then in the far-off mission of St. Labre's. It was an unfortunate time for her to be absent, no doubt giving Lenihan the impression that the superior of the Ursulines had little regard for his episcopal authority.

A week later, during his episcopal visitation of Miles City, the new bishop met the superior of the Ursulines for the first time. On November 8, Amadeus had arrived at Miles City, just in time to welcome Lenihan. Although the annalist made no mention of anything beyond the ordinary routine of an episcopal visitation, in fact, it was a stormy meeting. Lenihan, anxious to improve his diocese and always the sponsor of education, had determined to open a school in Great Falls as soon as possible. Since the Ursulines already owned property in the city, it seemed logical for them to assume responsibility for such a school; but when he proposed (or commanded?) this to Amadeus, she demurred. She had neither the money nor the nuns to begin such a project. Lenihan, unused to opposition, countered with the threat that unless she agreed to open a school by September 1905, she must sell the land to him so that he could bring in other sisters more deferential to his commands. Amadeus responded that what he asked was beyond her authority, that she did not have the power to make such decisions, which were reserved to their superior general in Rome.

This explanation, far from placating him, simply enraged Lenihan further. "He thinks because he is a bishop that he has unlimited power over us," Amadeus wrote later to Mother St. Julien. "I do not know the bishop of Helena yet but I think he is much the same as the bishop of Great Falls—colleagues of Bishop Ireland, so-styled American Bishop of the progressive order. I am not going to give in to these bishops on any points until after you have seen for yourself our situation,"[10] she concluded. With continued refusal, the battle lines were drawn.

At the same time that the nuns were experiencing their bishop's disapproval, they were also experiencing the practical consequences of their membership in the Roman Union. That fall, ten French Ursulines, exiled by France's anticlerical laws, arrived in Montana. The recently passed Laic Laws decreed that all French religious congregations were to be dissolved. Without an international organization to support them, the exiles' fate would have been even more difficult. Now, however, for members of the Roman Union, exile was at least mildly sweetened by the prospect of joining other Ursuline communities. America, that land of opportunity, opened its doors, and the refugees poured in.*

On October 17, the nuns at Miles City received a dispatch from Amadeus: "Expect ten exiles Thursday or sooner. Prepare beds immediately."

As usual, Amadeus gave scant attention to where the ten extra beds would come from or, even more problematically, where they would be put. Somehow Miles City, as always expandable, managed, and at 11:00 P.M. on October 21, they welcomed ten French sisters. Within the next months, nine more exiles arrived, bringing the number to nineteen.** They ranged in age from twenties to sixties, some knowing a little English, most knowing none. There were four from Bordeaux, five from Nevers, but most were alone, the single member of their community to volunteer for Montana when the prospect of exile could no longer be ignored.

Kindness was hardly sufficient to solace their fatigue and bewilderment at this strange life, where even though it was Sunday, they had no Mass, because the priest was needed elsewhere.

In addition to this deprivation was the daily work the sisters were engaged in. Nothing in the well-ordered French monasteries,

---

*Other countries also gave hospitality to the exiles, notably England, where whole communities were reestablished.

**Of these nineteen, only nine returned to France when the laws were overturned; the others remained on at the missions and died in Montana.

where manual labor was carried out by coadjutrix sisters, prepared them for the unremitting labor of Montana. "The poor exiles seeing us pressed with work offered to help us," the annalist wrote. "After we went to school they continued the washing which we began at 4:00 A.M. Some of them are also mending for us. Only two speak English. ... Everything is very hard for them. But they are beginning to adapt themselves a little to their surroundings."[11]

Less than a month later, the first ten were deemed sufficiently adapted to be sent out to the various missions: two to St. Ignatius's, two to St. Xavier's, two to St. Peter's, two to Holy Family, and one each to St. Labre's and the parish school at Anaconda.

St. Ignatius's had long been considered the queen of the missions, but by the turn of the century, its glory years were coming to a close. Frustrated by the unfair treatment of the government, in the fall of 1901, the Jesuit superior, Jerome D'Aste, wrote in anger to the Indian agent: "I see by another letter of yours that you are determined to crush our Mission. On vague and unfounded reports you act with us as if we were here only to break the laws and to make money. A very nice treatment, by an officer of the Government, of men and women sacrificing their lives for the good of these Indians for the last 50 years."[12] Father D'Aste was of a fiery temperament, and the series of letters he wrote to Snead could hardly have endeared the Jesuits to the agent.

In the years that followed, the mission became embroiled in controversy upon controversy. Both priests and nuns were accused of using their industrial school for financial gain—using the students to work on the farm, to take care of cattle, to do the baking, to help with the cleaning. This, the agent pointed out, was "distinctly against the rules of the school." The following year, a new regulation was inaugurated. Anyone with more than 100 head of cattle "must give $1.00 per head to the government which will then be distributed to the Indians." D'Aste clearly put no stock in such a regulation, denouncing it as "just a scheme to make money."[13]

In 1902, the Indians themselves, desperate over the high-handed decisions of the government, had sent a delegation to

Washington to present some of their problems. It was a fruitless trip. The secretary of the interior barely listened to their demands, and they came home empty handed. That same year, Father D'Aste's request that some allocation be provided for children in the kindergarten was refused on the grounds that the contract clearly stated that children must be six and over in order to receive an allocation.

The final straw was the government order that mission property was to be taxed. Such legislation, if passed into law, would be the end of the missions. This time, the Jesuits took the matter to court. They first appeared as plaintiffs against the County of Missoula. No verdict was reached and the case went to the Supreme Court of the United States. The Supreme Court's decision was that there was nothing in the constitution concerning this problem and that it must be settled according to Montana law. After two years of wrangling, the decision was finally handed down by the Circuit Court of the District of Montana that since tribal lands could not be taxed, and that since the mission was on tribal lands, it was exempt from taxation. It was a moment of jubilation in an otherwise bleak situation.

Even while the matter of taxation was being adjudicated, the government had initiated an act that authorized the allotment in severalty of lands within the reservation, "after which the remaining lands should be opened for settlement and entry." Thus the provisions of the General Allotment Act of 1887 were further executed and white settlers were enabled to flood into what had been promised to the Indians. What the missionaries had dreaded for years had become a reality.[14] A later historian described the consequences graphically. "Then between 1904 and 1910 a series of acts were passed by Congress which set aside and reserved a total of more than 60,000 acres within the reservation. ... Some of these were paid for. Some were not."[15]

While affairs at St. Ignatius's were more dramatic—or more carefully documented—all the missions were experiencing both the pinch of poverty and the loss of pupils in their schools. Although Mother Katharine still contributed generously, she could not compensate fully for the reduction of government allocations. The BCIM advised the Jesuits—and thus the Ursulines—that they needed to curtail the number of students. It was a hard decision, since it meant that the children would go to government schools or to those run by Protestant churches—both anathema to the Catholic missionaries, whose basic purpose was evangelization.

Thus through the first decade of the new century, they limped along, maintaining their existing buildings as well as they could, forced to close some of the industrial shops that they had worked so hard to establish and that, they rightly felt, were essential in preparing their pupils for suitable work when they left the mission. St. Xavier's continued its mission to the Crow, although without the initial enthusiasm of Fathers Prando and Van der Velden. At Holy Family, Father Aloysius Soer and Sister Irene Arvin did what they could to recover from their disastrous fire in January 1898. Of all the missions, St. Paul's was the most stable. Perhaps its very isolation was a help in keeping the children reasonably content and their parents away from the allure of Fort Belknap.

At St. Labre's, the runt of the litter, nothing seemed to change. While the fortunes of the other missions plummeted rapidly, at St. Labre's, they continued the precarious existence that they had come to accept as their way of life. From the beginning, they had been the least secure and the least appreciated by the Indians. With the departure of the Jesuits, they were subjected to several years of chaplains hopelessly inappropriate for their position. St. Labre's, more than most, was a mission that demanded zeal, energy, and resourcefulness; the clergy who arrived in sequence from Helena seemed to lack all three. It must be acknowledged that the task had little to recommend it. The mission was poor, badly supported, and unendurably lonely. The Jesuits had been trained for such work; the diocesan clergy had not.

Perhaps it was partially the tension between priest and people that made it increasingly difficult to keep the children in school. Because the mission was so close to the camps, the music of the night dances was more than the girls could resist, and no threat could keep them in. Runaways became weekly occurrences, encouraged by their parents, who threatened to remove their children entirely if their demands for increased rations were not met.

Although the nuns did their best to provide something festive at Christmas, it was not enough to placate the Cheyenne. On December 27, a large group arrived expecting a "big feast," but there was no feast to be had. Furious, Wooden Leg, one of the most aggressive males, threatened to shoot Sister Thecla Flood for ordering him out of the children's community room. Bad feelings between whites and Indians were augmented by accusations that the Indians had stolen ranchers' cattle. Although they had little evidence, the ranchers charged the Indians and swore to shoot them if they discovered the culprits.

Perhaps the worst of the difficulties at St. Labre's was the constant insecurity. From year to year, they were never certain if they would receive sufficient government help to continue. "We are sorely in need of money for this mission and I feel much anxiety about the future of the place," in June 1905, Amadeus wrote to Monsignor William Ketcham, who had succeeded Monsignor Stephan at the latter's death in 1901. "If we lose the contract for next year then we are truly to be pitied," she concluded.[16] But by September, she still had no definitive answer. "I regret to say that I can give no definite idea as to what you may expect for St. Labre," Monsignor Ketcham replied. "It will depend on the opinion of the attorney general who will be called upon to determine whether or not the funds of the Northern Cheyenne Indians can be used to pay for the care and education of Indian children in that school."[17]

Fortunately, with the installation of Bishop Lenihan, matters began to improve. While his relationship with the Ursulines was far from amicable, he showed himself a concerned pastor where the missions were concerned. The destitution of the Cheyenne and the laborious lives of the nuns moved his compassion. The energy and directness that had characterized him in Marshalltown was quick to the fore. Shortly after the bishop's visit to St. Labre's, the incompetent Father Aloysius Mueller received word that he was to be assigned to Miles City.

Lenihan was equally quick to contact Monsignor Ketcham at the BCIM to report that the mission at St. Labre's was hard-pressed for funds. "I am much relieved to know the special interest you are taking in this mission," he wrote. "It would be a great calamity to religion should this mission go down. The Cheyenne have been allotted less land and less provisions than any of the other tribes. ... Please send funds for St. Labre's to the local superior, Sister M. St. Thomas; she has many urgent bills to meet."[18] Ketcham's reply, praising the bishop for his interest in the missions, had a sentence that caught Lenihan up short. Although, Ketcham wrote, it was the regulation to send funds "to those who are in actual charge of the school and who reside at the schools," in the case of St. Labre's, the money had always been sent to Mother Amadeus. He had no record of Mother St. Thomas being the local superior.[19]

It was arbitrary conduct such as this that was to fan the conflict that had already ignited between Amadeus and Lenihan. From his first visit to the Ursulines, shortly after his consecration, Lenihan had indicated a certain displeasure. His first meeting with Amadeus at Miles City simply augmented his disfavor. It was abundantly clear by the winter of 1904—only two months after his consecration—that Lenihan had formed an opinion of Amadeus that was only to grow more hostile with time.

Several months later, Amadeus found herself not only at odds with the bishop, but with a full-scale revolt on her hands, a revolt made more painful and more dangerous because at its base was the discontent of her own nuns at St. Peter's, led by the woman to whom she had confidently entrusted her authority.

Chapter Fourteen

No joyous greeting awaited my return.

—*Mother Amadeus Dunne*

There is perhaps no more dramatic paradigm of the frequent clashes between American clergy and religious women than the events that played out in Montana between November 1904 and the end of 1906. By the time the conflict was moderated—one cannot say resolved—it had widened into a conflict between American authority and European religious traditions.

Although Amadeus must certainly have been aware of the growing discord at St. Peter's, her first mention of it came only in the spring of 1905. On her return to Montana, she spent little time at St. Peter's, anxious to travel to the missions she had not seen in several years. She felt no anxiety about conditions at the motherhouse, since she was confident of the efficiency and generosity of Rose Galvin, who was presiding in her place. But now, to her astonishment, Amadeus found that the very qualities that had led her to elevate Rose to a position of leadership—her decisiveness, her self-confidence, her determination—were marshaled against Amadeus herself.

It was not until March 1905 that she wrote at length to St. Julien in Rome, bewildered by the open antipathy of the bishop and grieved by the growing hostility of some of her own nuns, paramount among them Rose Galvin, her trusted assistant. There was no question, she wrote, that the bishop had been prejudiced by Father Van den Broeck, "who finds Mother Mary Rose more pliable than myself and therefore is anxious that she shall be in full authority." As for Van den Broeck himself, she found him acting far beyond his role as chaplain—trying to assume the control of the financial affairs of the mission as well as the spiritual welfare of the nuns.[1]

By the time Amadeus had confided her troubles to St. Julien, a full-scale accusation against her had reached Rome. On December 5, 1904, Van den Broeck, as spokesman for his bishop, had written at length to St. Julien. "I have a very delicate task to fulfill," he began, "that of speaking to you of complaints against Mother Amadeus." From the beginning, he continued, the bishop had heard these accusations, and when, in the month following his installation, he had visited St. Peter's, he saw at once that "things were in such a bad state that it was essential to have another superior."

Van den Broeck made his charges like a prosecutor who would brook no explanations. Amadeus had been absent for two years, traveling at great expense to California, Oregon, and Washington, he charged. Yet, despite her protracted absence, she continued to exert her authority as superior, demanding that all permissions come from her, although she was consistently negligent in responding to the requests she received. As a result, the community was left in a difficult state, unable to contact their superior but prohibited from acting without her permission. The novitiate, too, was badly managed, leading to discouragement and poor religious spirit. As for financial affairs, she had spent money so recklessly that she had incurred debts everywhere. Even the farm at St. Peter's, which could have been a source of income, was providing little return, since it was presently in the hands of an incompetent and expensive manager selected by Amadeus.

Bishop Lenihan was not alone in his displeasure, Van den Broeck continued. There was abundant evidence for the complaints made against Amadeus. He himself had had some opportunity to observe the problems she had created while he was chaplain at Miles City. In addition, he knew that she had had very unpleasant encounters with both the Jesuits and diocesan clergy. Even Bishop Brondel, her original patron, was at the end of his patience with her before his death. As for the present administrator of Helena, he had found her influence so injurious that he considered that the Ursulines would benefit if Amadeus were to leave Montana entirely. In contrast to his condemnation of Amadeus, Van den Broeck had nothing but praise, not only for Mother Rose, but for the entire Ursuline community: "the self-sacrificing spirit of these noble women, who, in spite of such misrule, labor with such devotion and such perseverance."[2]

Van den Broeck's condemnatory account may well have been the first hint to St. Julien that the charismatic woman who had charmed them all with her energy, her apostolic vision, and her fearlessness could also be a source of conflict and opposition. Although St. Julien kept Van den Broeck waiting several months for a reply, her response to Amadeus was immediate. She assured her at once of her support, but cautioned prudence, setting out three guidelines to direct her relations with Lenihan. First, she counseled, "You are the superior of the Ursulines of Montana with the power of provincial for all the houses in that area. It follows that you are also the superior of St. Peter's." Second, no election was to be held in any Ursuline house in Montana—at least for the present. St. Julien's third point touched what would become the crux of the conflict: "In your relations with bishops, of course be respectful but make them understand that *the government of your communities is dependent on another authority—that of the general administration.*"[3]

Nothing in Lenihan's priestly experience had prepared him for this opposition. The sisters he had dealt with in Iowa had been completely under his authority, but with the Ursulines, he found himself confronted with a different model. By joining an international union, the Montana Ursulines had placed themselves under the authority of a superior general resident in Rome, thus disengaging themselves from the immediate power of the local ordinary. Lenihan was not alone. In many dioceses, the disapproval of the bishop had been sufficiently strong to discourage the religious congregation from joining the union. Lenihan, however, had assumed his episcopal role too late to express his opposition. Brondel's generous compliance had made it easy for the Montana Ursulines to join the proposed union, but the new bishop of Great Falls was of a different persuasion. For a man who had lived on admiration and authority, he was poorly qualified to brook opposition. The Roman Union was to become Lenihan's bête noire.

He had seen nothing unusual in his command to Amadeus either to begin a school or sell their property in Great Falls. But instead of the obedience he had expected, he discovered, to his exasperation, that the Montana Ursulines, instead of submitting to his orders, had invoked a higher authority. Such an authority, based in Rome with close ties to cardinals, to members of the Sacred Congregation of Religious, and even to the reigning pontiff himself, might have daunted many an ecclesiastic, but it only entrenched Lenihan in his position.

Although of a choleric temperament, the bishop was, at base, not an unreasonable man. The disastrous events of 1905 to 1907, in which he was such a key player, may very well have been far less disastrous were it not for Victor Van den Broeck. By the time of Lenihan's installation, the role Van den Broeck had created for himself at St. Peter's was abundantly clear. He saw himself not merely as a chaplain, but as a superior, assessing the community's quality of life, giving orders, and directing the activities of the convent. Amadeus, whom he had rarely seen, he assessed as both incompetent and divisive, heaping on her head the responsibility for everything he decried at St. Peter's. Conversely, he saw Rose Galvin as peerless. Given authority, she could, he felt—perhaps with him to guide her—redress all the flaws of the community. With Van den Broeck's brief before him, Lenihan had been prepared for judgment before ever visiting St. Peter's.

While St. Julien had assured Amadeus of her unqualified support against the unjust accusations leveled again her, Amadeus made a decision that brought her judgment into question. The issue was the newly opened mission field of Alaska. Amadeus's passion for the missions of Alaska had begun almost as soon as the Jesuits had opened the territory to mission activity. As early as 1898, she had pleaded with Father Pascal Tosi, S.J., to accept Ursulines for the Alaskan work. Bishop Brondel, however, was quick to negate her request. While Brondel admired Amadeus's courage and dedication, he had learned to be wary of her unconsidered impulses. While she might have felt that she had accomplished all she could in Montana, he still saw Montana as a field for continued labor and had no desire to lose the Ursulines to another missionary field.

During her time in Rome, however, Amadeus had dazzled the members of the chapter with a description of this vast and desolate land awaiting the word of God. St. Julien, convinced of the value of the work, had given permission for Amadeus to begin work in Alaska. Were it not for her tragic train accident in 1902, she would probably have acted sooner, but it was the summer of 1905 before she was able to begin her plans, only to find herself facing the implacable Bishop Lenihan. He had refused categorically for any Ursuline to be moved from his diocese. Amadeus, not unwilling to be devious for a righteous cause, sidestepped his authority by choosing three nuns from St. Ignatius's—a mission belonging to the diocese of Helena, and thus outside of Bishop Lenihan's jurisdiction.

By early August, Sister Laurentia Walsh, Sister Claver O'Driscoll (both professed from Bedford Park, New York), and Sister Dosithée Leygonie (an exile from Bordeaux) were preparing to join the Jesuits at Akulurak, a bleak stretch of land that the Innuits described as "near the end of the world." Amadeus accompanied them to Seattle, and on August 13 bid them Godspeed as they boarded the ship that would take them to their promised land.

Lenihan's response to this subterfuge was a scathing denunciation:

> I have positive proofs that you have acted contrary to my
> personal orders in regard to the best interests of religion in
> Montana, and especially in regard to the welfare and good
> name and good government of the Ursuline Order in this
> state. In many instances you have violated the Sacred Canons
> of the Church and you have disobeyed the Constitution of
> the Ursuline Nuns.

I, therefore, command you not to interfere with
Mother Rose [Galvin], the local superior of St. Peter's Mission
in her government of that Mission. And, especially, you must
not interfere with the novitiate nor in the removal of any of
the members of said community.

Furthermore, you are commanded to pay all the bills
against St. Peter's Mission to the date of this letter. You must
not accept or use any of the funds from Mother Katharine
which are donated to said Mission. You must not borrow any
more funds on the credit of the Ursuline Corporation of
which you are president; but you must pay back at once, the
last amount you borrowed to improve the Ursulines property
at Anaconda.

Study the Constitution and SPIRIT of the Ursuline
Order and try, at least, in your old age, to live according
to same.

This do, and may God bless you.[4]

At the same time, he wrote to seven novices who had been
sent to Anaconda to make their retreat and to two sisters whom
Amadeus had sent to St. Ignatius's Mission, accusing them of violat-
ing their cloister and ordering them to return immediately to St.
Peter's, "even though you have received orders from Mother
Amadeus to the contrary."[5]

Following these letters, Lenihan took action, writing a document that he gave to Van den Broeck to be read to the community at
St. Peter's. With the nuns gathered in the chapel, the chaplain stood
at the altar steps and read Lenihan's letter denouncing Amadeus and
ordering the nuns, henceforward, to acknowledge Rose Galvin as
their legitimate superior. It was a moment of drama that left the community dumbfounded—caught between their loyalty to their
foundress and fear of transgressing this new order. With a flair for the
dramatic, De Merici Sheble sent a telegram to Rome: "Great disturbance Galvin rules!"[6]

Sometime later, Amadeus described at length the consequences of this histrionic moment:

> When I arrived in St. Peter's on September 5 it was like going into the house of death. No joyous greeting awaited my return—sadness, say coldness and fear, reigned supreme. Most everyone avoided me, very few had the courage to speak to me. With fear and trembling some stole into our room to ask what to do in their trouble. I counseled them all to obey the Bishop and told them I should also obey under protest until I could reach our Mother General. I think something should be done without delay to relieve the suffering of the nuns at St. Peter's and to remove the false impression that the house is to be closed and the nuns that do not adhere to Mother Rose and Father van den Broeck sent away. When I saw that my presence at St. Peter's only aggravated the situation and that there was no work left for me there, I retired to Holy Family Mission from which place I governed—St. Peter's excepted— all the other missions in Montana.[7]

A month earlier, St. Julien had received a long letter from Rose Galvin in answer to her request for an explanation of events at St. Peter's. Although, in many ways, the letter was a clear and judicious account of the trouble at St. Peter's, its tone was bitter and angry. Part of the reason that she had not informed St. Julien sooner, she wrote, had been her hesitance in complaining about someone who had been her superior for years and who had been kind and helpful to her. Even so, she had to acknowledge that Amadeus's decisions had always been arbitrary, that the advice of her councilors had never been taken seriously. "The rule of Mother Amadeus is totally arbitrary," she concluded. "She says one thing and does another. ... More than one person has heard her say that she is sorry they ever joined the Roman Union."[8]

If St. Julien found the letter disconcerting, she was discreet in her response, thanking Rose Galvin for her sincerity. "Distance makes it difficult if not impossible to resolve these delicate questions," she responded. "Since I am still not able to come to America I would like you to come to see me in Rome," suggesting that Rose and Amadeus come together in order to sort out the difficulties in which they were both involved.[9]

Amadeus responded at once, thanking St. Julien for her understanding kindness and assuring her that she was already making arrangements to come to Rome, probably arriving sometime in November with Sister Amata Dunne as her companion.

Several weeks later, St. Julien received a carefully worded reply from Rose suggesting another course of action. "The dissatisfaction here is not personal," she explained, "nor is it confined to one alone." Therefore, she felt, the only solution was to wait for a visit from Mother St. Julien. "The community would wish the investigation to take place here where all may have a voice even though the investigation be deferred another year." There followed the names of eight sisters who endorsed her position.[10]

The tone of the letter was deferential, but the message was intransigent: Rose Galvin would not come to Rome; she would wait for St. Julien to visit Montana.

St. Julien's astonishment was palpable. Unaccustomed to such obstinacy and determined to force Rose Galvin's submission, St. Julien resorted to a measure reserved for grave cases of disobedience: she sent a telegram ordering Rose "in virtue of holy obedience" to obey her order to come to Rome. The penalties of refusing such an order were sufficient to force Rose's compliance.

What had begun as a limited conflict between Amadeus and Lenihan had now broadened into an open battleground, and during that autumn, letters poured in to the generalate from several of the Montana houses speaking passionately in Amadeus's favor. From St. Xavier's, Sister Scholastica O'Sullivan wrote "in the name of all here ... expressing our grief at the complaints that have been written against our dear much loved Mother ... There are very few, if any, that could do what Mother has done under such trying difficulties, always courageous, cheerful, self-sacrificing and a model for all, her very presence being an incentive to good."[11]

From Anaconda came a further eulogy recounting "the struggles and trials that Mother has met, on every side, in the past twenty years; her heroic devotion to the welfare of the Indians, and her wonderful power that has held together the Montana Ursulines, a task that hardly another could accomplish."[12]

From Holy Family, there came not only an endorsement of their foundress, but a request that she be maintained in her position for life. "We your dear children come again to call on you for your usual kind considerations and heartfelt sympathies in our great affliction and beg of you to exercise your great influence in behalf of our dear suffering Mother to have her continued in office for life, or for such a time that this unexpected and surprising irreligious uprising may be quelled and proper religious discipline be restored in Montana."[13]

From the three Alaskan missionaries came a plea to take action against the troublemakers and restore St. Peter's to its proper state.[14]

It was perhaps a letter from one of the French exiles, Sister Clémence Viguier, stationed at Anaconda, that provided a more judicious evaluation of Mother Amadeus. At all the missions she had visited, Clémence noted, she had found a great veneration for the foundress. But, she observed, the difficulties of mission life were many: poverty, too few sisters, and too much work, which often made it impossible to live a life of prayer. In some ways, it had to be admitted that Amadeus contributed to the difficulties. She was frequently sick, and because she had no help, she could not take care of all that needed to be done; she was especially negligent in answering letters that required her response. It was inevitable that all of this caused dissatisfaction.[15]

By December, however, some of the letters that arrived in Rome were not simply testimonials in favor of Amadeus, but angry denunciations of Rose Galvin and her supporters. The letter from Holy Family, where Francis Seibert was superior, did not hesitate to voice serious accusations against those perfidious sisters who wished to usurp power and against Bishop Lenihan, who, in his ignorance of the work of the missions, was disdainful of the methods of the Jesuits as well as the Ursulines. Their most pointed accusations were made against Van den Broeck, whom they described as "a secular priest who could have no influence with our dear and best friend Bishop Brondel, but is playing his part in a new game and making the religious his tool."[16]

Rose Galvin it seemed, was his primary "tool." Flattered by his assessment of her talents, Rose Galvin accepted all his advice without question.

By the beginning of 1906, however, word was reaching Rome of a questionable personal relationship between Mother Rose and her mentor. In February of that year, Sister Philippa Seery wrote at length from Anaconda. The letter was direct and detailed: Mother Rose had less and less time for the nuns and for community business. Her morning hours were spent in private "conference." Her meals, too, were often spent with the chaplain, and evening hours found them "taking long walks out in the fields through the canyon and over the hills returning after dark." Although some other nuns or some children were with them, this did not dispel the shadow over their relationship. Sister Philippa's letter, unlike many of the others, was unemotional and factual. "I have only written what I saw or heard and have added nothing," she concluded.[17]

When Mother Rose arrived at the generalate two weeks later, St. Julien was surprised to find her accompanied not only by another religious—as Rule demanded—but shepherded by Father Van den Broeck himself. It was not an auspicious beginning. Van den Broeck came bearing a formal letter of introduction from the bishop, along with a list of complaints against Amadeus. "I received this priest with all the respect due to the mission with which he was charged," St. Julien responded later to Lenihan, but her disfavor was obvious. In addition to the bishop's letter, Van den Broeck brought a sheaf of papers that he presented as evidence of the charges made against Amadeus. The letters (mostly letters from the sisters to Amadeus as their superior), he explained, he had discovered during a search he had made of Amadeus's room. St. Julien was appalled, doubly appalled by his self-justification. "In his animosity toward Mother Amadeus," she continued in her letter to Lenihan, "this priest has taken papers, personal property of Mother Amadeus which she had left in her room at St. Peter ... I have not read these papers. I have returned them to their rightful owner."

Her outrage was manifest but controlled. She had been advised, she wrote, to bring all this to the Sacred Congregation in order to ensure that Van den Broeck be removed from his present position and be forbidden any contact with the Ursulines in the future, but she preferred a less public way. "I would prefer to show my deference and respect," she wrote to Lenihan, "by asking you to take this step yourself which seems to me essential for the peace and tranquility of Ursuline houses."[18]

The remainder of the letter (ten pages in length) responded fully to each of Lenihan's complaints. St. Julien's meticulous explanation of the fine points of religious administration and canon law left Lenihan with little ground for argument. Even Amadeus's debts, which could hardly be denied, found justification. "What is astonishing to me," St. Julien countered, "is that the amount of the debt is not greater when you think that in a period of twenty years and without any prior resources, she has founded such a great number of missions, enlarged her personnel from six to seventy persons, purchased land and raised buildings. ... And this debt of $30,000 she has contracted in spite of herself in order to obey the orders of her bishop, His Excellency Bishop Brondel."[19]

While St. Julien must have felt a certain satisfaction in her response to Lenihan, whatever she had hoped to accomplish in her interviews with Rose, she failed to achieve. The problem went far beyond the latter's animosity toward Amadeus: the basic source of contention was the Roman Union. It was Rose Galvin's contention that the Ursulines of Montana had never agreed either personally or collectively to affiliate themselves with this union. "The members of our community did not give to Mother Amadeus their individual right of vote nor empower her to act for us as a body, nor did we give her the power either tacit or expressed to enter our community in the union. For these and other reasons, Reverend Mother, I fail to see in you my lawful superior."[20]

Later, a letter from Mother Rose's colleague, Paula Slevin, affirmed this position: "When Mother Amadeus went to Rome in 1900 I understood it was merely to investigate what the union was, as others, but more honest superiors did. She had no right to bind her community without their individual right of vote or voice. This I never gave and I defy Mother Amadeus to say I did."[21]

These assertions ran directly contrary to Amadeus's insistent avowal that each sister had been given the form Brondel had sent and had had the privacy to complete it and return it to the bishop. In her formal statement, addressed to St. Julien, she wrote, "I hereby emphatically state that conformably to the orders of His Eminence Cardinal Seraphine Vannutelli each Ursuline Nun in the state of Montana, USA, sent in writing her opinion concerning the joining of the Union to the ordinary of the diocese, the Right Reverend J.B. Brondel, Bishop of Helena."[22]

In the light of two such passionate avowals, it seemed impossible to discover the truth. Rose Galvin and Paula remained implacable throughout their interview with St. Julien. A further interview with Cardinal Francesco Satolli, the Cardinal Protector, left them unswerving in their response. They demanded the right to leave the Roman Union, which they maintained they had never willingly entered. It was a stormy session that left the impression that they were willful, intransigent—and embarrassingly rude. Without returning to say good-bye, they left, leaving only a note at Villa Maria, where they had been staying: "Dear Reverend Mother, We have seen the Cardinal and we do not return to Villa Maria. Respectfully ... "

"Coup de théâtre," wrote Father Joseph Lemius, St. Julien's advisor; "the birds have flown. Yesterday evening when I went to see them as we had arranged, I found the cage empty. Where have they gone? Are they still in Rome, in some other house? In Naples? About to leave for America?"[23] In fact, they left for America, at once accompanied by their champion, Father Van den Broeck, angry and frustrated, and anxious to return to the promised protection of their bishop.

St. Julien, convinced that she could delay her visit to America no longer, sailed for New York on April 28, arriving on May 4. Although the trouble at St. Peter's was St. Julien's most immediate concern, she had other important affairs to deal with as well. The Roman Union had then been in existence six years, and by the end of 1905, the general council had made geographical divisions into provinces and begun to appoint provincial superiors. Despite the vast extent of the United States, it was divided into only two provinces: south and north. The southern province consisted of the houses of Texas and Illinois; the northern province encompassed the entire continent from New York to California. In late March, a circular letter was sent to North America appointing Mother Joseph Dallmer superior of the south, with a provincialate to be established at San Antonio, Texas, and Amadeus Dunne superior of the north, with a provincialate in Middletown, New York.

The appointment of Amadeus was both a bold and judicious move. It confirmed her authority and, at the same time, removed her from Lenihan's episcopal see.

The choice of Middletown as the center of power for this vast territory is more difficult to determine. Middletown was a small town, hardly more than a village, some sixty miles north of New York City. Inconveniently distanced from every other Ursuline house, it had little to recommend it, except that the New York Ursulines owned property there, having begun an academy in 1886. For the Ursulines of Montana, the choice was shocking. Middletown, a continent away, might as well be Arabia. Through the remainder of March and into April, they waited for the return of Amadeus and the promised visit of St. Julien Aubry, hoping for some relief from the turmoil that had overtaken them.

On May 18, St. Julien and Amadeus arrived at St. Peter's. Although this was the visit for which Rose Galvin had appealed, she had not waited for it to take place. Once again, the birds had flown, this time to Great Falls, placing themselves under the protection of their advocate, Mathias Lenihan. There were now three "birds." Elizabeth Arnheim had joined Rose Galvin and Paula Slevin in their flight. St. Julien wrote to them at once, asking them to return to St. Peter's and to give an account of their actions. In response, Paula Slevin wrote, curtly: "I am surprised that you expected me to return to St. Peter's. I left St. Peter's with the permission of my bishop and am now under his protection."[24]

It was a reply that demanded immediate action, and on May 23, St. Julien wrote directly to Lenihan, asking for the privilege of an interview in which she could present her respects and also discuss the case of the three religious:

> [They] have left the house to seek refuge, as I have been told,
> at Great Falls. ... I wrote to them immediately ordering them
> to return at once. ... They refused, entrenching themselves
> behind the permission and protection of their bishop. This is
> why I am writing to you, Your Excellency, to beg you to make
> these sisters understand the duty they have to obey me and
> come at once to give me an account of their conduct. ... I do
> not hide from you that if these sisters persist in their refusal
> to obey it will be my duty to denounce the entire situation to
> the Holy See. ... This letter is my last effort toward concilia-
> tion and if, God forbid, it should be without effect, I will
> immediately begin the process of canonical dismissal.[25]

Despite her avowal of conciliation, St. Julien's tone was far from conciliatory. Although during their meeting she stopped short of accusing the bishop of allying himself with the recalcitrant sisters, it was clear that she considered him responsible for their present position. As for Lenihan, his anger had been spurred by the appointment of Amadeus as provincial superior. In this, he was joined by Bishop Carroll of Helena. "Confidentially," St. Julien wrote to Father Lemius, "they are not completely at fault in this. It is obvious that Mother has been much too bold. I have tried to make her understand that bishops are necessary for us and that we have to work to make them our kind friends." But, even so, she could not help adding, in Amadeus's defense, "I have to say that these bishops are remarkably arbitrary. The one in Helena, although more formally correct, is no less authoritarian."[26]

By this time, it was clear that no reconciliation was possible and St. Julien began to carry out her ultimate threat. By June 16, she had completed an 8,000-word manuscript to be sent to the Sacred Congregation of Religious. It was a weighty and meticulous document. "I am taking the liberty of bringing before Your Eminence the sad and disturbing situation of the Ursulines of Montana," it began, and then continued with three main points:

> The attitude taken in their regard by Monsignor Lenihan, Bishop
> of Great Falls;
> The intrigues of a priest, the Reverend V.J. Van den Broeck,
> formerly cure of St. Peter's mission and chaplain of the
> Ursulines;*
> Finally, the revolt against the authority of the Institute by an
> Ursuline of Montana, Mother Rose, who led other sisters
> and even novices into her rebellion.[27]

The next thirty pages rehearsed in detail the history of the problems at St. Peter's under each of the major headings. Nothing was omitted: the intrigues of Van den Broeck, the irascible complaints and denunciation of Amadeus by the bishop, the arrogant and willful conduct of Mother Rose.

---

*By 1907, Van den Broeck was pastor at Lewiston, a town in central Montana. The following year, he was moved to Poplar on the northern border.

St. Julien's implacable demands had already forced Lenihan to remove Van den Broeck from St. Peter's. He now recognized that his patronage of the "rebels" was imprudent, at best. Although rumor had it that he had offered to establish them in Great Falls, where they could staff the school that he was determined to build, this project came to naught.

It was clear even to the intransigent Mother Rose that their situation was becoming increasingly precarious. If Lenihan were to withdraw his support, they had few other options. In an effort to provide some security for them, on March 23, Mother Rose wrote to Mother Stanislaus, superior in Toledo:

> Upon my return here I tried to obey our Bishop by assuming
> the position of Superioress, as he commanded me. I found
> two community nuns completely turned to the other side and
> the others are inclined to wait developments. ... There are
> now but six who would want to leave, at any and every cost.
> May we six (three professed and three white veils) still seek an
> asylum with you, till we are ready to start afresh? ... Will you
> please send me word soon, by letter, so that it will reach me
> by March 30th.[27]

Their petition to join the Ursulines of Toledo was rejected, however, leaving them without religious status. By now, the six "rebels" were reduced to three, and that fall, Rose, Paula, and the novice, Carmel McCabe, left Montana for Akron, Ohio, where they found temporary teaching positions.

Then, suddenly, in the middle of a bleak and uncertain winter, fortune smiled. In December 1907, Rome spoke. Mother Rose received an indult releasing them from the Roman Union, affirming their status as consecrated religious, and permitting them to affiliate with any Ursuline house. The following spring, with their status affirmed, they received more good news. Bishop Alphonse Glorieux of Boise, Idaho, was seeking nuns to establish an elementary school in his diocese. Still unaffiliated with any Ursuline group, but bolstered by hopes of a useful religious life, Mother Rose and Sisters Paula and Carmel arrived in Moscow, Idaho, in the summer of 1908, as Ursuline nuns in good standing, to open the first Catholic school in that city.

After so much turmoil and vilification, Mother Rose had won the battle. They were released from the Roman Union, they had regained their status as Ursuline religious, and she was now superior in her own right, the foundress of a new Ursuline community. It was probably not quite what Mother St. Julien had in mind. But there was still to be another unexpected turn. In 1915, Mother Rose, superior of a growing and successful community, recognizing the advantages of being associated with a larger group, asked to be affiliated with the Roman Union. For two years, she was kept waiting as a kind of penance for her rebellious actions at St. Peter's. Finally, in May 1919, the Ursuline community of Moscow, Idaho, was formally affiliated with the Roman Union. Mother Rose continued as superior until her death in 1934.

Chapter Fifteen

Our loved superior for twenty-five years and always our mother.

—*Annals of St. Peter's Mission*

The happy conclusion of the Rose Galvin affair was still far in the future as St. Julien prepared to depart from St. Peter's. On June 19, 1906, she wrote to Mother Angela Lincoln in Rome: "My time here is coming to an end. More than a month! But I have not wasted my time; I have nothing to regret."[1] She was convinced that had she not been present, things would have been far worse. Toward the end of the month, in the company of Amadeus, she left St. Peter's Mission. Amadeus, as the first provincial of the northern province, was traveling east to take up her residence in Middletown, New York. There are no records of that parting, and one can only conjecture the mingled emotions of loss and pride on the part of the community. Perhaps there was also a sense of relief that with Amadeus out of the diocese, the future might be less tumultuous than the past.

They stopped at Miles City, where, just twenty-two years earlier, the sisters had begun their work in Montana, and then continued southeast, stopping at Ursuline houses along the way to introduce the communities to their first provincial superior. While the journey had none of the pomp of a Renaissance royal "progress," it was, in its own way, a preeminent journey. It was a first in ways that would change the contour—and often the spirit—of the Ursuline houses that had voted in favor of the Roman Union. From small isolated units, free to determine their own destiny, they were drawn into a network that they would find both supporting and

231

demanding. While, in theory, they had understood and affirmed the alterations such affiliation would entail, only now with the formation of the northern province were they brought face-to-face with the modifications that would be required of them.

Their first stop was with the Ursulines of York, Nebraska, a community that already had ties with Amadeus, who as superior at Toledo had welcomed them some twenty-five years earlier, when they had come as exiles from Germany. The visit to York was all that St. Julien had hoped for: friendly, joyful, enthusiastic. Amadeus, now sixty-two—thin, small, with a decided limp—was welcomed not as an unknown superior, but as a benefactor and a fellow missionary. The visitors stayed on to celebrate Independence Day on July 4, a celebration that Mother St. Julien thoroughly enjoyed. In a letter to Angela Lincoln, she wrote, "This is the Fourth of July. ... Since yesterday evening we have heard nothing but bombs and firecrackers. ... I am enjoying this ... I think I have become an American! Hurrah!"

But, although she was enjoying the American spirit and the hospitality of the Ursulines, she was less sanguine about the clergy. As in Montana, she found them self-satisfied and ill-prepared theologically. In the same letter to Angela Lincoln, she continued, "Yesterday I gave a pastor a little course in philosophy and catechetics. He needed it badly. He's an Irishman who trusts more to feelings than to reason."[2]

From York, they traveled northeast into the green and prosperous country of Minnesota, where, in 1877, the Ursulines from Alton, Illinois, had founded a house in Lake City and then, eight years later, in Frontenac. At Minneapolis–St. Paul, they boarded the train for Chicago and the final eastern journey back to New York. By mid-August, they were at Middletown for the formal opening of the provincialate and provincial novitiate.

What was entailed in the administration of a province of an international order and what were the duties and responsibilities incumbent upon the provincial was clear to no one, least of all to the new provincial. With no one to guide her beyond a set of very general regulations, Amadeus sat in her office in Middletown with Mary of the Angels, her secretary and longtime friend, attempting to absorb the dimensions of her task. She was charged with administering a province, yet, so far, "province" was simply a concept, an idea created by a group of Ursulines in Rome. It was she, as the first provincial, who was tasked with bringing a concept to reality.

While St. Julien assured the Americans that she in no way wished to impose substantial changes on their mode of life, it was soon clear that things would be different for all of them. The vast reaches of the province inevitably changed their perspective. Although Amadeus was experienced in administering houses stretching across Montana, even she must have been staggered by the sweep of her responsibilities, extending from the Atlantic to the Pacific, a distance of well over 3,000 miles. In contrast to the physical scope of the province, the site of the provincialate itself was far from imposing, consisting of a suite of rooms in a wing of the Middletown convent, the same building that also housed the recently established novitiate.

Nothing had more immediate impact on the American houses than the establishment of a central novitiate. Prior to the union, each convent received its own novices, trained them according to the Rule and their local traditions, and, following their profession, inserted them into the teaching ministry of the house. The central novitiate changed everything. Now, all novices had to be sent to Middletown, where they would be trained under a novice mistress appointed by Roman authority.

It was a hard saying, and no house found it more difficult than the missions of Montana. The train fare from Montana to New York was a prohibitive item. The postulants who came to St. Peter's could not depend on their families for such expenditure, nor for the monthly board that was expected of novices. Certainly, the Montana mission houses, reduced to penury since the government's retraction of contract schools, were in no position to scrape such funds together.

Beyond the question of money, however, was a more fundamental consideration. From the beginning, Amadeus had

determined that the young women volunteering for work with the
Indians should receive their formation within the culture where they
would be ministering. Such ministry was a special vocation and had
to be fostered as such. Thus, one of her first acts at St. Peter's was to
establish a novitiate. Despite some initial opposition, her decision
had been proved right, and, by 1888, almost all vocations at St.
Peter's were coming not from other Ursuline communities, as they
had at the beginning, but from young women entering directly into
the novitiate at St. Peter's. Now, in bitter irony, it was Amadeus herself who had to close the doors of the novitiate at St. Peter's and
enforce the new regulations.

It was soon evident that much of what was demanded of
Amadeus was drawing on her weaknesses rather than her strengths.
Letters had never been her forte. When she wrote them, they were
vivid, detailed, full of her compassionate spirit, but as she grew
older, her letters became fewer. Father Lindesmith she never neglected, and there were occasional letters to Mother Drexel, usually
begging for money. But letters to the sisters—giving permissions,
settling questions, making decisions that only she had the power to
do—were rare indeed.

Now she found herself in a position where correspondence was
at the heart of her responsibilities. Superiors, unsure of their authority, nervous of making decisions outside their jurisdiction, needing a
strong hand to guide them in unknown paths, sought advice from
their provincial superior. Since the telephone was still a rare com-
modity, the letter was everything. In addition to letters seeking
counsel were the more formidable letters from Rome: letters asking
for information, for lists of sisters, lists of professions, lists of schools,
numbers of children in the schools. For such requests, she had neither the energy nor the inclination.

Within a year, it was clear that Mother St. Julien, who had had
high hopes for Amadeus once she was beyond the hostility of Bishop
Lenihan, was recognizing another side. Again and again, Amadeus was
reprimanded for having acted independently, for acting counter to her

superior's judgment, for having submitted documents incorrectly or too late, for using questionable judgment in dealing with sisters.

Lost in the welter of letters, regulations, and reprimands that surrounded her, Amadeus solaced herself by planning a trip to Alaska to visit the three sisters she had sent to Akulurak in 1905, and possibly to establish another mission. On January 17, however, she received a telegram reminiscent of so many she had received in the past: "FIRE AT ST PETER'S!" The beautiful stone building that she had built with so much pride had been destroyed. She cabled immediately: "Most sincere sympathy. Intensely pained at our great loss. Mother Katharine Drexel has insurance policy. Thank God the Blessed Sacrament and all were saved. Write me full particulars."[3] If such a letter was sent, it has not survived, and the account provided by the annals is the only description left of those defeating hours.

> At noon today just as the nuns were assembled in the chapel
> for examen, a little Indian girl ran in and cried, "Fire, Mother,
> Fire!" All ran to the rescue; no flames were to be seen but from
> the roof, just over the Boys Dormitory issued a dense smoke.
> The priest immediately took the Blessed Sacrament from the
> Seminary Chapel and carried it to the convent. In the mean-
> time all the nuns on the place were in the building trying to
> extinguish the fire but the density of the smoke was so great
> that they could do very little. The Sacred Vials, some of the
> vestments and altar linens and three statues, the Sacred Heart,
> the Blessed Virgin, and St. Joseph, were saved. Also some of the
> Indian children's bedding. In less than a half hour entrance to
> the building was impossible by reason of the smoke. The wind
> blew the sparks eastward and one straw stack took fire and
> burned to the ground. The cow sheds—the only protection for
> our cattle in the winter—burned to the ground.[4]

The following day, the annalist continued her account, describing how Sister Sebastian Finnegan, crippled with rheumatism,

was moved to safety to the community room, and their resident
chaplain given a bed in the convent parlor.

> The white boys on straw ticks on the floor in the music room.
> The Indian girls slept in the loft of the wash house. Today the
> boys are having meals in the basement hall and the Indian
> girls take their places at the end of the meal. The boys school
> is closed and the parents are asked to come and take their
> sons home; the homeless boys will go to St. Ignatius.[5]

The report in the *Great Falls Daily Tribune* added few details
beyond indicating that the fire was probably caused by a defective
flue, that the loss was estimated at $25,000, and that, so far, no plans
for rebuilding had been made.[6]

In the next weeks, the nuns received donations of clothing and
bedding to help them through the freezing nights. As always with such
a loss, it was not simply the matter of "making do" in the immediate
aftermath of the event, but even more important, how to determine the
future. Was it possible to keep the schools in operation? Was it possible
to find the monies necessary to rebuild? And, in the last analysis, was it
advisable? Had the fire occurred five years earlier, the decision to rebuild
would have been less problematic. Even with the loss of government
subsidies and with the withdrawal of the Jesuits in 1898, St. Peter's had
continued successfully with Indian schools for both boys and girls, as
well as a boarding school for the children of white settlers—"an academy"—the only such institution in that bleak landscape. Although the
schools flourished, with the development of the Roman Union, the
status of St. Peter's had changed dramatically. It had lost its place as
motherhouse of the Montana missions. Amadeus, who, for most of the
sisters, had been at the very heart of their missionary vocation, was no
longer theirs. And the preceding summer, the novitiate that had always
sustained them had been closed. The unquenchable fire that roared
through the buildings of St. Peter's Mission on that freezing January day
was perhaps a visible symbol of something already lost.

The coming of spring added its own difficulties. In April, a dam near Helena gave way, damaging the railroad tracks and stopping the westbound trains. In June, torrential rains destroyed two bridges between Cascade and St. Peter's. The force of wind and rain not only flooded the convent basement, but brought down the skeleton chimneys, remnants of the burned school, and commencement took place amid the destruction. The reporter from the *Great Falls Daily Tribune* who wrote of the event, "The recent rains added a touch of emerald to the hills," wrote out of a sanguine spirit the nuns did not share.

The immediate responsibility for St. Peter's rested with Francis Seibert, the recently appointed superior—the only one of the original six still remaining in Montana. Opposite in temperament from Amadeus, Francis's spirit was less visionary than practical. Amadeus's maxim—God will provide—brooked no opposition. Francis was of different mettle. Wise and experienced, she knew they could not long continue as they were. At least for the time being, she decided, they would not rebuild. Meanwhile, she hoped that when Amadeus arrived for her promised visit, she would be able to make some firm decisions.

But when Amadeus finally arrived, on September 2—seven months after the fire—it was clear that her primary concern was not for St. Peter's, but for a new mission she was planning at St. Michael's, Alaska. She brought with her Angela Lincoln (recently returned from Rome) and De Merici Sheble along with two other nuns who were to serve on the Alaska mission: Sister Bartholomew from Bryan, Texas, and Sister Margaret Mary of Malone, New York. Although Amadeus had written earlier to Father Lindesmith that her time at St. Peter's would be spent "developing plans for the rebuilding of the old Mission," in fact, she spent no more than a single day at St. Peter's, hardly sufficient time to discuss the future of the mission. On September 3, Amadeus and her companions boarded the westbound train at Cascade for Seattle and then the steamer for Alaska.

Two months later, she returned, exhausted, in company with Angela Lincoln, having caught the last boat to leave Alaska before the ice set in. The four-page letter that she wrote that Christmas to Katharine Drexel is solid proof of where her heart lay:

> As our ship was twelve days late in leaving Seattle, I was
> debarred the pleasure of getting to Akulurak where three other
> brave Ursulines have been teaching the Innuit Indians since
> 1905. The tundra was not sufficiently frozen to permit travel
> by dog-team whilst the running ice in the great Yukon
> prevented navigation. So I was obliged to do violence to my
> heart and take the last steamer back to Seattle without seeing
> those dear children, but I hope to make up for this great
> sorrow next May, when ... I shall lead another band of
> missionaries to the dear Indian field in the North.[7]

Alaska had replaced Montana. One vision had replaced another. For Amadeus, Montana was a goal of the past, and neither the past, nor even the present, could ever constrain her spirit. Only the future—that vast unknowable adventure—pulled her inexorably into its orbit. When in the spring of that year Amadeus was replaced as provincial by Mother Irene Gill, then superior of the Ursulines of New Rochelle, it seemed that she would soon be free to devote herself completely to Alaska.

A greater contrast in personality and experience would be hard to find. There is no evidence that Mother Irene had ever traveled farther west than the Hudson River. Irene (née Lucy) Gill was preeminently an educator. Born in Ireland, she had been schooled in New York City, where she entered the Ursuline convent. Convinced that education was the most valuable tool for an immigrant population, she devoted herself to improving Catholic school curriculum and training young women for their roles as teachers. In 1904, she put her dream into action by opening a college for women in New Rochelle, New York. When, in 1909, she was appointed superior of the northern province, she was already fully occupied by her role as superior of the growing community in New Rochelle and foundress of the nascent College of St. Angela. For her, Montana was a far and distant land. That she was replacing a woman whose activities had already given her the stature of a myth was clear to her.

Despite Amadeus's long absence, Montana clearly still thought of her as their own. "Today's mail brought us the sad news that our beloved Rev. Mother is no longer Provincial Prioress," the annalist at St. Labre's wrote on May 15, 1909. "Words fail to express our grief ... Reverend Mother Irene of New Rochelle is our Provincial. No one can take the place of our own dear precious Mother who has been a real Mother to each of us since our arrival in Montana."[8]

It is clear evidence of Irene Gill's sense of responsibility that, four months after her appointment, she arrived in Montana to acquaint herself directly with their situation. Although transportation had improved since the Ursulines' arrival twenty-five years before, it was still an exhausting journey. The weather was bitterly cold and the wagon trip from Cascade to St. Peter's left Irene and her companion, Mother Dominic Weiss, half frozen. October was already a winter month on the Great Plains.

Her reception must have been, even at best, cautious. Despite their frequent exasperation at Amadeus for her procrastination, her imperious judgments, and her erratic behavior, she was, in a unique way, "their own." That month, St. Peter's was celebrating its silver jubilee of foundation and a telegram was sent to Amadeus: "Jubilee Greetings to the Reverend Mother Amadeus, Foundress of the Montana Ursuline Missions, our loved superior for twenty-five years and always our mother."[9] The tone was significant of their affection and trust. Irene Gill could never replace Amadeus. Irene was not only an unknown, but she was everything that western pioneers had a tendency to distrust. She was not only from the East, but from what was quintessentially East: the city of New York. In terms of personality, Amadeus and Irene represented two poles—Amadeus: responsive, exuberant, spontaneous; Irene: measured, reserved, deliberate.

Except for the dates of her arrival and departure and a detail about the weather, the annals contain no comments about Irene's visit. On October 21, however, five days after her arrival, accompanied by Francis Siebert, she traveled to Great Falls to present herself to Bishop Lenihan. Again, no details exist of the meeting, but in the light of future events, one may safely conjecture that the subject of a school in Great Falls, a consistent desire of the bishop, was discussed. Such a discussion would never have been possible under Amadeus's leadership, but now Lenihan was able to dismiss his hostility toward the Ursulines and look to a valuable partnership. In a way, it was an episcopal triumph. Lenihan, since the year of his consecration, had been determined to build such a school in his diocesan see.

It was a fitting moment for the Ursulines as well, since some decision had to be made about St. Peter's. Either it would have to be rebuilt or else a fundamental reorganization of the schools would have to be made.

There is no record of the response of the nuns to such a dramatic turn. The Montana Ursulines had been founded for a specific purpose: to educate and evangelize the native population. While they had maintained a school for white children in Miles City and taken on the responsibility for diocesan schools in Anaconda and Roundup, their avowed purpose was their work with the Indians. Although St. Peter's included a school for the children of white settlers, none of the nuns would have considered this their primary goal. Now, however, they were being asked to set their sights on something radically different. An academy in an urban setting was far from their foundress's initial vision. Had Amadeus continued as provincial, there could be little doubt that such a plan would never have been considered. If an academy were to be built in Great Falls, the position of St. Peter's would be diminished considerably, with only the Indian girls' school still functioning. The majority of the sisters would be needed at Great Falls, and whatever resources they had would be devoted to the new project. Perhaps they were wise enough to see the value of a new direction in the light of the changing status of mission schools, but, even so, such surrender could not have been made without pain.

Less than six months after the initial interview with Bishop Lenihan, Mother Francis and her council made a formal petition to the provincial council "to transfer from St. Peter, Montana, to Great Falls, Montana, the Boarding School called Mount Angela Academy; and to open also in Great Falls, a Day School in connection with the Boarding School."[10] At once, plans for the academy were set in motion. The land—two entire blocks—at Central Avenue and Twenty-Third Street, had been donated by the Townsite Company, which saw the academy as a valuable asset in the development of the city. Steps were taken to remove some small buildings and narrow lanes that surrounded the property so that the view from the academy was unimpeded and majestic.

"Majestic" was certainly the word to describe the proposed academy. The architect, George Shanley of Great Falls, drew up blueprints for a building in Gothic Revival style. It would consist of four stories with a five-story tower, centered between two wings, replete with crenellated parapets and eight winged gargoyles. For a town such as Great Falls, which had only been established in 1883 and whose first schoolhouse had been built in 1885, this extraordinary building, the use of which was devoted to the education of their children, must indeed have seemed a wonder. But Great Falls had an advantage that few Montana towns had. Unlike such cities as Miles City, which had grown from a cow town with little planned development, Great Falls was a carefully architected city. Planned by Paris Gibson, a native of Minneapolis, the town was designed by Gibson with the help of his partner and wealthy railroad magnate, James Hill.[11] Despite its recent origin, Great Falls seemed ready for this extraordinary educational project.

As they watched the plans unfold, the townspeople were in awe, as indeed were the nuns, who must have wondered how this elaborate building would ever be paid for. Although many of the companies involved had generously contributed services and materials, it remained an extraordinarily expensive venture. The original estimate, $100,000, had soon risen to $150,000. But Lenihan was a determined advocate and, his hostility toward the Roman Union set aside, he urged Irene Gill to convince the Roman authority to help them borrow the necessary funds.

The contractors began work with uncommon speed, and on September 17, 1911, the cornerstone of the new school was laid at an elaborate ceremony presided over by Bishop Lenihan, assisted by many priests of the diocese. Lenihan was at his rhetorical best, speaking eloquently of the value of education and the contribution of the Ursulines. The cornerstone itself was carved in the Ursuline tradition: on one side a cross with the legend "St. Angela pray for us" and on the other "Suffer the Little Children to come unto me."

Meanwhile, the schools at St. Peter's continued as best they could in their vastly reduced space. The following year was spent in the bittersweet aura of excitement and loss as decisions were made about who would stay and who would go. Once the academy opened in Great Falls, all white pupils would be transferred there, enabling the Indian pupils to move into the vacated space.

But even this decision was called into question. In a letter to the council in Rome, Irene Gill reported a discussion she had had with the Jesuit superior, George De la Motte, who had advised her to close the mission entirely and sell the property. Once the boarding school was moved, there would be only a small Indian school left. While, in the past, Mother Drexel had provided funds for this, it would no longer be advisable to continue it. The suggestion seemed like a practical one to Irene, especially since they needed all possible funds for the new building. Although, she wrote, the nuns raised stock and ran a farm, this did not really pay, and, with a typically eastern bias, she concluded, "It does not seem appropriate work for Ursulines although they may have had to do it at the beginning."[12] On this score, however, Irene's opinion did not hold, and the Indian school continued for another six years.

On June 19, the closing exercises of St. Peter's schools were held, with the bishop in attendance. Four days later, June 23, thirty-nine Ursulines gathered for the final annual retreat. The month of July, insufferably hot, was spent in sorting and packing. On July 24, the final break came. Mother Francis and her council moved into Great Falls. The once imposing motherhouse, now lying in ruins, was left with a few nuns to continue the reduced Indian school.

During the second week of August, the public was invited for an inspection of the completed Mount Angela Academy. The *Great Falls Daily Tribune* wrote a glowing report, replete with photographs of the imposing building. After details of its length and breadth and the various companies responsible for its construction, the paper continued:

> The strong appeal made by the interior is the convenience of arrangement and the modern methods of heating, ventilating and lighting used. It is a building which will be the pride of the citizens of Great Falls because it is one of the best educational buildings in the entire northwest. It will give fine accommodations for 175 girls as boarders and 375 as day pupils. The work will begin with the kindergarten and carry the pupils through all the grades till they are prepared for college work. Music and the arts, too, will be given much attention. ... The completion of the handsome new building has caused unbounded joy in the hearts of the Ursuline nuns who made the building possible and second only to their delight in its completion is that which comes to the bishop in having the substantial structure added to the equipment for educational work in his diocese.[13]

On August 15, 1912, the dedication of the new school was solemnized by a pontifical High Mass. Two weeks later, on September 3—ready or not—Mount Angela Ursuline Academy opened its doors to its first pupils.

Chapter Sixteen

Our schools
must be kept up at any cost.
—*Father Louis Taelman*

As the nuns in the newly established academy tried to adjust their energies to the vast reaches of their new building—with its four stories, its extensive wings, and its immense kitchen, equipped to cook for an anticipated 300 boarders—the remnant of sisters and children left amid the ruins of St. Peter's were adjusting to a condition of increased poverty and desolation.

Once the decision had been made not to rebuild St. Peter's, it was clear that little was expected of the school that remained. By 1912, everything that had made St. Peter's exceptional was gone. The statues, the beautiful pieces of hand-carved furniture, whatever would beautify the academy at Great Falls had been packed into wagons and taken to the train at Cascade. While there was no thought of abandoning their Indian pupils, no one doubted that the old St. Peter's was irretrievably gone. What remained was simply a matter of "making do." The nuns essential to the upkeep of the mission stayed on, moving the Indian girls into the space abandoned by their white pupils, keeping their classes going as best they could, dependent on the whim of Bishop Lenihan for a priest to minister to their spiritual needs. It was only a distance of some forty miles to Great Falls, but the space was as vast as a continent.

While conditions at St. Peter's were more dramatic than at the other missions, by 1912, all the missions served by the Ursulines experienced a sense of blight. Although following the disastrous fires at St. Ignatius's and Holy Family the missions had been rebuilt, the confident zeal with which they had been initiated had never been fully restored. The old missionaries, such as Cataldo, Damiani, and the Bandini brothers, had come out to Montana in the full flush of missionary enterprise. Everything was before them, and the Ursulines who came to work with them shared that vision. The vast scope of the work, the dangers that surrounded them, the sheer drudgery that their daily lives demanded could not dishearten them: the prize was too glorious. They would bring comfort to a comfortless people, a people betrayed by white men's lust and government subterfuge. They would bring them what, to their eyes, was the most precious gift that anyone could offer: the grace of Christianity, with its civilizing powers. That Christianity might be offered without the sacrifice of the native's essential culture was beyond their imagination.

The comfortless people, however, were not always the grateful recipients they were expected to be. Even those who accepted the gift of baptism did not always accept the discipline the missionaries demanded. The efforts to bring children into the missionary boarding schools, to separate them as soon as possible from the "barbarous" customs of their tribal life, did not meet with unqualified success. Once they returned home, their pious prayers and Christian discipline were often abandoned before the more natural routine of family life.

While, for the missionaries, the beginning of the new century was a period of diminishment, for most Americans, it was a golden era. Everything was on the move: railroads, telephones, and the automobile had transformed isolated communities into urban centers. The country was peopled with new settlers seduced by the "amber waves of grain," by the "purple mountain majesty" by "America the beautiful" with its limitless expanses stretching from "sea to shining sea." That all that glorious land that they hoped to claim as their own had once belonged to a proud people now displaced and impoverished did not concern them.

The missionaries had watched through the years as the design of bilateral treaties was replaced by executive orders and the system of reservations superceded by the well-meaning but disastrous Severalty Acts, which initiated a regime of personal property into a society built upon communal organization. The foreboding prophecies of those who understood the native people soon came true. Henry Teller, senator from Colorado, had spoken ominously from the Senate floor: "When thirty or forty years shall have passed and these Indians shall have parted with their title, they will curse the hand that was raised professedly in their defense to secure this kind of legislation."[1] But there was no need to wait forty years before the folly of the Severalty Act became apparent. The land apportioned by the government to individual Indian families was neither tended nor farmed, but was soon sold to acquisitive whites for absurdly inadequate sums. The money lasted but a short time, spent on immediate enjoyment, leaving Indians more destitute than ever.

At the same time, the money to sustain missionary schools, which might, at least, have provided Indians with the basic education for coping in an inevitably white world, diminished yearly. Contract schools were a thing of the past. The BCIM remained a sustaining source, and such philanthropists as Mother Katharine Drexel continued to extend what support they could. But it was never enough. The schools were often primitive, lacking essentials in both housing and educational resources. The industrial schools, which the Jesuits had built so proudly, had, in many cases, to be dismantled, the fathers unable to provide the requisite equipment for the mills, the carpentry shops, and the printing presses on which they had built such hopes.

The paramount problem of these years was the changing nature of the schools. The goal of mission schools had, from the beginning, been clear and direct: to evangelize the native people through the education of the children. They would be taught elementary subjects and skills to prepare them for a life increasingly influenced by a white culture, but, primarily, they would be evangelized. It was the logical conclusion of a religion that believed that there could be no salvation outside the Church. For years, the federal government, despite the acknowledged separation of church and state, had happily used the work of the missionaries to do what they lacked the will or the means to do.

As the resources of the Catholic boarding schools diminished, two other groups of schools developed: government schools and those initiated by various Protestant churches. Having slept during the early part of missionary expansion, the latter had now awakened with an energetic desire for evangelization, offering generous funds for the establishment of new missions. In an era when ecumenism

St. Paul's Mission, nuns on holiday excursion. Courtesy of Ursuline archives, Great Falls, Montana

was not yet on the horizon, the centuries-old hostility between the churches inevitably developed into rancorous jealousy, with Protestants accusing the Catholics of coercing children into their schools by means of threats of eternal damnation, and Catholics responding with accusations that the Protestants forced Catholic children into their religious services. The scurrilous arguments hardly provided evidence to the Indians that Christianity was the great religion of peace and brotherly love.

In addition to the Protestant schools—and often condemned even more harshly by the missionaries—were the schools initiated by the government. Such schools were anathema to the Catholic missionaries, who saw them as the very antithesis of everything they considered essential elements of education. That these schools provided no religious teaching, that boys and girls mixed frequently—to the moral detriment of both—that the lay teachers employed were inadequately prepared with little personal devotion to their pupils, all were charges leveled with greater or less ferocity, depending on the zeal of the missionary.

Such schools asserted proudly that they were free of religious indoctrination, forming the children instead in patriotism and moral

St. Paul's Mission, calisthenics class. Courtesy of Ursuline archives, Toledo, Ohio

development. This hardly satisfied the Blackrobes. How could moral development exist without religion? And what moral development could take place in an environment where the sexes were allowed and encouraged to mingle? Worse still was a system where children, instead of being kept in the protection of the mission compound, were allowed to return each evening to their pagan families.

Since all Catholic mission activity was based on the assumption that only in separating the child from his deplorable home environment was it possible to Christianize him, the concept of a day school was worse than meaningless. But to the Indian parents and their children, it seemed the very summit of successful education, and they put all their influence into petitioning for more day schools.

All the mission schools where Ursulines served were forced to confront—more or less dramatically—these inevitable changes.

Even St. Paul's, although spared the turmoil of some of the missions, struggled arduously to maintain adequate facilities for its pupils. In 1909, the Jesuit superior listed a litany of disasters: continued drought, which ruined their crops; blizzards in which some of their cattle died; a disease that killed four of their horses. Meanwhile, they had a record number of children—154—to feed and clothe. They already owed $1,800 to the local store, and $900 more for wages. "I beg of you to do something," Father Joseph Piet wrote to the BCIM.[2]

While government reports on the education provided by St. Paul's had been generally satisfactory, it was becoming increasingly difficult to meet the demands of the Indians, who coveted the greater freedom and wider curriculum of the government schools. At the same time that the superior at St. Paul's was denouncing the school at Fort Belknap as a "regular hell; no education of any kind given," his own school was under attack. In 1909, a pamphlet was circulated criticizing the scope of the mission schools: "Their chief aim was religious training and consequently did not cover the entire scope necessary to the highest degree of efficiency," the writer claimed.[3]

Although the source of the pamphlet was never established— Carlisle denied any involvement—it touched a nerve. The nuns at

St. Paul's were well aware that they were not sufficient for its needs. The superior, Mother Thomas, was in her mid-sixties; two members of the community had suffered severe accidents; the sister cook, too, was growing old, and, despite her "ardent zeal," could hardly be expected to provide meals for more than 150 children. When, in 1911, Mother Irene Gill came to visit the mission, she saw at once the need for additional help, but she could do no more than assign a single additional sister. Every mission, she had come to recognize, was stretched to the limit.

Nothing provided a clearer picture of the daily burden of work at St. Paul's than the encomium for Sister Teresa Abair on her departure for St. Labre's. "Mother Teresa was the Mother Superior here at the mission for seven years," wrote the Jesuit annalist. "All the children loved her for she was a true mother. Order was kept perfectly, cleanness likewise ... Besides being the Superior she was the teacher of the higher classes, taught music and several instruments, took care of the church, did the washing and was the infirmarian during measles and chicken pox. May she be for St. Labre's what she has been for Holy Family."[4]

The problems at St. Paul's were replicated on all the missions with more or less severity. Although Holy Family had recovered remarkably from the devastating fire of 1898, by 1910, the mission found itself in deeper debt than ever. "I am completely out of money and necessary supplies and there are some firms anxiously waiting," wrote Joseph Bruckert to Ketcham. Two months later, another letter pleaded, "How long shall I have to wait for the account?"[5]

Although Holy Family was designated a "ration agency," indicating that the children at the mission were entitled to rations, just as though they were living at home, in fact, the rations were often withheld or cancelled for reasons that were never made clear. Soon, rumors were circulating that at the mission school the children were not getting enough to eat.

It was a rumor not far from the truth. Providing for clothes and shoes as well as food for more than 100 boarders was always a struggle, but deprived of rations, it became an impossibility. "Without meat the Indians will starve," wrote old Father Damiani in despair, pointing out that if they were forced to slaughter their cattle, they would be destitute. As it was, their crops had failed because of the weather, and they were left with nothing but cabbage and rutabagas.

Despite letters to the Department of the Interior explaining the plight of the mission, they received no answer beyond a letter explaining, "It is deemed inadvisable that the system of rations continue at Holy Family." By way of solution, the letter continued, "They [the Blackfeet] must be helped to grow crops such as alfalfa and oats so that the land will be put to use. ... Labor is the salvation of the human race."[6]

It was hardly a comforting aphorism to a school of hungry children. It was already midwinter before the privations of the Blackfeet were finally presented to the Committee for Indian Affairs and the system of rations reestablished.*

While Damiani did all he could to reverse such injustice, it was the nuns who bore the full weight of the problem as they tried to make the limited supply of flour last longer and to find ways of making the inevitable rutabaga more palatable to children whose bodies longed for the meat so essential to their diet.

Like Holy Family and St. Paul's, St. Xavier's, among the Crow, suffered from the problems common to all the missions. In 1906, the irrepressible Peter Prando, who had founded St. Xavier's and had drawn the Crow to Christianity, had died, and, although other Jesuits continued his work, no one had quite his combination of optimism, geniality, and devotion that the Crow had found so compelling. By 1911, Thomas Grant had taken over the mission and put his analytic mind to work in assessing its condition and in finding means to improve it. Like all the missions, St. Xavier's lacked funds, lacked adequate accommodations, and lacked sufficient personnel. Despite

---

*In fact, the problem of rations at Holy Family was never conclusively solved; it emerged again and again over the years.

the hard work of the sisters, Grant wrote, they failed to maintain "a sufficiently high standard" to satisfy the demands of Indian parents who were easily wooed by the promises of government schools that could provide advantages beyond anything the mission schools could offer.

In early February 1911, Grant wrote at length to his provincial with a proposal that would make a dramatic change at St. Xavier's:

> It looks to me that the Indian school here cannot continue
> much longer as a boarding school owing to the general
> tendency toward day schools on the reservation. ... What is
> to be done? I have a plan in view which, if it meets with
> your approval, will throw the whole burden of the school
> here on the sisters, free the priest from the care of material
> things, and allow him to attend much more to the spiritual
> side of the work.[7]

Grant's reasoning was the most overt statement of the philosophy on which missions were organized: the sisters would be

St. Xavier's Mission, girls' graduation. Courtesy of Ursuline archives, Great Falls, Montana

responsible not only for teaching, but for all material needs, thus leaving the priests free for the superior tasks of spiritual ministry.

The plan Grant had in mind was that of establishing a hospital at St. Xavier's. The reason for a hospital, he explained, was the increasingly poor health among the Crow. Of the forty older pupils in the school, no more than twelve were in actively good health; all the others were suffering from some serious disease—mostly tuberculosis. Infant mortality was also high, though a little less among those of mixed blood.[8] Unless something intervened, he predicted ominously, he anticipated that the Crow nation would die out.

Taking into account the decreasing number of boys in the school, Grant wrote, "Our school is morally sure to go out of existence as a boarding school within the next two or three years."[9] Why not, therefore, put the building to a more profitable use? The few boys remaining could be given space in the sisters' school. In a letter to the Indian agent, Grant listed the specific responsibilities to be undertaken by the sisters: "[The hospital] would be under the direct management of Sisters. Besides the building, the sisters would furnish all the requisites in the line of bedding, heat, light, water, food, all the necessary accessories for the comfort of the sick, also the nurses to wait on the patients and the help needed around the building and premises."[10] While Grant assumed that government funds would be provided to cover the finances of the undertaking, it was very clear who would bear the ultimate responsibility.

Grant's only problem—one he seemed certain could be solved—was finding a community of sisters willing to undertake such responsibility. When the Ursulines were consulted, their answer was an unequivocal no. Since, despite a flurry of correspondence with sisters of various congregations, the proposed hospital never became a reality, one can only conjecture that no group of nuns could be found foolhardy enough to assume such an ill-balanced commission.

While suffering the same debilitating poverty as the other missions, St. Ignatius's continued to enjoy—for a while—the success of schools filled with reasonably satisfied children. "We have a house full of children well and happy," the Sisters of Providence wrote to Monsignor Ketcham. And Father De la Motte reported that he was pleased with the good spirits and "piety" of their pupils. But such dispositions were hardly enough to balance their increased expenses. In addition to all the usual costs, they now labored under a multiplicity of government taxes—property tax, water tax, grazing tax. Such additional expenses were putting their mission schools in peril. In the spring of 1909, Father Louis Taelman, then stationed at St. Ignatius's, wrote, describing their situation, to Monsignor Ketcham:

> I must inform you that some help is needed. Without it, the Ursuline sisters are stuck, unable to pay their bills and their workmen, etc. They have over 60 Indian children to support. The Sisters of Charity are struggling to support the 105 Indian girls they have in their schools. Neither can I make ends meet caring for 55 Indian boys. We have never refused children in the past, but under the circumstances we shall soon be forced to do so. And this is a sad prospect when I see the immense amount of good done in our schools.[11]

Sometime later, the nuns themselves wrote to Monsignor Ketcham, affirming Taelman's assessment: "This year we are caring for at least 80 Indian children and refused at least fifty on account of not having accommodations for them. This has been a very hard year as our crops failed. ... Can you not come to our aid and send us some money?"[12]

Ketcham, well aware of the seriousness of the requests, wrote at once to the secretary of the interior, explaining, "I beg to state that the Fathers and sisters of St. Ignatius's Mission are now and have been for the past ten years caring for, educating and clothing, in these three schools from 175 to 200 Flathead Indian boys and girls without a dollar of expense to the Government or the Indians."

This was but one of dozens of complaints pouring into Washington concerning the situation of the Native Americans. The folly of government policy was evident on all sides. The Severalty Act had destroyed, not assisted, Indians in sustaining their dignity and sense of worth. "I am trying to urge our excellent agent to do something for the temporal welfare of our old Indians," Father De la Motte wrote to Monsignor Ketcham. "They have land allotted to them it is true but many of them are utterly unable to do anything more than look at it and in the meanwhile they are starving or freezing or both." As for the bestowal of citizenship, from the missionaries' point of view, it was meaningless.[13]

While De la Motte was hardly able to redress the injustices he found everywhere, he was able to provide some assistance. In the spring of 1913, he encouraged the Sisters of Providence to establish a small hospital at St. Ignatius's. As at St. Xavier's, such a facility was badly needed and Father De la Motte had the advantage of having the Sisters of Providence, who were, essentially, nursing sisters. De la Motte's plan was simple and practical: he offered to renovate the old church—now abandoned—and help equip it for basic hospital care. Less than a year later, he wrote proudly to the commissioner for Indian affairs:

St. Xavier's Mission, nuns with girls' division. Courtesy of Ursuline archives, Toledo, Ohio

I wish to inform you that we have at last carried out a project
which was dear to all of us. We have built a nice little hospital
at the Mission, St. Julian's Hospital, which is under the care of
the Sisters of Providence. The hospital is primarily devoted to
the Indians and half-breeds of this Reservation, and secondar-
ily to the white settlers who are too poor or too sick to be
transported to Missoula. The hospital is well equipped with all
that is necessary and is admired by all. It has been in operation for ten months and is well patronized by Indians and
half-breeds.[14]

De la Motte was particularly pleased that the maternity ward
was saving many young girls who often lost their lives and their
babies in childbirth. The need and value of the hospital was unques-
tionable, yet no government funds toward its upkeep were made
available. "It was thought that the Commissioner of Indian Affairs
might compensate the Sisters for the actual expenses of the Indians
who are cared for in the hospital," Ketcham wrote in exasperation.
Ironically, the BIA continued to discuss the need for establishing a
medical facility on the reservation while offering no help to the "nice
little hospital" that already existed at St. Ignatius's.

During its long history, St. Ignatius's Mission had grown into a
small city, with an extensive farm and a sizable herd of cattle. Now,
recognizing that a major reorganization was necessary if they were to
continue, De la Motte began a serious restructuring. Everything was
to be reordered so that the priests would be freer for spiritual duties.
The farm was to be substantially reduced and the sisters asked to
assume more of the daily burdens of the school and the domestic
labor of the mission. "I approached the Sisters of Providence," he
wrote to his superior, "and asked them whether they would be willing
to board the Fathers and the [work] men. They are perfectly willing."

Thus encouraged, De la Motte approached the Ursulines. Here,
the request was more inclusive: the Ursulines would undertake to
instruct and board the boys of the Jesuit school—some forty in

number. Although the boys would continue to live in their present dwelling, under Jesuit supervision, all the rest of their care—cooking, washing, mending, classroom instruction—would be provided by the Ursulines. The sisters would receive $10 per month for each boy in addition to his clothing. A small building, abandoned by the Jesuits, would also be available to them. Already overworked, with too few sisters and a house bulging with children, they found little appeal in the proposal. To Father De la Motte's chagrin, his offer was rejected.

But Father De la Motte was a determined man and he was willing to adjust his terms. Thus, after a series of letters and compromises, a satisfactory document was drawn up and signed. Although the Ursulines agreed to undertake the boys' education, the amount of domestic labor was curtailed, and, in place of the abandoned Jesuit building originally offered them, they were to receive $4,000 to build as they saw fit.

While St. Xavier's and St. Ignatius's were attempting a reorganization that was better suited to the changing conditions of mission life, St. Labre's stumbled along, too burdened with the grim business of daily living to think about the future. When, in 1898, Amadeus had made the decision to maintain St. Labre's despite the departure of the Jesuits, she had done so with her usual penchant for the heroic. At the time, the nuns shared her exultation at being faithful to the Cheyenne, while their masculine counterparts forsook them. It was not long, however, before the cost of that decision became vividly clear.

With the departure of the Jesuits began ten years of spiritual poverty. The first priest sent to St. Labre's by Bishop Brondel could hardly have been less suited for mission work. Aloysius Mueller had been ordained only a year when he was sent from the cathedral at Helena to the mission at St. Labre's. Whatever he had expected from his life as a priest, it was not found at St. Labre's, with its ugliness, its poverty, and its unendurable loneliness. He could find no point of contact with the Indians, whose language fell on his ear in a meaningless jumble, or with the nuns, who lived their contained lives within the school and their community. With no other avenues open, he found his refuge in the casks of wine kept for the celebration of Mass.

Frightened of the Cheyenne, he stayed in his room, refusing to visit them, even when in sickness they called for him. He came less and less frequently to offer Mass, even on Sundays, when the Indians were gathered. The demoralized condition of the mission had its impact on the children and their parents. There were more and more runaways, more insolence, more complaints about their food, their clothing, their lessons. Cattle stealing—always a problem—increased with accusations leveled by both Indians and whites. For five years, the mission struggled along, until finally the nuns' reiterated complaints were heard by the bishop, and Father Mueller was removed.

The nuns' joy at the thought of his replacement was tempered when they heard the rumor that the day before taking up his post, Reverend Paul Gallagher had spent the night in the Forsyth saloon, from which he had to be carried by his friends. Father Gallagher, it must be admitted, was a man of many parts. He was sincerely interested in the plight of the Cheyenne and was articulate in espousing their cause. His correspondence with Ketcham and the BIA was voluminous. He was concerned over the shifting boundaries of the reservation, over the encroachments of ranchers on Indian land, over the fact that the mission was considered outside the reservation, and thus not entitled to rations. He found time to write articles for *The Indian Sentinel* and to undertake repairs needed in the boys' school. In many ways, he was ideal for his job.

Unfortunately, like Aloysius Mueller before him, Gallagher found strength in alcohol. Less retiring than his predecessor, he often spent his nights in what the Indians in contempt called "The Drunk House." While the Indian agent and the Ursulines were doing their best to curtail the raucous dances that took place not far from the school, Father Gallagher, in full Indian dress, was seen to dance away the night.

There was no secret about his activities, and the mission bore the humiliation of another drunken chaplain. "The Indians say they would like to have a priest who is able to pray," the Ursuline annalist wrote;

"they want to write to Father Van der Velden and ask him to come back to pray with them. This priest is too often in bed, they say."[15]

It was as close to despondency as the sisters had ever come. Always before, despite the difficulties, there had been something to hold them steady, but the last ten years had been years of unrelieved endurance. Although, in February 1909, the nuns had done their best to celebrate the anniversary of their twenty-five years among the Cheyenne, it was but a glimmer of light in a dark winter. Amadeus had arrived "very cold, tired, bespattered with mud," yet, even so, a jubilant figure. On February 7, they had Mass for the first time in weeks. Following this, they offered a dinner for everyone. "We cooked meat, coffee, and rice in washtubs. 125 Indians came ... They took dinner home in pails to the old and sick people." Amadeus had gifts of dresses for the Indian women, who talked with her for hours, "telling all their troubles, wants, and dislikes."[16]

The celebration was no more than a momentary lull. Once the feast was over, Father Gallagher abandoned the bright promises he had made to Amadeus and, once again, the Cheyenne began their endless litany of complaints. Whatever reverence for religion Father Van der Velden had inspired in the Cheyenne had been erased by his successors. The Indians, finding nothing admirable in these drunken Blackrobes, retreated into their own familiar rituals, relying on their medicine men to cure their sicknesses.

Despite the overt scandal, it was five years before the bishop responded to the nuns' petitions. Finally, in August 1910, the annalist wrote in relief, "Father Gallagher leaves on the stage for Forsythe. Our fervent wish is may he never return."*[17] Bishop Lenihan was not insensitive to the problems at St. Labre's, but he was hard-pressed to find a priest who could sustain the desolation of St. Labre's. Following Gallagher's departure, a young Augustinian priest volunteered to

---

*In fact, Father Gallagher continued to drop in during the next few months, staying a day or so and then moving on. The following March, he was hospitalized in Anaconda, and eight months later, news was received of his death.

undertake the post of chaplain. His residency, while free of scandal, was short-lived, and, by the fall of 1911, Father Grant in a letter to Ketcham expressed his concern about the survival of St. Labre's:

> I thought it well to mention to you that there are serious prospects for the Srs. being withdrawn from St. Labre. The priest has left there and I don't believe the Bishop can find one to replace him. No secular priest of the diocese wants to go there. No doubt it is a very hard place for a secular priest. The prospects do not seem good for the Jesuits to undertake the charge again. ... We can't blame the sisters for leaving if they can get no priest to stay there. On account of so many scandals the Indians there have lost all confidence in the ... clergy.[18]

The Indians' contempt extended beyond the clergy to the mission school. What, they questioned, was to be gained from these sisters who could not give them enough to eat and punished and frightened their children? The annalist noted in despair the increasing number of runaways. Even those remaining in school were never content. No matter what they were given, it was never enough. The boys, especially, did not obey, and their impudence was encouraged by their elders. They laughed and talked during prayers. During Christmas festivities, not a single Indian received Holy Communion. Meanwhile, the sisters were worked to death trying to provide for the children's needs and worried to death by the mounting pile of unpaid bills. Small wonder that the entry ended with a cry of anguish: "Oh, why are we at St. Labre's!"[19]

Their frustration was heightened when, in the fall of 1911, the superior, Mother Thecla, received a letter from Ketcham explaining that a delegation of Cheyenne had come to him to "make a number of complaints and charges against your school. Complaint was made as to the food, clothes, etc." Their complaints ranged over everything: their children had to eat from cracked plates, the knives and forks were bent, the clothing was not sufficient. Far more serious were the accusations that the children's health was neglected and that several children had died at the school. Many of these grievances the nuns had often heard before, but this time, they were faced with a searing accusation: that the contract money the nuns received for the mission school—never enough to cover their needs—had not been used for the children but had been put to other purposes.

Ketcham was well aware of the seriousness of the accusation, and the tone of his letter to Sister Thecla was uncompromising: "That money should be spent on their clothing, food, and on keeping up the buildings, and if any portion of it has been sent away a great mistake has been made. ... I want to know the truth, however, because if St. Labre's school cannot be up to the satisfaction of the Indians, it will be absolutely necessary to discontinue it. ... "[20]

Thecla's answer was immediate and indignant: "I can say that every cent received has been spent right here for the food and clothing of the children of St. Labre," she responded. "I assure you, Father, it is used conscientiously for the good of the children."[21]

Ketcham's reply was more reassuring, explaining that the Indians who had come to him were those who were always opposed to the mission schools, troublemakers who would never be satisfied. They must not forget the others, he consoled her, who were well aware of the benefits of St. Labre's, such braves as James Yellow Hair, who had written to Ketcham in defense of the mission: "They have nice dishes and forks and knives and good beds, too. And when I see them eat, they have plenty food to eat. ... I never see sisters do any bad things to the children. And I am all true what I say, no lies in it."[22]

Ketcham, however, recognized that conditions at St. Labre's were far from satisfactory. In October 1912, he wrote at length to Bishop Lenihan concerning the state of the missions in his diocese. While all of them suffered from lack of resources, it was St. Labre's that cost him the greatest concern:

> The reports that reach me from St. Labre's are far from
> reassuring and I must urge your Lordship to help me out at

once in making a success of this mission, otherwise it is
doomed. You know how much interest I have taken in St.
Labre's. When the Indians came to Washington this spring
and made their complaints I would not sympathize with
them, although in view of the fact that they have really never
had a missionary [priest] since the time of Father Van der
Velden, I felt that allowance ought to be made for them.

   ... I went out there this summer. I found St. Labre's in a
great state of dilapidation. ... The buildings are worn out,
uncomfortable and unsafe. I could not promise [the Indians]
new buildings but I did promise them that these buildings
would be fixed up ... and now I have found that they have
not been fixed up, even to this day. ... It shows that the
management is wrong and ought to be changed radically.[23]

The problems at St. Labre's were more than a question of dilapidated buildings. The five nuns in residence were totally inadequate
for the work involved. Sister Thecla, although devoted to the Indians
and revered by many of them, was an ineffective administrator. Two
of the nuns were French exiles who had never mastered English—a
serious concern since the mission contract stipulated that all teachers must be fluent in spoken and written English. Two years earlier,
Father Gallagher had spoken with Frances Seibert on the subject. "I
gave her fits about the staff she has here," he wrote to Ketcham. "Two
English speaking sisters in the whole lay-out and the govt demanding that the employees should all speak English fluently."[24] Neither
Gallagher's warning nor the request for a sister skilled in music, able
to preside at church functions and teach the children hymns in their
native language had been answered.

   Powerless to act, the nuns limped along, well aware that St.
Labre's was, in every way, below the standard the Cheyenne had a
right to expect. The concluding sentence of Ketcham's letter to
Lenihan sounded like a death knell: "This is the year of grace for
St. Labre's Mission—the mission is on trial.[25]

Chapter Seventeen

It is surely the land of "perhaps."

—*Mother Amadeus Dunne*

In contrast to the situation of the Indian missions, Mount Angela was proving itself. The registration had increased, both parents and children seemed delighted, and even the irascible Lenihan had nothing but praise for the venture.

But in December 1913, the harmony with the bishop came close to a rupture. On November 29, Amadeus—no longer restrained by her office as provincial—accompanied by Angela Lincoln, arrived at Great Falls to begin a visit of the Montana missions with the specific purpose of soliciting sisters for the Alaskan missions. In light of Lenihan's unremitting hostility, it was a foolhardy venture.

Even the Ursuline authority in Rome, once so impressed by Amadeus's zeal, had begun to question her judgment. As early as 1909, Mother St. Julien had written to Irene Gill asking her to keep Amadeus from returning to Montana for "good reasons which you understand." A month later, she wrote again, affirming her position. It seemed important that she did not return immediately to Montana; there had been too much trouble with the bishops. "I am telling you all this in confidence. I love and admire this sister; but I do not believe her capable in the present circumstances of being in charge without it having some drawbacks."[1]

Despite such hesitation, the permission for Amadeus to undertake missions in Alaska was reaffirmed. "In consideration of almost a lifelong work in those missions which she founded and spent her best years, Rome deems that it would not be exactly right to refuse

263

her request and restrict her to a life of inactivity," a member of the Roman Council wrote to Irene Gill by way of explanation.[2]

Despite Amadeus's waning energies, her vision was still vast. She could not comprehend that others did not share that vision, especially those with whom she had worked for so long. In the summer of 1912, she wrote a long letter of grievances to Angèle de Notre Dame, who had succeeded Mother St. Julien as superior general. "Like dwellers in a beleaguered city, we are walled in and left to starve or die unless help comes to us from without," she wrote dramatically. "I feel it very keenly that Reverend Mother Irene and Mother Francis and the Montana community refuse to help me after my many years of labor there. Many nuns would be willing to help us in Alaska but they will not be allowed."[3]

By this time, Amadeus had established three schools in Alaska. The sisters she had sent off in the summer of 1905 had arrived at the mission at Akulurak in September of that year, welcomed by the Jesuits who had just reopened the school after several years of absence. Built on a swampy tundra, Akulurak offered few advantages. In summer, it was besieged by mosquitoes, and in the winter, it was rocked by winds off the Bering Sea. Despite the obstacles, St. Mary's mission school prospered. By the end of the first year, they had fifteen boarders and a number of day students, necessitating additional buildings.*

Unlike the mission at Akulurak, the second mission, begun in the fall of 1908, never prospered. In many ways, St. Michael's was a strange choice for a mission. Located on a little island off Norton Sound, it had originally been a Russian stockade; the dome of the old Russian church still marked its origins. In 1867, with the sale of Alaska to the United States, St. Michael's became a military installation. Situated on the Yukon, it became an important port for the Jesuits heading for the interior.

---

*St. Mary's Mission at Akulurak was the most stable of the Alaskan foundations, lasting until 1950, when it was moved to a more favorable site at Andreafsky.

It is curious that Amadeus was so quick to accept the Jesuits' invitation, since St. Michael's had never been a native settlement. The original strategy was for the nuns to take over the public school and thus reach the increasing Catholic population. In fact, the three Ursulines who arrived there in the fall of 1908 found that they had little to do. There was no place for them in the school and, beyond weekend catechism classes for white children, they exercised little influence. St. Michael's, with its lyrical name, "St. Ursula's-by-the-sea," was soon closed, although the modest building was kept as a resting place for Ursulines on their way to Akulurak.

Undaunted by the failure of St. Michael's, in the summer of 1912, Amadeus responded to Bishop Raphael Crimont's appeal to open a school for white children in Valdez. Situated on Prince William Sound, at the turn of the century Valdez was a thriving little town. Not only had gold been discovered nearby, but the area became a source for large deposits of copper. Men came to explore, but many stayed on to raise families. By the time the Ursulines arrived, Valdez boasted a bank, a newspaper, a public library, along with the usual number of saloons. The town, it seemed, was ready for education.

With three missions activated—and surely more to come— Amadeus began her plan for a novitiate where young aspirants could be trained expressly for the Alaskan apostolate. Seattle, she decided, was the ideal setting, since it was the port of embarkation for Alaska.

From the beginning, the Alaskan novitiate was a source of contention. There was a certain deviousness in Amadeus's explanations of who had originally sanctioned the enterprise. To Rome, she affirmed that the Jesuits had asked her to open a novitiate. To Bishop Edward O'Dea of Seattle, she indicated that it was the Holy See that confirmed her plan: "Our Holy Father ... has authorized the opening of an Ursuline Novitiate in Seattle; as soon as your Lordship's full consent is obtained," she wrote to the bishop in October.[4] O'Dea, however, already wary of the rumors he had heard about Amadeus, at first refused his permission. Six months later, however, he acceded to her repeated requests. In July 1913, a house was rented, and the following month, the novitiate was formally opened.

That fall, Amadeus and Angela Lincoln arrived in Montana, triumphant over their successes. Although aware of Bishop Lenihan's ban on taking sisters from Montana, Amadeus set out to allure volunteers, confident that where she beckoned, sisters would follow. Her appeal was a source of serious concern for Francis Seibert. She could not afford to sacrifice a single sister from Great Falls or from the other missions. Even more disturbing was the thought of Lenihan's anger when he learned he had been disobeyed.

Her fears were not unfounded, for when he heard of Amadeus's presence in Great Falls, his fury was unleashed. Determined to put an end to her influence for once and all, he wrote at length to Irene Gill, condemning the conduct of both Amadeus and Angela:

> This woman ... visited our academy at Great Falls last month
> and as usual caused a disturbance by telling that she had it all
> fixed to take away some of the best teachers—and try and
> break up the institution which has been her intent. ... I am
> sure that your Mother General and consultors do not know
> the real state of affairs and the wicked schemes of M.
> Amadeus or they would not permit her to run around the
> country, collecting money under false pretenses and bringing
> disrespect on the venerable Ursuline Order ... I do most
> deliberately and emphatically denounce the bad conduct of
> M. Amadeus and her companion and I hereby appeal to the
> highest authorities at Rome to forbid her taking away any
> more of the sisters that belong to Montana.[5]

Meanwhile, Francis, fearful of the consequences of Lenihan's wrath, wrote directly to Angèle de Notre Dame in Rome. "The letter I am now writing to you I find very painful," she began as she outlined the difficulties of Amadeus's brief visit. "Mother's visit was anything but pleasant," she continued. "She fully intends returning next June for help, I hate to say anything but I heartily wish you could put some barrier in the way to hinder her return as I know what an upset it will make in all our houses; even now she has made disturbance where she has been and many are upset and wanting to go."[6]

The following week, Irene Gill wrote to Rome, seconding Francis's complaints and questioning not only Amadeus's activity in Montana, but even her fitness to undertake the Alaska missions. "The Vicar Apostolic of Alaska [Raphael Crimont, S.J.] I do not think trusts Mother Amadeus as he came to me to ask what were her powers, etc."[7] Impressed by what she had accomplished in Montana, Bishop Crimont had originally encouraged Amadeus in her plans for Alaska, but by the end of 1914, he had begun to question her ability.

Father John Van der Pol, S.J., the regional superior, was even more dubious. Hearing of the plans for a novitiate, he wrote warningly to O'Dea: "I understand that [Amadeus] would like to open a novitiate in your diocese ... those two sisters, and I refer more particularly to Mother Angela, are entirely and totally unfit to upbuild the kingdom of Christ."[8] His language was blunt, but his assessment was not far from the mark. Although both Amadeus and Angela spoke of Valdez as another successful establishment, in fact, Angela Lincoln, in the short time she was there, had succeeded in alienating the people so that from Father Van der Pol's perspective, there was little possibility for the Ursulines to carry on a successful mission.

Angela, despite her initial charm, had rarely brought peace where she went. She had an imperious quality that often angered and alienated the people she dealt with. Mother St. Julien, at first so impressed by her zeal and international spirit, had soon discovered another side. Now Irene Gill admitted that she found it impossible to work with her, suggesting darkly that she could not count on her to tell the truth. Amadeus, however, was blind to all this. As she grew older, she was increasingly dependent on Angela, grateful for her solicitous care, her unflagging affection, and devotion. Their needs fitted into each other without a wrinkle. If Amadeus gave thought to a successor, she had one ready at hand.

By this time, Amadeus was a woman close to seventy, "an old lady," as one of the priests at St. Labre's had described her. Increasingly frail, constantly in pain from her broken hip, her spirit fought against her body as though she were trying to outwit it. "She is astonishing," wrote Sister Marie de Debusschère in admiration of her dynamism when they met in Montana. But, in the end, her body was taking its relentless toll, weakening not only her physical strength, but her ability to reason and judge. "She has lost her judgment," Crimont noted sadly.

Always a visionary, she now seemed blinded to everything but the goal she had set. Her rapturous vision of Alaska—its desolate tundra, its glaciers, its tumultuous seas—obscured the reality of daily living. Bishop Lenihan had accused her of vanity, ridiculing her dream of Alaska as no more than "a foolish exhibition of false zeal." But such a judgment trivialized her.

Vanity was far from her spirit; vanity was too superficial, too concerned with a need for flattery. Whatever the "mar in the marble," whatever that dark vein that made her such a contradictory spirit, it was far deeper than vanity. When she was younger, that compelling need to control, to shape reality to her design, had been tempered by a keen perception of what path would best lead to her goal. But now, like an astronomer peering through a telescope, her vision was limited to what that narrow circle of glass revealed. The ground around her had dropped away. She could see Alaska, and nothing else.

As soon as the permission to establish a novitiate was received, she accepted nine young women who had responded to her call, with Angèle Fouyer, a French exile, as novice mistress. It was a spartan atmosphere into which they were welcomed. The sources of alms on which Amadeus had always presumed were no longer available, and there was little money for even the most basic needs. When they were offered teaching positions in a neighboring parochial school, Amadeus accepted at once.

Since church law prohibited the novices from teaching during their year of training, she unhesitatingly sent for three sisters from Montana, explaining to Francis Seibert that she had permission from Rome—an explanation that did nothing to curb Lenihan's wrath at such flagrant disobedience to his commands. "The bishop is greatly incensed," Irene Gill wrote to Rome, begging for the sake of peace that no additional nuns be allowed to go, despite Amadeus's pleas for help. Francis, too, wrote at once to Angèle in Rome, protesting Amadeus's action. The letter she received in reply did little to assuage the situation: "In permitting the two French nuns and Sister Immaculata to give their services to Mother Amadeus I do not think any injustice was done to the Montana houses, dear Mother ... Let us regard all this in a spirit of faith and submit to the decisions of a supreme authority."[9] Angèle not only justified the assignment of the three sisters, but affirmed that the novitiate was established with the full permission of the Holy See.

In a short time, the "charming little house" that Amadeus had rented so hastily proved unsuitable. Not only was it too small, but, as she wrote to Katharine Drexel, "the rented house proved unsanitary from seepage of water in which our dear hard-working sisters stood ankle deep."[10]

Despite their impoverished situation, she succeeded in scraping together enough money to make a down payment on a larger house in a better environment at St. Helen's Place. Where she would get the balance of the money, she did not know. Once more, following a lifetime habit, Amadeus was plunging recklessly into debt.

Ultimately, it was not debt but the management of the novitiate that brought down her plans. Angèle Fouyer, at a loss as to how to handle the situation, wrote frequently and at length to Rome attempting to describe the impossible situation in which the novices were forced to live. Even their most essential needs went unheeded. When they attempted to explain their difficulties, they were told that they were not fit for mission work. Even worse was the lack of spiritual formation. Angèle's directions were often countermanded, humiliating her in front of the novices. "There is no order in the house," she wrote, explaining that there was little observance of Rule and that the novices were constantly interrupted in their spiritual exercises in order to obey Amadeus's peremptory orders.[11]

The novice mistress's assessment was seconded by Father John Carroll, S.J., their confessor, who deplored Amadeus's conduct, which he found volatile and irrational. "I'm considerably disappointed in Reverend Mother Amadeus. She seems to be no longer capable of managing affairs and she has treated her postulants in so shameful a manner that they will not remain unless conditions be remedied," Father Carroll wrote.[12]

Even the novices themselves, perhaps encouraged by Father Carroll or Angèle, took courage and wrote to explain their position, affirming that although they were unswerving in their desire to work in Alaska, they could not in conscience continue in a house in which there was such criticism and confusion.

When Bishop O'Dea came for a formal interview with the novices, he found the information he had received more than justified. When, in addition, he learned that Amadeus was a defendant in a lawsuit with the city for establishing a novitiate ("an institution") in an area zoned for private dwellings, he acted at once. On August 18, after a discussion with Irene Gill, who had traveled west to assess the situation, he wrote to Rome. His denunciation was candid and direct: "[Amadeus] is not a fit person to be at the head of a religious house, much less of a novitiate. ... I beg of you in the name of God and Holy Church to remove her."[13] It could not have been a more damning judgment. Had the superior general not heard so much from other sources, she might have dismissed O'Dea's request as the unreasonable demand of an autocratic bishop. This time, however, the bishop seemed well within his discretion.

On September 21, Mother Angèle de Notre Dame wrote to Amadeus, a letter remarkable for its integrity and its diplomacy:

I am perfectly sure of your good will to make any sacrifice for
the prosperity of your great work. I have admired your
courage and patience. ... You know that the house in Seattle
was founded exclusively for the Alaskan Novitiate and for the
Italian parochial school. No other Ursulines but those
employed for these two missions may reside there. It would be
contrary to the agreement made with the bishop and we must
scrupulously carry out his wishes; even you, dear mother and
Angela Lincoln must not remain in Seattle. I ask you this, my
very dear Mother, to spare me the pain for giving you an
express order since the Rt. Rev. Bishop requires it. ... You can
take up your residence in Valdez and still direct the mission as
you have hitherto done.[14]

For the second time in her life, Amadeus found herself exiled
from her home. Ten years earlier, she had been exiled from St. Peter's
through a conspiracy of hostile forces. Once again, unable to understand the grounds of the criticism, she saw only the shadow of
conspiracy. "It is most painful to be placed in the hands of persons
so inimical to us and to our interests," she had written earlier, after
an interview with Irene Gill. All the trouble, she explained, was
caused by "six rebellious postulants," who were engaged in "a conspiracy against me to get rid of me."[15] It was the bewildered
accusation of a woman old beyond her time who could not understand why the world had turned against her.

While Angèle de Notre Dame had done her best to couch her
demand in compassionate terms, her suggestion that Amadeus take
up residence in Valdez was adequate proof of how little she understood of the actual situation and the problems involved. Although
three sisters still remained at Valdez, Van der Pol had written the preceding summer, "For the last year, the Convent of Valdez is a
hopeless and fruitless burden on the parish." It was certainly not a
residence from which Amadeus could carry out the government of
the Alaska missions. Yet with both Seattle and Montana closed to her,

Alaska was her only refuge. The order to leave Seattle was far more terrible in its consequences than Mother Angèle could have realized.

With the departure of Amadeus and Angela, the house in Seattle needed a superior, and in the spring of 1916, Francis Seibert received word from Rome that this difficult position was assigned to her. On April 14, Mother Perpetua, the newly appointed superior at Great Falls, went with Mother Francis to inform the bishop of the news. "No words of mine can express the abuse we received," she wrote to the provincial, Mother Regis McMahon. "We were—so to say—paralyzed and could not realize that a human being could so speak. He said 'the whole order had no more regard for him then it would have for a dog; that those people in Rome say one thing and do the contrary.'" He concluded by saying he would write to Rome and that Mother Francis was not to move from Great Falls until he had received an answer.[16]

The letter he wrote to Angèle de Notre Dame was a masterpiece of invective. He gave no quarter, including in his condemnation not only of Amadeus "and her ambitious companions," but of the entire concept of the Roman Union, which refused to recognize his ecclesiastical authority. Following his final salvo, he signed the letter with a flourish, "Yours in faith and charity." This time, his voice was heard and the order rescinded. Francis would remain in Montana.

The preceding January, Amadeus, in obedience to Angèle de Notre Dame's command, had left for Valdez, accompanied by Angela Lincoln. They weathered the winter, and in May wrote to O'Dea asking permission to return to Seattle to prepare for a trip east to solicit vocations in response to Bishop Crimont's demands for more Ursulines. At the beginning of August, Amadeus visited Toledo, her original convent home. The nuns were shocked by her frailty, and the annalist noted, "She was unaccompanied and it seemed sad to see a person as old and infirm as she traveling alone. We felt bad for her and wondered how she could manage with only a cane to support her. ... It seemed she had an idea she must go on to New York on some business; however she got letters that removed the necessity."[17]

By the middle of August, she was back in Seattle, leaving for St. Michael's on August 23 and returning on the last boat, two months later. Thus began a pattern of superhuman and often useless voyages that would continue until her death three years later. While in a technical sense Amadeus had acceded to the order to leave Seattle, in reality, she was frequently in residence, continuing to exercise her authority over the novices.

Throughout the spring and summer of 1917, Sister Angèle Fouyer wrote to Rome begging that some steps be taken to regularize life in the novitiate. "They cannot continue much longer," she warned. Her pleas were augmented by those of Father Carroll, who wrote to Mother Regis: "I beg you to do something for the Seattle novices. ... It is my firm conviction that all of them have a true religious vocation. They are most anxious to persevere in the religious life ... I cannot in conscience urge them to bind themselves to such a tyranny. [Amadeus] is totally unfit to exercise authority any longer. In fact, it is a crime to keep religious subject to her cruel caprices."[18]

This time, their pleas were heard, and in August 1917, just two years after Bishop O'Dea had initially expressed his dissatisfaction with the novitiate, the novices were transferred to the Ursuline novitiate in Alton, Illinois. Amadeus, bewildered and resentful, wrote to Rome seeking an explanation for why her vision was being disregarded. Sister Angèle Fouyer was an easy target for her indignation. "The novice mistress has no missionary spirit and did not understand what was involved," she wrote of her disparagingly.[19] It was a sad little letter, unsure and petulant, the small, cramped penmanship far from the graceful, expansive hand that had once covered the pages so easily.

For many, such action would have been conclusive, a sign that it was time to put a dream to rest. For Amadeus, opposition was simply an obstacle that must be cleared away. She was now seventy-one. A small, frail woman, bent and crippled, but as determined as she had been when, thirty-three years before, she had set out for Miles City. In those thirty-three years, she had beguiled, cajoled, and coerced her followers and ridden roughshod over the opposition. Her methods had won her money (never enough) and followers (always too few), but she had built her missions, befriended the Indians, established a motherhouse, and frequently alienated both priests and bishops who could not keep pace with her. They quoted church law to her, and she responded with the needs of the poor. For thirty-three years, she had succeeded; she saw no reason why it should be different now. Clouded by infirmity, she did not see that what she was

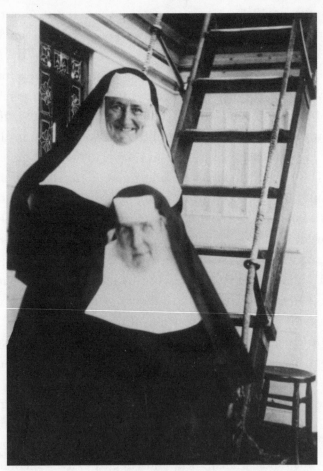

Amadeus Dunne and Angela Lincoln on the way to Alaska, circa 1912. Courtesy of Ursuline archives, Great Falls, Montana

doing was often unreasonable and imprudent. She had become deaf to advice, even from such devoted friends as Bishop Crimont. She saw only Alaska and could not understand why obstacles were being placed in her way.

Angela Lincoln was now her constant companion and her only confidante. Once Amadeus's devoted helper, Angela had now become her unquestioned support. Nothing Amadeus demanded was to be denied her; no decision she made was to be questioned. Criticism was stamped as perfidy and the critic dismissed out of hand. With Amadeus no longer her steadying force, Angela's passionate temperament had free reign. Always impelled by emotion rather than moderation, she had now entered a state where her passions ran counter to reason.

There is no other way to understand how she could have endorsed those grueling trips from Seattle to Alaska with Amadeus so unsteady that she often had to be carried onto the ship; or how she could have affirmed her determination to remain during the terrible winter months in the inadequate little dwelling at St. Michael's, where the winds almost tore the roof from their house. She never minimized the difficulties, narrating them in full harrowing detail in the newsletters she sent out. The greater the perils, the more they enabled her to present Amadeus as the heroine of the cross, the missionary nonpareil. It was as though Angela, along with Amadeus, had passed the boundaries of reality where human lives have ordinary limits—a dangerous country where it is hard to distinguish the saint from the fanatic.

In March 1918, shortly before her final voyage to Alaska, Amadeus wrote to Bishop Crimont, revealing how deeply wounded she had been by the events of the last years:

> I present myself before you in confusion on account of my
> long silence caused by inability to write. I lost control of my
> muscles—ill body and soul. During a time of great depression
> your most kind letters reached me. Your words were doubly

appreciated and your financial help very consoling. ... I have
many trials and sorrows to meet—all too painful to write
about. If I could see you I would place them all in your soul
for guidance and protection. I think my darkest hour has
come. I beg your dear prayers.[20]

The strain had affected her health, and for weeks she was incapable of any activity, yet that July, although still not fully recovered, Amadeus, accompanied by Angela and Sister Rose Miller, set out for the last time for Alaska. Too weak to climb aboard, she had to be lifted onto the deck of the *Victoria*. The voyage was unusually stormy for a summer crossing, and on one tumultuous night, Amadeus was tossed from her berth, further injuring her hip and increasing the constant pain in her back. At last, on August 1, they docked at St. Michael's, St. Ursula's-by-the-sea as she had optimistically named it when it had been founded ten years before. The hopes for a true mission had already failed, and there was nothing left for the Ursulines except a little house, hardly adequate for a stormy winter. The Jesuits were still there, as well as a small contingent of military at the old Fort, who did what they could to make the nuns comfortable.

Unfortunately, we have only the memoirs of Mother Angela to help us reconstruct those winter months, and Angela, even at her most temperate, was far from accurate. Her biography of Mother Amadeus, written several years after the latter's death, is nineteenth-century hagiography at its most elaborate. Sparing of dates and facts, Angela is lavish in her descriptions of her subject's sanctity. Her heroine, she affirmed, brought joy and admiration everywhere, endearing herself by her sacrificial spirit and unfailing smile. The last months in Alaska provided Angela with an unparalleled opportunity for presenting her subject in stained-glass colors. There could be nothing more heroic than radiant tranquility under trial and suffering, and the months at St. Ursula's-by-the-sea gave full scope to Angela's talent for hyperbole.

Amadeus, despite her failing health, was resolute in her decision to remain at St. Michael's for the winter, faithful to her ultimate mission. Forced into exile by those who had failed her trust, she was determined to experience during the bleak winter months the only consolation left her: prayer and the grace of attending Mass daily at the nearby Jesuit church. In fact, she was rarely able to make even that short trip. On October 28, while leaning over to pick up something from the floor, she fell from her chair, severely injuring the broken hip. While it was not a life-threatening injury, in Amadeus's case, it might well have become one, and the doctor at St. Michael's urged Angela to make arrangements to return to Seattle on the last boat, which was soon to depart. But both Amadeus and Angela were beyond prudence, and together they assured the doctor that they would remain for the winter as they had planned.

During November and into December, Amadeus stayed on in their unsubstantial house, confined to bed, listening to the winds sweeping in off the sea, and totally dependent on Angela for all her needs. Then, in the early hours of December 9, they woke to the disaster that plagued the Alaskan missions: their house was on fire. With everything frozen solid, there was no chance of dousing the flames. Wrapped in blankets, Amadeus was carried to the officers' quarters in the empty military barracks, while Angela and Rose stumbled along beside her.

The following week, Father John Sifton wrote to Bishop Crimont at some length regarding the fire and its aftermath. "I am not surprised they were burnt out. It was due to carelessness, pure and simple. Sister Rose wishes me to tell you that she did not burn the house. I know the others tried to throw the blame on her. I think that but for Sr. Rose the thing would have happened sooner. Only a few weeks previous, I wanted to clean the stove pipes; of course it meant that the fire in the heater must be out for an hour or so. Angela objected. ... She trusted St. Joseph ... Angela needs a guardian."[21]

Despite Father Sifton's sardonic comment, he did his best to find suitable lodgings for the nuns, aware that the doctor found Mother Amadeus so frail that he did not expect her to last through the winter.

For the next seven months, the nuns stayed there, helped by the Jesuits and a few remaining members of the military, their situation made more perilous by the ravages of the Spanish influenza, which raged around them. No place was spared, both towns and native villages were stricken, and St. Michael's lived in terror of the onslaught of the plague.

In April, Father Sifton wrote again to Crimont, reporting that the plague had caused forty deaths on the island but that Amadeus, increasingly feeble, lived on: "Mother Amadeus is a baby again—physically altogether, and mentally quite often. She may live to go out on the first boat. Still there is no telling."[22] Mother Angela's dream of a heroic life had descended upon them in full reality. The fire had consumed not only their house, but all their possessions, including the precious papers that Angela hoped would some day form the basis of a history of their Alaskan missions. Amadeus's spiritual maxim that God would always provide was tested to its limit. She had once written to Angèle de Notre Dame, "I have been kept from writing to you for such a long time by the great and most perplexing uncertainties of life in Alaska. It is surely the land of 'perhaps.'"[23]

Now, with no other course opened, they continued to live in the "land of perhaps" until the faithful *Victoria*—called by some "the grand dowager of the northern Pacific"—arrived in mid-June 1919. Unable to stand, Amadeus was carried aboard the little launch that brought them out to the ship and then, with great difficulty, was hoisted aboard the *Victoria*.

The voyage sapped her remaining strength, and on their arrival in Seattle, she was brought at once to Providence Hospital. There was little that could be done for her, however, and after a few days, she was brought "home." The nuns who welcomed her to the convent at St. Helen's Place knew they looked on someone close to death. Angela Lincoln was there, of course, and Sister Amata Dunne had recently arrived, sent by Mother Perpetua to help with Amadeus's care. The nuns from Valdez—Sister Mary of the Angels Carroll and

Sister Dosithée Leygonie—had closed the Valdez house and were expected momentarily.

Mother Perpetua, with the bishop's approval, had offered them the hospitality of Montana, where she felt Amadeus could be better cared for, but Angela, who had assumed full responsibility for Amadeus's care, rejected the proposal. It soon became clear, however, that it was too late for Amadeus to be moved at all.

On July 8, Sister Amata wrote at length to Angèle de Notre Dame, explaining their situation:

> I reached Seattle yesterday and found Mother Amadeus very ill indeed. She is perfectly helpless—not being able even to turn herself in bed; while she is conscious at times, at others she lapses into a state resembling coma or semi-coma; she seems to be unable to read; and cannot attend to her own mail, to business affairs or community affairs. ...
>
> In sending me here, my superior, Mother Perpetua of Great Falls, told me to beg Mother Amadeus to come home to Great Falls. Mother Amadeus replied that she would be very happy to do so. But Mother Angela objects. ... She argues that if Mother must be moved, it will be to Valdez and not to Montana. We, Mother's Montana daughters, want Mother to come to us and we shall be happy to care for her. However, dear Reverend Mother, it is very doubtful if it would now be possible to transfer poor Mother to any place without causing her death in transit.[24]

Amadeus's primary illness was diagnosed as an enlarged heart, but a more comprehensive diagnosis would have included thirty-five years of unrelenting activity, of poor and insufficient food, of travel in unendurable discomfort—and, most of all, years of anxiety: Where would the money come from—to feed the children, to clothe them, to keep them warm, and to provide the medicines they so desperately needed? Who would protect her from the creditors who encircled her? And, most recently, who would uphold her against the conspirators who threatened her? Prudence would have demanded that she attempt less, reduce the projects she had set her heart on, listen to the advice of her councilors—but she had dismissed prudence as unworthy of her calling.

As the weeks passed, the expectation of an immediate death diminished, and throughout the heavy dampness of the summer, Amadeus lingered on. She lay motionless, her eyes closed, her breathing sometimes labored. Angela had had her bed moved so that on days when they had Mass, Amadeus could "attend." It was a pious thought beyond reality. Amadeus had passed beyond attention. That powerful will that had believed that her determined faith could move mountains was no longer conscious. Having directed the lives of so many, she now lay without direction, dependent on others for even her most basic bodily needs. By September, the brief moments of awareness had ceased. She lay as one dead, as one of the sisters wrote.

In October, Mother Perpetua, concerned about the situation in Seattle, traveled west to see for herself. It was not simply Amadeus's health that concerned her; she was also worried about their financial affairs. Who, in fact, owned the property at St. Helen's Place and at Valdez? She understood that a corporation had been formed but was unsure of what that meant and who was involved. With Amadeus in a semicomatose state, authority would pass to Angela Lincoln, and Perpetua had no faith in Angela's financial discretion or ability. Her trip, however, provided her with little help. Angela had assumed full authority and refused to discuss the affairs of Seattle and Alaska.

On October 15, Mother Perpetua, frustrated by her reception in Seattle, wrote to Angèle de Notre Dame and also to Bishop Crimont, who had already expressed his own concern:

> I have just returned from a rather fruitless trip to Seattle.
> Though I remained there a week I did not get either yes or no
> from Rev. Mother Amadeus. She is not able to speak at all. She
> is simply living and that is all. She does not seem to be

suffering much but I think she is kept in this semiconscious state more by drugs than by disease. Mother Angela is paying a physician $25.00 a week and he makes a visit every evening and gives Mother four tablets in a hypodermic, digitalis for her heart, etc., etc., and opium, I presume to deaden the pain; but my opinion is that it keeps her faculties dulled, so you can readily understand that I had no success in getting any information from Rev. Mother Amadeus and Mother Angela absolutely refused to give me any insight into Mother's affairs, said Mother had given her full power of Attorney and that she will keep her confidence in trust.[25]

Three weeks later, on November 10, at eleven o'clock in the morning, Amadeus died. She was surrounded by her sisters and two priests, Father McGrath and the Jesuit missionary Achilles Vasta, who led the prayers for the dying. She was seventy-three years old.

Mother Amadeus had expressed her wish to be buried at St. Ignatius's Mission, and two days after her death, accompanied by one of the earliest Montana missionaries, Sister Mary of the Angels, and her niece, Sister Amata, her body was placed aboard the east-bound train for Ravalli, a station stop only a few miles from the mission. Mother Angela, whose passionate devotion had kept her at Mother Amadeus's side day and night for months, announced that she would not be part of the funeral cortege. She would remain in Seattle to attend to business. Even those who had grown accustomed to Angela's erratic decisions found this one beyond comprehension. Was she so fearful that financial affairs be taken from her hands that she could not afford to be absent even for Amadeus's funeral? Or was she unable to acknowledge this ultimate act of death of the person who had absorbed her life?

From Ravalli, the body was brought to the mission at St. Ignatius's. That night, the coffin remained in the Jesuit chapel while the nuns kept vigil according to custom. The following day, a procession of Flathead Indians, children, Jesuits, and Ursulines accompanied the coffin to its final resting place in the cemetery at the foot of the Mission Range. The setting was Montana at its most glorious: the miles of unbroken plains, the encircling sky, and rising dark and forbidding, the sharp peaks of the distant mountains. Although Angela was not present, she did not hesitate to write a dazzling account of those last moments: the sudden appearance of the sun from behind the clouds, the tears of the nuns, the beat of the Indian drums, and the death chant for heroes sung by the Flathead warriors.

Like much in Mother Angela's life, her effort at embellishment only weakened the reality. Mother Amadeus's life needed no hyperbole. Her reputation rose larger than life. While her accomplishments never matched her vision, they were quite sufficient to give her a place in the pantheon of heroic women. But beyond that was the woman herself, and there it is hard to plumb the depths, for Mother Amadeus provided little help. The simple truth of her final hours carried its own mysterious drama. Later that month, Mother Perpetua wrote to Rome: "Our dear Mother Amadeus has been laid to rest among her dear children, Nuns and Indians, at St. Ignatius's Mission. She died without speaking."[26]

Chapter Eighteen

*I cannot tell you how much
I admire the spirit of courage ...*
—*Father William Hughes*

Mother Amadeus Dunne had outlived her dream. There was little in her last years that spoke of anything but defeat and diminishment. In November 1918, just three weeks before St. Michael's had burned to the ground, the remaining buildings at St. Peter's had gone up in flames. No news could have reached Alaska in those winter months, and there is no record of when Amadeus received word of this final destruction of her initial dream. It is possible that she never knew, for by the time she had reached Seattle the following June, she was barely conscious. Within a month of her burial, fire struck again, and the Sisters of Providence at St. Ignatius's watched the fiery destruction of their beautiful school. The Ursulines opened their doors, taking in sisters and children as far as they were able, mercifully unaware that within two years, fire would claim their own house.

Fire had always been the terrifying agent of destruction for the Montana missions. Defective flues, overheated chimneys, and carelessly tended lamps had all contributed. No mission had escaped; everyone had been besieged in varying degrees. "Bowed under the mighty hand of God," the missionaries accepted their fate—and rebuilt. The decision to rebuild had never been a question. It was part of the inevitable cycle of death and rebirth. With their buildings still smoking, they made plans for the future. They housed the children where they could, moving them from building to building, doubling up in dormitories and refectories, the difficult demands of daily life now doubled. Yet, whatever the hardships, school life hardly lost a beat.

In the second decade of the twentieth century, however, missionaries were faced with agents of destruction less dramatic but more pervasive than fire. Fire had not cowed them. Something new could always be built on its embers, but now the world was changing and the old order no longer met the needs of a new society.

Adequate funds had always been a mission concern, but there had been sources they could count on: the BCIM, diocesan collections, philanthropists such as Mother Katharine Drexel, fervent Catholics willing to sacrifice for a worthy cause. Now, even these sources were failing them. Government funds had stopped years earlier, and the new system, which made mission schools dependent on tribal funds, only added to the insecurity.

Monsignor Ketcham, in a letter to the superior at St. Xavier's, had made it clear that he could not continue to fund the missions, reminding him that the original understanding had been that, ultimately, the missions would become independent. How that was to be accomplished had never been clearly delineated. The ideal was undoubtedly to develop the Indians into successful farmers and ranchers, an ideal hardly encouraged by government enactments that opened increasing amounts of reservation land to white settlers, leaving the Indians poorer, more dependent, and, justifiably, more distrustful.

In many ways, it was the missionaries who bore the brunt of that distrust. They had promised the Indians great things—that if they let the Blackrobes pour water over them, that if they came to church and said their prayers, a god who loved them would bless them. But the blessings the priests had in mind were far different from the blessings the Indians longed for: the restoration of their native lands, the return of the buffalo, freedom from the rapacious white man. These blessings were farther away than ever.

Staffing the missions—even inadequately—had become an increasing problem. For the older missionaries, the sense of failure was augmented by the disinterest of younger men in the work of the Indian missions. For the daring and adventurous, the Rocky Mountains had lost their appeal. St. Xavier's, with its automobile, St. Paul's, with its telephone, St. Ignatius's, with steam heat and indoor plumbing had no attraction for the young missionaries. Montana was no longer the last frontier, and they yearned for something more rugged. They longed for Alaska. While there were few volunteers for the Montana missions, there were growing lists of Jesuits awaiting the opportunity to bring Christianity to the "frozen north."

With fewer young men available, the work of the schools was left increasingly to the sisters. The Ursulines, however, were experiencing the same frustrations as their male counterparts. There was never enough money to pay their bills or to buy necessary materials for the classrooms, nor had they ever received compensation for their long years of service.

It was, however, not privation, but the changing nature of the schools that drove St. Xavier's to the brink. Government schools were cropping up in increasing numbers. For years, the mission schools had been the only available sources of education. In some areas, they were woefully inadequate; in others, they were remarkably sophisticated. No matter what their value, however, they never became popular with the Indians, who resented the fact that their customs and traditions were never acknowledged or honored. Even those parents who admitted the value of education found the price of separation from their children far too high.

With the development of government day schools, parents began to reclaim their rights over their children. They would send them to school, since that was required of them, but not to the Blackrobes' boarding schools, where their children were even forbidden to speak their own language. If the Blackrobes wanted to educate Indian children, they would have to provide day schools for them.

The storm over schools was already in full force by the fall of 1912, and in October of that year, Father Grant wrote at length to F. H. Abbott, acting commissioner of Indian affairs, explaining the moral issues involved in permitting Indian girls, especially those over twelve years of age, to attend day schools. All Crow girls, he affirmed, should be in boarding schools at that age in order to guarantee them the "physical protection" they needed. "There is a preconcerted effort among the boys and young men to entrap the girls," he averred, although acknowledging that, on the other hand, the girls "seek out occasions for being entrapped."[1]

Father Grant's arguments made no impression on the Indians, however, who were strong in their endorsement of day schools, which enjoyed many advantages that the poverty-ridden school at St. Xavier's could ill afford. When Father Taelman arrived as superior in 1913, he was amazed at the deterioration of the mission. On September 9, he wrote to Monsignor Ketcham, "Now, as to temporal affairs, I find that this Mission is indeed very poor. ... Although the Mission has been 26 years in existence, the Mission people, that is the Fathers, Brothers, Sisters and schoolchildren, are still deprived of the ordinary modern conveniences, found nearly everywhere. After twenty-six years, there are no bathtubs at all nor toilets, either in the Fathers' house and school or the Sisters' house and school."[2]

Father Grant had already written at length of the difficulties, especially of the privations suffered by the sisters.

> The few sisters we have are almost worked to death. Besides, Sisters are not getting any salary from this Mission ... and the resources of the Mission are not sufficient to give the sisters all the necessary conveniences they should have for their work. ... We cannot reasonably expect them to take all the expense on themselves without any remuneration and at the same time sacrifice the health of their subjects by overwork and privation of many very necessary conveniences to which they were accustomed in many other places. I must say that I admire them for having stood it so long; but I would not be surprised if a good chance came along they would be but too willing to drop this place.[3]

When, in fact, the Ursulines did withdraw, it was not because "a good chance" had come along, or even because, at long last, the privations had became more than they could bear, but rather because it had become impossible to maintain a boarding school. By 1915, the cry for day schools could not be ignored.

Although Father Taelman was jubilant over the Indians' participation in the Easter ceremonies that year, this was his single source of comfort. He had no money to pay his bills, a terrible hailstorm had destroyed their crops, and the health of the Indians was an increasing concern. Along with the usual diseases, they had been attacked by infantile paralysis, which had put the whole mission in quarantine.

In the fall of 1918, however, they were struck by an even more dangerous epidemic: the so-called Spanish influenza. Although it was most virulent in the East, Montana was not spared. The Indian population around St. Xavier's and St. Labre's was especially vulnerable. At St. Xavier's, three nuns, infected while nursing the children, died in a short space. Bernard Vervacke, of Belgian birth, the oldest of the three, died the last week of August. Two weeks later, she was followed by Scholastica O'Sullivan. A few months later, after the epidemic had peaked and they had begun to breathe easily, Ursula Yunck, St. Peter's first postulant, succumbed. The mission was devastated.

Taelman, embattled by disease, by lack of resources, by the renewed movement to further open the Crow reservation to white ranchers, was forced to acknowledge that the mission school, despite the unremitting work of the five remaining Ursulines, could not continue without a miracle. In July 1919, he wrote at length to Ketcham, summarizing the events that had led to their present failure:

> You know that the Crow Indians are opposed to any school
> whatsoever. They have always considered a Boarding school as
> a jail. The government in former years allowed no other
> schools but boarding school and the Indians perforce gave in.
> Some years ago, the government allowed the Baptist Minister
> at Lodge Grass to put up a day school. ... The movement thus

inaugurated was the ruin of the Boarding school on the
reservation—for the Crow day school is the nearest to no
school. Little insignificant day schools then came into
existence everywhere and are known to be a farce and not a
word can be said in their favor from an intellectual, educational, moral or sanitary standpoint.[4]

Even Father Taelman, in his feisty battle, must have realized
that the handwriting was on the wall. In July 1921, a letter from
Mother Drexel forced him to recognize how desperate his situation
was. She informed him that the insurance on their buildings had
expired and, because of so many other demands, she could not
renew it. Father Taelman, aware that he had already tapped all available sources, wrote at once to Francis Dillon, S.J., provincial in
Oregon, asking advice. The "advice" he received, less than ten days
later, was peremptory: close the school. "I have notified Monsignor
Ketcham as to this determination; I have also notified the Mother
Provincial of the Ursulines," Dillon wrote.[5]

While Dillon apparently considered that such notice was sufficient, both Monsignor Ketcham and Mother Xavier Gavigan, the
Ursuline superior at Great Falls, found his actions unconscionable.
Four days later, an angry letter went out over Mother Xavier's flourishing signature: "Your letter of the 12th inst. came as a great
surprise. The Council regrets very much not having earlier knowledge of your decision, as it could have saved Community the
expense of hiring lay teachers for some of our schools. ... Whenever
you decide to close St. Paul and Holy Family kindly let us know six
months in advance."[6]

The tone was justifiably acerbic. The Ursulines had worked at
St. Xavier's for thirty-three years; to be dismissed now, without a
word of appreciation and without notice, as though they were inter-
mittent day workers, was intolerable. Monsignor Ketcham, who had
received a similar letter, was further outraged to find that not only
had no advice been asked of the BCIM, which had supported the mis-

sion for years, but that the ordinary of the diocese, Bishop Lenihan himself, had not been advised. He wrote at once to Father Dillon, expressing his indignation and asking for further explanation.

> The St. Xavier School has been closed without any consulta-
> tion with the Bishop of Great Falls or Mother Katharine
> Drexel or the Bureau of Catholic Indian Missions, and almost
> without prior notification, although for more than twenty
> years the St. Xavier school has been carried on under an
> understanding which amounts to a contract, and which has
> always been referred to as a contract, between the Jesuit
> Fathers, Mother Katharine and the Bureau.
>
> It is possible that if the situation had been discussed by
> you and the Bishop and the Bureau, the Bishop and the
> Bureau might have agreed to the closing of the school—I do
> not know; but there would have been some understanding as
> to the care of the buildings and the mission property and as to
> whether some Sisters would remain among the Indians ... [7]

The Ursulines left almost at once—relieved, perhaps, to escape a rancorous situation and aware that the boarding school could not have continued with its diminishing number of pupils. For a time, the Jesuits conducted a day school, but with limited success. There was some thought among the Jesuits that the Ursulines might be willing to administer the day school, but it was clear that the Ursulines had no intention of returning to St. Xavier's.

St. Labre's, the mission geographically closest to St. Xavier's, although spared some of St. Xavier's acrimony, experienced all of its hardships. From its beginning, St. Labre's had a unique status. Unlike the other Ursuline mission schools, which had been established by the Jesuits, St. Labre's had been founded by Bishop Brondel, then bishop of the entire Montana Territory. Hardly had the mission started when it became clear that this line of authority would create difficulties. Brondel had none of the resources that the Jesuits could draw on, and his efforts to find a priest to serve in this lonely and desolate country were largely unsuccessful. With his death, the responsibility for St. Labre's was passed to Mathias Lenihan, now bishop of Great Falls. Ill-suited for missionary work, Lenihan was quick to remind Ketcham that St. Labre's had been established long before his episcopate. The Cheyenne Indians, whom he had never seen, stirred little zeal in his heart, and the constant requests of the nuns for funds to continue their dilapidated school only added to his annoyance. The fact that he could find "no sober priest" willing to be chaplain on the reservation was a further source of frustration.

The ideal, he wrote to Ketcham, would be to turn the mission over to a congregation of priests, and from 1912 on, he actively sought such a congregation, but without success. Although the Jesuits had originally served at St. Labre's, they were no longer willing to assume that responsibility. For a while, a Canadian priest, Theodore Rocque, took on the work. He was young, energetic, devoted to the Indians, and, he averred, would have gladly stayed on—were it not for the nuns! The problem was one of authority. The nuns, who for years had been "the whole mission," had had no need to be concerned with the division of authority. Monsignor Ketcham was quick to recognize the source of the problem. No mission could ever succeed, he wrote to Father Rocque, unless some harmony among the priests, the sisters, and the bishop could be established.

But Rocque felt he had endured enough and, frustrated by the ambiguity of his position, threatened to resign unless he could be assured of full administrative responsibility. To his chagrin, Lenihan accepted his resignation, leaving St. Labre's once more without a priest. In the summer of 1914, however, Lenihan's search for a religious congregation was successful at last, and in August, two priests, Fathers M. J. Trigory and William Arendzen of the congregation of St. Edmund, came to serve the mission. Father Arendzen, in particular, delighted the nuns by his success with the Cheyenne. "The Indians like the new Father very much. They call him a second Van der Velden," wrote Mother Thomas. But it seemed that at St. Labre's, every blessing was matched by a disaster, and the following summer, just as they were congratulating themselves on the prospect of a good harvest, of healthy cattle, and a hundred chickens, they were struck by a tornado. "Hail, wind and cloudburst gave a total loss of all," wrote Sister Theresa. "The water was over two feet around the house and fields ... 146 panes of glass shattered. Roof so battered that it leaked in all places."[8]

The tornado was only a harbinger of further disaster, however, and on January 12, 1917, fire, that pervasive demon, destroyed their principal building. "We have been blessed with crosses," the superior wrote to Monsignor Ketcham, "but we will not give up."[9]

Within two weeks of the fire, they had reorganized the church so that it could be partitioned into classrooms. Dormitory space was more difficult to arrange. The girls were huddled together without proper beds—most of them had been destroyed in the fire—and the five nuns squeezed into two "rooms" no larger than closets.

It was an unendurable situation, and Mother St. Thomas began at once to draw up plans for a new building. She had not anticipated, however, the stoic opposition of Lenihan. He rejected her arguments for a brick building and then further directed her to put off all plans until she had in hand the full sum for rebuilding. It was an impossible directive from which Lenihan could not be moved. "If something is not done," Ketcham wrote warningly, "the sisters will have to leave ... I wonder that they have had the courage to persevere even as they have."[10] It was to be over two years, however, before a brick school was finally opened, and only after a liberal donation from Mother Katharine Drexel and other faithful benefactors. As for Bishop Lenihan, he never visited the mission to assess the results of the fire nor did he make any contribution to its rebuilding.

The privations and frustrations of life at St. Labre's would have been sweetened had there been signs that the mission was succeeding in its goal, but it seemed that time, instead of softening the resistant spirit of the Cheyenne, confirmed their hostility. Mother Theresa, who had served earlier at St. Labre's, wrote sadly to Monsignor Ketcham,

"After spending these three months at St. Labre I have unfortunately lost much confidence in the fact that these poor people can ever be converted to the faith or even become half-civilized ... to gain the goodwill of the old Cheyenne seems impossible." Her discouragement was confirmed when one morning she woke to see, written in plain English, on the mission buildings, "God damn this mission."[11]

Yet even while they deplored the response of the Cheyenne, the nuns recognized the degradation to which they had been reduced. They had been robbed of their way of life, and what was offered in its place had little to attract them. The Cheyenne were intelligent people, well aware that they were mocked as lazy, ignorant, and stupid. Whites usurped their land and were not punished. The food rations on which they were compelled to depend were used as bait to force them into obedience. Even the mission schools, where the nuns professed to love their children, had no understanding of who these children were, but made them conform to arbitrary white men's regulations. The only weapon the Cheyenne had left was their contempt and hostility.

By 1920, although the fathers of St. Edmund had, at Bishop Lenihan's request, assumed the financial responsibility of the mission, there was still some serious question of the nuns being withdrawn. When, three years later, these priests were recalled permanently to their headquarters in Vermont, there seemed little future for St. Labre's. In 1924, Mother Xavier Gavigan, then provincial superior, wrote in anger to Father Hughes (who had replaced Ketcham at his death in 1921) of the circumstances in which the nuns were living and of the indifference of the bishop concerning the work of the mission. It was clear from her letter that her intent was to close St. Labre's unless conditions changed dramatically.

That dramatic change, which she could scarcely have presumed, began in 1924, when Lenihan engaged in negotiations with the Capuchin Fathers (a branch of Franciscan friars) to assume full responsibility for St. Labre's Mission. In 1925, a formal contract was signed, and by summer 1926, the Capuchin Fathers arrived at the mission, which its first missionary, Peter Barcelo, had appropriately named "The Mission of Sorrows."

The Capuchins who arrived that summer had the energy born of zeal and single-mindedness. Although the spiritual descendants of "the poor man of Assisi," they were astonished at the poverty and desolation of St. Labre's.

They were astonished, but not overwhelmed. Both self-sacrificing and resourceful, within a year, they began to attract Indian boys to the school. Girls followed, and in two years, St. Labre's had outgrown its buildings. While the Ursulines had been powerless to provide the Indians with what was needed, the Capuchins had the authority and the resources to move ahead. Within a few years, new buildings were completed for both boys and girls. Recognizing the need to contact Indian families, the friars traveled into the reservation, visiting the Indian homes, conducting religious services at convenient locations, building small chapels wherever feasible, and preparing catechists who could work with their own people.

Meanwhile, the school expanded, offering training in crafts, trades, and industrial skills, as well as classroom learning. On October 15, 1932, another Capuchin dream was fulfilled: the first Indian high school was opened at St. Labre's. For the first time since the Ursulines had arrived, forty-eight years before, the four remaining sisters saw their dream taking shape. Yet, before the year was out, they received a letter that dismayed and bewildered them: the Ursulines were to be withdrawn from St. Labre's. There was little explanation except that the decision had been made by their major superior in Rome.

Despite the protests of the Capuchin superior, who regretted the change, praising the ability of the sisters to deal with children who were often difficult and willful, the order remained. The Ursulines would be replaced by the School Sisters of St. Francis. Neither the remonstrance of the Capuchins nor the demur of Bishop Edwin O'Hara, who had recently succeeded Bishop Lenihan, changed the decision made in Rome. That August, the four Ursulines (Sisters

Regina Kiernan, Bernadette Walthers, Magdalen La Tronch, and Gonzaga Seilnacht) returned to Great Falls. They left just a year before the celebration that would commemorate the fiftieth anniversary of the founding of St. Labre's Mission and without the consoling prevision that in time the mission that had cost them so dear would become the most successful mission enterprise in Montana.

St. Paul's Mission, tucked away at the foot of the Little Rockies, escaped many of the problems that dogged the other missions. They had children in abundance, grieving that they could not take all who came to them. With never enough money to buy the food they needed, they had attempted to supplement their income by establishing an apiary with two colonies of bees, contributed by the brother of one of the Jesuits. They also stacked a pond with fish from the government hatchery. But these small measures were hardly enough to counter their poverty. After almost twenty-five years of mission labor, neither the girls' school nor the

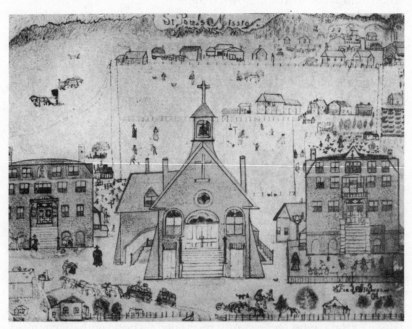

St. Paul's Mission, line drawing by a pupil. Courtesy of Marquette University Libraries, Bureau of Catholic Indian Missions Records

convent had bathtubs or toilets. The boys' building was little better, but every plan to improve the mission was countered by their limited finances.

Meanwhile, the Indians grew increasingly restless as they heard rumors of plans to open further reservation land to the ranchers, who were always clamoring for more. The situation was hardly helped by an optimistic agent, who gave them false assurance that they could count on government support. Now, wrote Father Hubert Post, the superior, they are waiting in vain for the government promises to be made good. "The Indians are absolutely starving and I am unable to help them," he wrote to Ketcham. "Where is the government now with all its fair promises? The Indians will be desperate if they are not helped. Would you say a little word for them in Washington."[12]

But even Ketcham was able to do little. In September 1912, he wrote: "I am sorry to say that we can only give in the future as we have been giving in the past. When the Indian schools were originally established the idea was on all sides that in the course of time they would become self-supporting. This was the impression of this Bureau, of Mother Katharine, of the Government and of those who, at that time, were in direct charge of the work." But "that time," with its optimistic goals, was past, and Ketcham concluded sadly, "But experience shows that no Indian school ever became self-supporting and I have given up the idea that any ever will."[13]

For another decade, St. Paul's scrabbled along, determined to provide an education for the children who came to them, crowding them into inadequate space, well aware that the conditions of the school were, in many ways, inferior. In May 1921, Sister Aloysius Bailey, the superior, wrote to the Indian agent:

> May I ask you in your kind charity for a little help to repair our convent roof that is leaking dreadful, without your kind aid I can simply do nothing to repair it, as this poor mission is simply struggling for its existence. We have a great many

children and obliged to refuse many for want of means to support them, much to the loss of our holy faith.[14]

After ten more years of struggle, their efforts were brought to a close when fire, that demon that St. Paul's had escaped throughout its forty-four-year history, destroyed them at last. The sisters, priests, and students were all in chapel when fire struck the kitchen at 6:30 A.M. on November 5, 1931. As always in such cases, there was little that could be done. It was already winter, with a high wind blowing in from the canyon, and no water was available. The kitchen and the refectories went up at once, then the girls' dormitory, followed by the stone church, with its elegant frescoes of which they were so proud. A few priestly vestments were saved from the sacristy, but everything in the girls' school was lost.

That night, they slept where they could, on tables, on piles of robes, wrapped in blankets against the increasing cold, while the Jesuits reorganized the boys' dormitory so that it would be available for the girls. Mother St. Henry Perret, who was visiting at the time, wrote the following week:

> The Reverend Jesuit Fathers are giving their home to our Nuns
> and girls for the winter and until the religious get a new
> convent. The building is large enough to have refectories for
> both Communities and also class-rooms for the two schools.
> The Fathers and boys will have to accommodate themselves
> for sleeping quarters wherever they can find room in the old
> buildings.[15]

Almost at once, plans were made to rebuild, first the church and then the girls' school. But it was not to be the Ursulines who would continue at St. Paul's. Five years after the fire, the decision was made to withdraw; there were no longer sufficient sisters to continue the work that would be carried on by the School Sisters of St. Francis. On the last page of the St. Paul's annals, it reads:

June 18, 1936: It will be fifty years since the Ursulines came to
the Mission, since the Mission opened. Now our work is done
here. May the new sisters do good work here.

Left July 9: M. Veronica Leuschen, Marie Field, Ursula
Marie Johnson.[16]

Like St. Paul's, Holy Family Mission, which had been started for
the Blackfeet in 1890, had no difficulty in filling the school, but like all
missions, they were desperate to find the funds to maintain it. In 1916,
they reported that they had registered over 100 and had been forced to
turn away a dozen girls. The same year, they were reproached by
Charles Lusk, secretary for the BCIM, with the "matter of cleanliness"
in the girls' school. The Jesuit superior was exasperated that they
should be criticized, despite all his efforts to improve the buildings. "I
put up new toilets and shower baths for the Sisters' school and a new
building for laundry and bakery in stucco and cement with concrete
floors. I expect to have power laundry machinery installed before the
next two months. You see we have not been idle."[17]

While the bureau was well aware of the needs, there were no
extra funds for the repairs the school so urgently needed. Still more
desperate the following year, Grant wrote again that without some
assistance, he could not pay his bills, nor could he afford even the
most basic foodstuff—$7 per day for flour was beyond their means,
he noted. The government was worse than useless, often failing to
provide the rations of meat promised to the Indians and now levy-
ing a water tax on the mission. His requests for clothes for the
children (heavy cotton hose, heavy undershirts, sturdy shoes) often
went unmet. Most alarming of all, he wrote, "The sisters are asking
for salaries from the Mission. I don't know how I am going to meet
their demands."[18]

Perhaps it was this demand for salaries on the part of the
Ursulines, along with their inability to provide additional sis-
ters, that led Grant to look for another religious congregation.
In June of that year, he wrote to the provincial of the Franciscan

Missionaries of Mary in New York, explaining their work and soliciting their help.

> Ordinarily we have about 50 girls and 50 boys as boarders. All the cooking, etc., is done at the Srs. building and is under the direction of the Srs. The class rooms for the girls are in the Srs. Building. ... All running expenses are met by the Mission and the Srs. are allowed $200 each year to meet their personal expenses. ... There are only 5 Srs. here now but there should be seven Srs. in order to carry on the work properly. I feel sure that if you get started here your work will increase and spread. ... [19]

The Franciscans, however, declined his offer, and the Ursulines continued at Holy Family, understaffed but somewhat eased by their newly acquired yearly stipend.

As funds diminished yearly, and as government schools opened in the area, it became clear that Holy Family, despite all its good work, would soon be unable to continue. Perhaps, as the criticism was later made, a more provident or efficient administration might have saved the mission from the welter of debt that finally overwhelmed it. It was an inglorious end. Accusations over unpaid bills and squabbles over fiscal responsibility lay heavy over the mission, which had sacrificed so much and for so long.

Holy Family Mission, preparing for procession. Courtesy of Ursuline archives, Great Falls, Montana

In October 1939, the Marquette League published an article in
the mission magazine *The Calumet*: "One of the most discouraging
letters that has reached the office of the Marquette League in the past
few years came a few days ago, bringing the news that the Holy
Family Mission School was closing its doors due to the lack of financial help."[20] Eight months later, the buildings, already shabby and
weather beaten, were finally abandoned. The Ursuline annals at
Great Falls reported bleakly: "The truck sent out to Holy Family to get
furniture, etc. from the Mission. Rev. Mother named a few nuns who
are out there packing household articles to be sent here and to St.
Ignatius's Mission as Holy Family is to be closed or sold. Sad days for
we poor missionaries."[21]

Farther to the west, St. Ignatius's Mission, although experiencing the same difficulties—poor crops, a plague of grasshoppers,
increased poverty among the Indians, inability to raise sufficient
monies to support the boarders—managed more successfully. The
reorganization of the mission resources and a more efficient administration kept the mission on an even keel. Even so, the Jesuit
superior had to admit that their situation was tenuous: "The Ursuline

St. Ignatius's Mission, preparing for procession. Courtesy of Marquette
University Libraries, Bureau of Catholic Indian Missions Records

sisters have had several successive crop failures," he wrote to Monsignor Ketcham. "This coupled with the high cost of everything and the high wages they have to pay for help has made their financial condition precarious. ... Last winter the Ursuline sisters were obliged to sell their cattle because they had no hay and are now obliged to buy meat."[22]

The following year, however, the ordinary difficulties of daily living were forgotten as the sisters struggled beneath the weight of that tragic moment that all missionaries had learned to dread. On December 9, 1919, fire destroyed the buildings of the Sisters of Providence. On December 11, Father Joseph Bruckert, the Jesuit superior, wrote to Ketcham, "I must send you some very sad news. ... The day before yesterday at noon a terrific conflagration destroyed within two hours every building belonging to the Sisters of Charity."[23]

To the Jesuits' surprise, the sisters' immediate decision was not to rebuild, but to devote themselves to the hospital work in which they were already engaged. They agreed to continue a small day school but nothing more. The Ursulines, despite their inadequate staff, were left with little choice but to double their work.

Within the year, Mother Perpetua Egan, superior at St. Ignatius's, recognizing the inadequacy of their present buildings, began a series of costly improvements. She installed a steam heating plant, enlarged the laundry, and made basic renovations on the dilapidated sections of their old house. Such improvements put her in debt for over $10,000. "I admire her courage in undertaking this work in these hard times," the Jesuit superior wrote.*

Her courage, however, was not to be rewarded. On February 19, 1922—even before the debts were paid—the Ursuline buildings burned to the ground. The following day Father Sullivan wrote to Father William Hughes who had replaced Monsignor Ketcham as director of the Catholic Bureau:

---

*Their full title is the Sisters of Charity of Providence.

Fire broke out about midnight in the Ursuline Convent. ... Fire
spread very rapidly. In about half an hour it had enveloped the
whole quadrangle of the buildings. A wind was blowing and it
carried the fire along the porches of the buildings. There was
very little time to save anything. ... The chapel furniture,
school furniture, Sisters' and children's personal effects, beds,
bedding, etc., etc., were destroyed. ... No one knows for certain
how the fire began. No stoves were burning, as the building
had been heated for the past few months by a fine steam plant
recently installed. No lamps were burning, as the house is
lighted by electricity. ... The loss I would estimate at about
$80,000 and the insurance amounts to $14,000.[24]

Although in the initial commotion it seemed that all had been
saved, soon they realized that Sister John of the Cross, one of the
French refugees who had come to Montana in 1904, was missing. At
first they thought she was among those who had been taken to the
hospital. Their search was in vain, however, and by noon her bones
"among red hot debris" were located amid the ruins. Two days later
her remains, enclosed in a small white casket, were carried to the
chapel for a requiem Mass.

Father Hughes's response to the catastrophe was instanta-
neous, mailing a check for $1,000 "to meet the immediate
emergency" and promising $10,000 as soon as possible. "I cannot tell
you how much I admire the magnificent spirit of courage, faith and
charity of the Ursuline Sisters," he wrote. "I am sure that your uncon-
scious heroism will impress the people of the country and that they
will come to your rescue."[25]

Already heavily in debt, it seemed impossible that the Ursulines
would plunge into further financial hazard, but within weeks, the
decision had been made to rebuild—and to rebuild on a larger and
more commodious scale than before. The old frame buildings were to
be replaced by three-story, sturdy brick structures, as fireproof as possible. Plumbing and electricity were to be modernized, and a heating

plant installed. The cost was estimated between $80,000 and $100,000. Mother Perpetua, well aware of the enormous debt she was incurring, was also aware that they must provide a modern school if they were to draw the Indian children.

For the next two years, appeals for money went out in all directions—spearheaded by the Catholic Bureau, by Bishop Carroll of Helena, by loyal mission benefactors. Construction had begun at once. By June, half the bricks were ready and the brick layers had begun work. On July 19, they had a ceremony for laying the cornerstone. "The new building is going up," wrote Father Sullivan, "but I don't think any part of it will be ready by September." It was an accurate prediction, and on September 5, Mother Perpetua wrote to Father Hughes, "I wish you could see us today, Father. We're putting up beds everywhere in order to accommodate at least one hundred girls. 'Tis no little task to find sufficient space for these dear children

St. Ignatius's Mission, girls' school, circa 1905. Courtesy of Ursuline archives, Great Falls, Montana

and ourselves on the third floor [of the Jesuits' building]. Many more children applied but I have had to refuse them. School is to open next Monday."[26]

Although the actual building was ready by the beginning of 1923, it was months before they could assemble the necessary furniture so that the children could move in. Their debts had escalated to a level that was making it impossible to cover the basic interest payments, and there were those who were quick to criticize Perpetua's expenditures, suggesting that less expensive furnishings would have been adequate. But Perpetua, in the spirit of Amadeus before her, wanted St. Ignatius's to be a model school that would indicate the value of education, not some poor makeshift structure unworthy of its calling.

In this, she succeeded. The school, which was fully open by the fall of 1924, could not be faulted. Whatever the Ursulines' anxiety over their debts, they took pride in refounding their mission at St. Ignatius's. Begun in 1890 as a kindergarten, the least significant part of the Jesuits' extensive enterprise, it had grown to include the whole educational system—from kindergarten through high school.

But even this new mission school, reported by a local paper to be one of the finest buildings of its kind in Montana, could not withstand the inevitable shift of time. With the increase of day schools and the relocation of some of the native people, boarding schools were no longer necessary, and by 1962, the Ursulines decided to close the boarding school. For another ten years, a day school continued, with dwindling numbers of children. By 1972, it was clear that even the day school was no longer needed. That year, the Ursuline school was finally closed, and the land returned to the Indians. A few sisters stayed on to work on the reservation, but the mission school begun so modestly eighty-two years before had come to an end.*

---

*Neither Miles City nor Mount St. Angela Academy in Great Falls was considered part of the mission work, since they were established for white children. The academy in Miles City continued until 1954. Mount Angela high school closed in 1950, and the elementary school in 1966.

Conclusion

The era of the Lady Blackrobes was over. Amadeus Dunne had never succeeded in bringing to reality her golden dream of fifteen missions. But, with her companions, she had done more than anyone could reasonably expect. In April 1884, just three months after their arrival in Miles City, the sisters had established a mission for the Cheyenne on the Tongue River. By October of that same year, they were in residence with the Jesuits at St. Peter's Mission for the Blackfeet. In those few months, the number of sisters had doubled to twelve. Three years later, in 1887, they established schools for the Crow at St. Xavier's in southeastern Montana and St. Paul's Mission at the foot of the Little Rockies. In 1890, two more missions were established (Holy Family and St. Ignatius's), just south of the Mission Range. By the turn of the century, there were more than sixty-seven Ursuline sisters working on eight missions.

The golden age of missionary endeavor was short-lived, blazing like a meteor and plunging into darkness. Like so many human endeavors, it succeeded for only a time, replaced by other golden dreams. Whatever judgment more-enlightened generations will pronounce on these activities, it will be hard to contemn the unswerving fidelity and courage that inspired them.

Endnotes

AAC: Archives of the Archdiocese of Cleveland
AAS: Archives of the Archdiocese of Seattle
ACU: Archives of the the Catholic University of America
ASBS: Archives of the Sisters of the Blessed Sacrament
AUG: Archives of the Ursulines of the Roman Union Generalate
AUW: Archives of the Ursulines of the Roman Union Western Province
AUQ: Archives of the Ursulines of the Canadian Union at Québec
AUT: Archives of the Ursulines of Toledo
AUTR: Archives of the Ursulines of the Canadian Union at Trois Rivières
BCIM: Bureau of Catholic Indian Missions
JOPA/NWMC: Jesuit Oregon Province Archives, Northwest Mission Collection
MMWH: *Montana Magazine of Western History*
TIS: *The Indian Sentinel*

Chapter One

1. Laura Zook, *Miles City Memories*, ed. Amorette F. Allison (Miles City, Mont.: Miles City Preservation Commission, 2002), 42.
2. John Baptist Brondel to Richard Gilmour, Oct. 1, 1883, AAC.
3. Gilmour, *The Catholic Universe*, Oct. 18, 1883.
4. AAC.
5. For more information on the history of the Ursulines of Cleveland, see Sister Michael Francis Hearon, O.S.U., *The Broad Highway* (Cleveland, Ohio: 1957). For more information on the Ursulines of Toledo, see Sister Lelia Mahoney, O.S.U., ed., *A Tree in the Valley: Ursuline Sisters of Toledo 1854–1979* (Toledo, Ohio: Ursuline Sisters of Toledo, 1979).
6. Gilmour to Stanislaus Duffey, Oct. 24, 1883, AUT.
7. Ibid.
8. Gilmour, *The Catholic Universe*, Dec. 13, 1883.
9. Brondel to Gilmour, Dec. 31, 1883, AUT.
10. See the excellent article on Father Eli Washington John Lindesmith by Louis L. Pfaller, O.S.B., "Eli Washington John Lindesmith: Fort Keogh's Chaplain in Buckskin," *MMWH* 27 (1977): 14–25. See also James R. Kolp, *The Amazing Father Lindesmith* (Canton, Ohio: 2004) and *Centennial Roundup: A Collection of Stories Celebrating the 100th Anniversary of the Incorporation of Miles City, Montana* (Miles City, Mont.: *Miles City Star*, 1987).

11. Gilmour to Duffey, Dec. 31, 1883, AUT.
12. Carlos A. Schwantes, "The Steamboat and Stagecoach Era in Montana and the Northern West," *MMWH* 49 (1999): 3.
13. Amadeus Dunne's memoirs, AUT.
14. Sacred Heart Meilink to Duffey, Feb. 2, 1884, AUT.
15. *MMWH* 3 (1953): 17.
16. *Centennial Roundup*, 6.
17. Ibid.
18. Dunne to the Ursulines of Toledo, Jan. 19, 1884, AUT.
19. Francis Seibert to the Ursulines of Toledo, Jan. 28, 1884, AUT.
20. Dunne to the Ursulines of Toledo, Jan. 19, 1884, AUT.

Chapter Two

1. *Yellowstone Journal*, Jan. 19, 1884, AUT.
2. Amadeus Dunne memoirs, AUG.
3. Dunne to the Ursulines of Toledo, Jan. 22, 1884, AUT.
4. Francis Seibert to the Ursulines of Toledo Jan. 28, 1884, AUT.
5. Dunne to the Ursulines of Toledo, Jan. 22, 1884, AUT.
6. Ignatius McFarland to Ursulines of Toledo, Feb. 17, 1884, AUT.
7. *Centennial Roundup*, 82.
8. Dunne memoirs, AUG.
9. McFarland to the Ursulines of Toledo, Feb. 16, 1884, AUT.
10. Dunne to the Ursulines of Toledo, March 29, 1884, AUT.
11. Ibid.
12. Ibid.
13. Sacred Heart Meilink to the Ursulines of Toledo, April 27, 1884, AUT.
14. Ibid.
15. Ibid.
16. Angela Abair, *A Mustard Seed in Montana*, unpublished manuscript, AUW.
17. Series 1, Reel 13, BCIM.
18. Abair, *Mustard Seed*.
19. Series 1, Reel 13, BCIM.
20. McFarland to the Ursulines of Toledo, April 27, 1884, AUT.
21. Meilink to the Ursulines of Toledo, June 8 and 14, 1884, AUT.
22. John Baptist Brondel to Dunne, July 9, 1884, AUW.
23. Series 1, Reel 13, BCIM.
24. McFarland to the Ursulines of Toledo, April 27, 1884, AUT.
25. Meilink to Dunne, June 22, 1884, AUT.
26. Brondel to Dunne, July 9, 1884, AUW.
27. Dunne to the Ursulines of Toledo, June 19, 1884, AUT.
28. Richard Gilmour to Dunne, July 28, 1884, AUW.
29. Brondel to Dunne, Aug. 5, 1884, AUW.

Chapter Three

1. Amadeus Dunne to the Ursulines of Toledo, May 29, 1884, AUT.
2. Dunne to the Ursulines of Toledo, July 14, 1884, AUT.
3. John Baptist Brondel to Dunne, June 13, 1884, AUW.
4. Dunne to Stanislaus Duffey, Aug. 31, 1884, AUT.
5. Brondel to Dunne, Aug. 20, 1884, AUW.
6. Dunne to Brondel, undated, AUT.
7. Dunne to the Ursulines of Toledo, Oct. 18, 1884, AUT.
8. Dunne to Miles City, Oct. 29, 1884, AUT.
9. Dunne to the Ursulines of Toledo, Jan. 15, 1885, AUT.
10. Dunne to the Ursulines of Toledo, Nov. 1, 1884, AUT.
11. For two accounts of the Italian priests working in the Rocky Mountains, see Andrew F. Rolle, "The Italian Moves Westward," *MMWH* 16 (Jan. 1966): 13–19, and Gerald McKevitt, S.J., "Northwest Indian Evangelization by European Jesuits, 1841–1909," *Catholic Historical Review* 91 (Oct. 2005): 688–713.
12. Francis J. Weber, ed., "Grant's Peace Policy: A Catholic Dissenter," *MMWH* 19 (1969): 60.
13. Howard H. Harrod, "The Blackfeet and the Divine Establishment," *MMWH* 22 (1972): 48.
14. John C. Ewers, *The Blackfeet: Raiders on the Northwest Plains* (Norman: University of Oklahoma Press, 1958), 290.
15. Lawrence B. Palladino, *Indian and White in the Northwest* (Baltimore: John Murphy & Co., 1894), 225.
16. *Historia Domus, 1884–1886*, Roll 8, JOPA/NWMC.
17. Frederick Eberschweiler, "Sketch of the History of St. Peter's Mission," Roll 8, JOPA/NWMC.
18. Dunne to the Ursulines of Toledo, Dec. 8, 1884, AUT.
19. Dunne to the Ursulines of Toledo, Dec. 19, 1884, AUT.
20. Dunne to the Ursulines of Toledo, Nov. 1, 1884, AUT.
21. Dunne to the Ursulines of Toledo, Dec. 19, 1884, AUT.

Chapter Four

1. Angela Abair, *A Mustard Seed in Montana*, unpublished manuscript, 11–13, AUW.
2. Ignatius McFarland to Amadeus Dunne, Dec. 23, 1884, AUT.
3. John Baptist Brondel to Richard Gilmour, Jan. 1885, AAC.
4. Charles Lusk to the commissioner of Indian affairs, Feb. 5, 1885, Series 1, Reel 13, BCIM.
5. Brondel to Joseph Stephan, Feb. 14, 1885, Series 1, Reel 13, BCIM.
6. Brondel to McFarland, March 28, 1885, AUT.
7. McFarland to Lusk, March 25, 1885, Series 1, Reel 13, BCIM.
8. Stanislaus Duffey to Gilmour, March 1885, AAC.
9. Duffey to Gilmour, May 10, 1885, AAC.

10. Mary of the Angels to the Ursulines of Toledo, undated, AUT.

11. Sacred Heart Meilink to the Ursulines of Toledo, July 27, 1885, AUT.

12. Dunne to the Ursulines of Toledo, Aug. 31, 1885, AUT.

13. Dunne to the Ursulines of Toledo, Aug. 12, 1885, AUT.

14. Dunne to Duffey, Aug. 12, 1885, AUT.

15. Abair, *Mustard Seed*, 17.

16. Ibid., 14.

17. Ibid., 15.

18. Ibid., 15.

19. Ibid., 17.

20. McFarland to Lusk, Oct. 11, Oct. 26, Series 1, Reel 13, BCIM.

21. Brondel to Gilmour, Nov. 7, 1885, AAC.

22. Stanislaus to Gilmour, May 10, 1885, AAC.

23. Meilink to the Ursulines of Toledo, July 27, 1885, AUT.

Chapter Five

1. Amadeus Dunne memoirs, AUG.

2. Dunne to Stanislaus Duffey, March 8, 1886, AUT.

3. Sacred Heart Meilink to Dunne, March 7, 1886 AUT.

4. Dunne to Duffey, March 8, 1886, AUT.

5. Dunne to Duffey, March 18, 1886, AUT.

6. Ibid.

7. Duffey to Richard Gilmour, April 17, 1886, AAC.

8. Amadeus to Gilmour, June 17, 1887, AAC.

9. Eli Washington John Lindesmith diaries, March 9, 1886, Page 40, AUT. The originals of Lindesmith's letters and diaries are in the archives of The Catholic University of America, Washington, D.C.

10. Lindesmith to Duffey, May 26, 1886, ACU.

11. Lindesmith diaries, March, Page 49, ACU.

12. Dunne to Lindesmith, May 24, 1886, AUT.

13. Ibid.

14. Ibid.

15. Gilmour to the Ursulines of Toledo, Feb. 28, 1886, AUT.

16. Mary of the Angels Carroll to the Ursulines of Toledo, Oct. 28, 1886, AUT.

17. Dunne to the Ursulines of Toledo, Nov. 9 and Nov. 17, 1886, AUT.

18. Brian W. Dippie, *The Vanishing American: White Attitudes and U.S. Indian Policy* (Middletown, Conn.: Wesleyan University Press, 1982), 15, 48.

19. Ross K. Toole, *Montana: An Uncommon Land, Second Edition* (Norman: University of Oklahoma Press, 1959), 115.

Chapter Six

1. Amadeus Dunne to Richard Gilmour, Jan. 18, 1886, AAC.

2. Frederick Eberschweiler to Joseph Cataldo, July 28, 1885, Roll 13, JOPA/NWMC.

3. Dunne to the Ursulines of Toledo, Sept. 9, 1887, AUT.
4. Dunne to the Ursulines of Toledo, Sept. 20, 1887, AUT.
5. Eberschweiler to Katharine Drexel, Oct. 13, 1887, ASBS.
6. Dunne to Sr. Raphael, Jan. 24, 1888, AUT.
7. Seibert to Assumption Seibert, Feb. 7, 1888, AUT.
8. Eberschweiler to Drexel, March 13, 1888, ASBS.
9. Seibert to Assumption Seibert, July 15, 1888, AUT.
10. Eberschweiler to Drexel, Oct. 1, 1888, Jan. 1, 1889, ASBS.
11. Leopold Van Gorp to Joseph Cataldo, July 4, 1889, Roll 12, JOPA/NWMC.
12. Eloise Whitebear Pease, "The Crow Indians," *MMWH* 94 (1994): 53.
13. M. L. Blake to Cataldo, Feb. 26, 1886, Roll 14, JOPA/NWMC.
14. Joseph Bandini to Amadeus Dunne, June 1884, JOPA/NWMC.
15. Dunne to Gilmour, June 17, 1884, AAC.
16. For a full account of this uprising, see Colin G. Calloway, "Sword Bearer and the 'Crow Outbreak' 1887," *MMWH* 36 (1936): 38–51.
17. Peter Prando, *Helena Catholic Sentinel*, Feb. 3, 1887, Roll 14, JOPA/NWMC.
18. Ibid.
19. Oct. 1887, Roll 15, JOPA/NWMC.

Chapter Seven

1. Amadeus Dunne to the Ursulines of Toledo, Oct. 23, 1887, AUT.
2. Peter Bandini to Joseph Stephan, April 17, 1889, Series 1, Reel 19, BCIM.
3. Ignatius McFarland to Richard Gilmour, Jan. 22, 1888, AAC.
4. Aloysius Van der Velden memoirs, undated, Roll 11, JOPA/NWMC.
5. Stephan to McFarland, Feb. 15, 1888, Series 1, Reel 17, BCIM.
6. Joseph Cataldo to Van der Velden, July 1888, Roll 11, JOPA/NWMC.
7. McFarland to Stephan, Oct. 10, 1888, Reel 17, BCIM.
8. From the superior in Toledo to Ignatius McFarland, Dec. 30, 1887, AUT.
9. Dunne to Katharine Drexel, Jan. 11, 1888, ASBS.
10. Eberschweiler to Drexel, June 4, 1888, ASBS.
11. *Great Falls Daily Tribune*, Sept. 15, 1888.
12. Dunne to Stephan, May 7, 1889, BCIM.
13. Leopold Van Gorp to Drexel, Jan. 26, 1892, ASBS.
14. *Great Falls Daily Tribune*, July 1, 1889.
15. Bandini to Drexel, Oct. 31 and Nov. 17, 1887, ASBS.
16. Bandini to Drexel, March 9, 1888, ASBS.
17. Magdalen Cox to Gilmour, Jan. 24 1888, AAC.
18. Cox memoirs, AUT.
19. Cox to Stephan, Dec. 8, 1888, Series 1, Reel 17, BCIM.
20. Eberschweiler to Stephan, July 12, 1889, Series 1, Reel 19, BCIM.
21. Gilmour to Dunne, Jan. 13, 1889, AUW.
22. Van der Velden to Stephan, Feb. 20, 1889, Series 1, Reel 19, BCIM.
23. Reprinted in the *Fifty-Eighth Annual Report of the Commissioner of Indian Affairs to the Secretary of the Interior* (Washington, D.C.: Government

Printing Office, 1889).

24. Dunne memoirs, undated, AUW.

25. For the material concerning the Sisters of Providence, I am indebted to
    Suzanne H. Schrems's *Uncommon Women, Unmarked Trails: The Courageous
    Journey of Catholic Missionary Sisters in Frontier Montana* (Norman, Okla.:
    Horse Creek Publications, 2003).

26. Office of Indian Affairs to Van Gorp, 1888, Series 1, Reel 17 BCIM.

27. E. D. Bannister to the secretary of the interior, Oct. 22, 1888, Series 1, Reel
    17, BCIM.

Chapter Eight

1. *Litterae Annuae*, 1889–1926, Roll 4, JOPA/NWMC.

2. Peter Ronan report to the Indian commissioner in Washington, D.C.,
   1890, AUW.

3. Amadeus Dunne memoirs, 1906, AUG.

4. See the interesting article by Margaret Connell Szasz, "Listening to the
   Native Voice: American Indian Schooling in the Twentieth Century,"
   MMWH 39 (1989): 42–53. See also Michael Coleman, "Motivations of
   Indian Children at Missionary and U.S. Government Schools, 1869–1918,"
   MMWH 40 (1990): 30–45.

5. "Article of Agreement," Roll 1, JOPA/NWMC.

6. Peter Prando, 1912, *TIS*.

7. Stephan to the commissioner of Indian affairs, 1890, Series 1, Reel 21,
   BCIM.

8. This magazine article, written anonymously by an Ursuline, repeated the
   myth propagated by Angela Lincoln herself that her family was related to
   the family of Abraham Lincoln. Later family documents indicate that there
   is no evidence for this. *The Messenger of our Lady of Prompt Succor* (Nov.
   1937): 5.

9. Amata Dunne memoirs, AUG.

10. Philbert Turnell to Katharine Drexel, Nov. 24, 1890, Reel 19, BCIM. All doc-
    uments in both BCIM and the Drexel archives cite "Father Turnell." Jesuit
    documents list him as "Philbert Tornielli."

11. Turnell to Joseph Stephan, Feb. 23 and Jan. 7, 1891, Series 1, Reel 23,
    BCIM.

12. Dunne to Stephan, May 16, 1890, Series 1, Reel 21, BCIM. See also Joseph
    Damiani's report to his superior, Aug. 20, 1890.

13. Newspaper clipping in St. Peter's Mission scrapbook, AUW.

14. St. Peter's annals, June 28, 1891, AUW.

15. Ibid.

16. Ibid.

17. For information on the establishment of Pryor Mission, see the account of
    Prando, "Pryor Mission, 10 April, 1893," Roll 14, JOPA/NWMC.

18. For the full text of Thomas Stoeckel's reminiscences, see *TIS* 1 (July 1916):

23–25.

19. Dave Walter, "Chief Charlo, Trail of Tears," *MMWH* 47 (1997): 99–105.

20. Ellen Baumler, ed., *The Girl from the Gulches: The Story of Mary Ronan as told to Margaret Ronan* (Helena: Montana Historical Society Press, 2003), 150.

21. John Baptist Brondel to Richard Gilmour, Feb. 14, 1891, AAC.

Chapter Nine

1. Annals, II, 649, AUQ.

2. The narration that follows is from a document called "*Les Ursulines Missionnaires de St.-Pierre (Montana); Missions indiennes,*" preserved at AUTR.

3. Most of the details that follow are taken from the diary of Marie de l'Espérance Tessier, AUTR.

4. St. Bernard Trudeau to the superior at Trois Rivières, Aug. 31, 1893, AUTR.

5. Ibid.

6. St. Félix Talbot to the superior at Québec, Aug. 1893, AUQ.

7. Ibid.

8. Pélagie Gosselin to the superior at Québec, Sept. 10, 1893, AUQ.

9. Trudeau to the superior at Trois Rivières, Sept. 17, 1893, AUTR.

10. Trudeau to the superior at Trois Rivières, April 15, 1894, AUTR.

11. Talbot to Philomène, Dec. 27, 1893, AUQ.

12. Ibid.

13. St. Peter's annals, Dec. 24, 1893, AUW.

14. Ibid., Jan. 5, 13, and 14, 1894.

15. Ibid., Jan. 22, 1894.

16. Talbot to the superior at Québec, March 17, 1894, AUQ.

17. Gosselin to the superior at Québec, Feb. 4, 1894, AUQ.

18. Trudeau to the superior at Trois Rivières, April 15, 1894, AUTR.

19. Mission register and annals, Feb. 5, 1894, AUW.

20. St. Peter's annals, July 27, 1894, AUW.

21. The public library at Cascade has an excellent collection of material on Mary Fields.

Chapter Ten

1. Aloysius Van der Velden to Joseph Stephan, May 2, 1894, Series 1, Reel 24, BCIM.

2. Luke Van Ree to Katharine Drexel, Nov. 29, 1893, BCIM.

3. *Litterae Annuae,* 1893–1895, Roll 11, JOPA/NWMC.

4. Notes of Aloysius Van der Velden, S.J., edited by Sister Eustella, O.S.F., Roll 11, JOPA/NWMC.

5. *Litterae Annuae,* Roll 11, JOPA/NWMC.

6. Scholastique Lajoie to Philomène, Sept. 1893, AUTR.

7. Marie de l'Espérance Tessier to the superior at Trois Rivières, Sept. 24, 1893, AUTR.

8. St. Bernard Trudeau to the superior at Trois Rivières, March 1894, AUTR.

9. Balthasar Feusi to Katharine Drexel, summer 1894, ASBS.

10. Elisabeth Sirois to the superior at Québec, Aug. 9, 1894, AUQ.

11. Félix Talbot to the superior at Québec, Nov. 4 and 11, 1894, AUQ.

12. Sirois to the superior at Québec, Aug. 8, 1895, AUQ.

13. Talbot to the superior at Québec, Nov. 11, 1894, AUQ.

14. Ibid.

15. Pélagie Gosselin to the superior at Québec, May 1, 1894, AUQ.

16. Gosselin to the superior at Québec, April 6, 1894, AUQ.

17. St. Peter's annals, Dec. 4, 1894, AUW.

18. Ibid.

19. Gosselin to the superior at Québec, Dec. 26, 1894, and Feb. 17, 1895, AUQ.

20. Trudeau to the superior at Trois Rivières Feb. 22, 1896, AUTR.

21. Trudeau to the superior at Trois Rivières, June 15, 1896, AUTR.

22. Trudeau to the superior at Trois Rivières, Oct. 25, 1896, AUTR.

23. Trudeau to the superior at Trois Rivières, July 12, 1896, AUTR.

24. Lajoie to the superior at Trois Rivières, Nov. 17, 1896, AUTR.

25. Amadeus Dunne to an anonymous priest, Feb. 5, 1897, UATR. Since this letter is preserved in the Ursuline Monastery at Trois Rivières, it is possible that the addressee is the bishop of the diocese whom Dunne had met in the summer of 1893.

Chapter Eleven

1. Francis Andreis, S.J., winter 1894, Series 1, Reel 24, BCIM.

2. Joseph Stephan to John Baptist Brondel, Sept. 8, 1896, Series 1, Reel 25, BCIM.

3. Amadeus Dunne to Katharine Drexel, Feb. 2, 1897, ASBS.

4. Genevieve McBride, O.S.U., *The Bird Tail* (New York: Vantage Press, 1974), 166.

5. *Litterae Annuae*, 1893–1895, Roll 11, JOPA/NWMC.

6. St. Labre's annals, Aug. 8, 1897, AUW.

7. St. Labre's annals, Aug. 10, 1897, AUW.

8. Dunne memoires, UAG.

9. *Yellowstone Journal*, Dec. 2, 1897.

10. Dunne to Eli Washington John Lindesmith, Dec. 18, 1897, Lindesmith diaries, ACU.

11. Dunne to Lindesmith, Feb. 7, 1898, Lindesmith diaries, ACU.

12. Leopold Van Gorp to Drexel, Jan. 26, 1892, ASBS.

13. William N. Bischoff, S.J., *Jesuit Missions in Montana* (Caldwell, Idaho: The Caxton Printers, Ltd., 1943), 103.

14. *Historia Domus*, Holy Family Mission 1898, Roll 10, JOPA/NWMC.

15. "Holy Family Mission School, Blackfeet Indian Reservation, Montana," unsigned, undated manuscript generally ascribed to Peter Prando, Roll 10, JOPA/NWMC.

16. R. C. Bauer to the commissioner of Indian affairs, Jan. 9, 1899, Box 1619, No. 3323, Department of the Interior, Indian Service.

17. Thomas Morgan to James Rebmann, S.J., March 22, April 30, and June 11,

1892, Roll 2, JOPA/NWMC.

18. "Indian parents have no right to designate which school their children shall attend," Browning Ruling, *TIS*, Sept. 30, 1896.

19. "A percapita payment was made to 1510 Agency Indians, aggregating $21,458, the funds from which this payment was made was obtained from the Northern Pacific Railway Company," Roll 4, JOPA/NWMC.

20. St. Bernard Trudeau to the superior at Trois Rivières, April 6, 1895, AUTR.

21. St. Ignatius's Mission house diary, Feb. 25, 1896, Roll 3, JOPA/NWMC.

22. Ibid., Nov. 16, 1896.

23. Ibid., Dec. 3, 1896.

24. Ibid., June 8, 1898.

25. Ursulines to Stephan, Jan. 26, 1900, Series 1, Reel 29, BCIM.

Chapter Twelve

1. For the origin of the Roman Union, see the excellent study by Marie Andrée Jégou and Marija Jasna Kogoj, *Journey Towards Unity*, 2 vols., (Rome, 1998).

2. Amadeus Dunne to St. Julien Aubry, May 20, 1899, AUG.

3. Ibid.

4. John Baptist Brondel to Dunne, Aug. 25, 1899, Helena, Diocesan Archives. See also Jégou, *Journey Towards Unity*, I, 235, and II, 20.

5. St. Peter's annals, AUW.

6. Dunne to Katharine Drexel, Jan. 18, 1900, ASBS.

7. St. Peter's annals, Nov. 21, 1900, AUW.

8. Ibid., Dec. 21, 1900.

9. Ibid., Feb. 4, 1901 (date received).

10. Ibid., April 25, 1901.

11. Dunne to Eli Washington John Lindesmith, March 1901, CUA. There is clearly an error in this date, since, according to the St. Peter's annals, Dunne did not arrive back in Montana until April.

12. Angela Lincoln to Drexel, May 24, 1898, ASBS.

13. Dunne to Lindesmith, March 1901, CUA.

14. For the history of Carlisle, see Louis Morton, "How the Indians came to Carlisle," *Pennsylvania History* 29 (Jan. 1962): 53–73.

15. For more on this controversy, see Series 1, Reel 21, BCIM, and Roll 12, JOPA/NWMC.

Chapter Thirteen

1. *Centennial Roundup: A Collection of Stories Celebrating the 100th Anniversary of the Incorporation of Miles City, Montana* (Miles City, Mont.: *Miles City Star*, 1987), 49–54.

2. Amata Dunne, "Memoir of the Re-opening of the Ursuline Convent at Miles City," *Billings Daily Times*, Saturday, Oct. 4, 1902, AUW.

3. Amata Dunne memoirs, AUG.

4. Amadeus Dunne to St. Julien Aubry, Sept. 16, 1903, AUG.

5. Marie Andrée Jégou and Marija Jasna Kogoj, *Journey Towards Unity*, vol. II (Rome, 1998), 168–170.

6. Aubry to Dunne, Feb. 6, 1904; Dunne to Aubry, Aug. 18, 1904, AUG.

7. For the material on Mathias Lenihan, I am indebted to George Fox's unpublished manuscript.

8. St. Peter's annals, AUW.

9. Ibid.

10. Dunne to Aubry, March 24, 1905, AUG.

11. Miles City annals, AUW.

12. Jerome D'Aste to Snead, 1901, Roll 1, JOPA/NWMC.

13. D'Aste to Snead, Roll 3, JOPA/NWMC.

14. See John H. Holst, "Observations on the Former Flathead Reservation," 1943, Roll 4, JOPA/NWMC.

15. C. C. Wright, Roll 4, JOPA/NWMC.

16. Dunne to William Ketcham, June 21, 1905, Series 1, Reel 36, BCIM.

17. Ketcham to Dunne, Sept. 8, 1905, Series 1, Reel 36, BCIM.

18. Mathias Lenihan to Ketcham, Series 1, Reel 35, BCIM.

19. Ketcham to Lenihan, Series 1, Reel 35, BCIM.

Chapter Fourteen

1. Amadeus Dunne to St. Julien Aubry, March 24, 1905, AUG.

2. John Victor Van den Broeck to Aubry, Dec. 1904, AUG.

3. Aubry to Dunne, April 10, 1905, AUG.

4. Mathias Lenihan to Dunne, Aug. 23, 1905, AUG. Unfortunately, very little of Lenihan's correspondence concerning this controversy is available at the Diocesan archives at Great Falls. Much of it is available at the Ursuline Generalate in Rome.

5. Lenihan to Ursulines, Aug. 12, 1905, AUW.

6. St. Peter's annals, Sept. 11, 1905, AUW.

7. Dunne to Aubry, Dec. 1905, AUG.

8. Mary Rose Galvin to Aubry, Aug. 1905, AUG.

9. Aubry to Galvin, Sept. 1905, AUG.

10. Galvin to Aubry, Oct. 28, 1905, AUG.

11. Scholastica O'Sullivan to Aubry, Oct. 5, 1905, AUG.

12. De Merici Sheble to Aubry, Sept. 27, 1905, AUG.

13. Francis Seibert to Aubry, Dec. 8, 1905, AUG. This letter, sent from Holy Family, was signed by representatives of all the missions.

14. Laurentia Walsh, Dosithée Leygonie, and Claver O'Driscoll to Aubry, Feb. 12, 1906, AUG.

15. Marie Clémence Viguier to Aubry, Sept. 26, 1905, AUG.

16. Holy Family Mission to Aubry, Dec. 8, 1905, AUG.

17. Philippa Seery to Aubry, Jan. 6, 1906, AUG.

18. Aubry to Lenihan, March 17, 1906, AUG.

19. Ibid.
20. Galvin to Aubry, May 21, 1906, AUG.
21. Paula Slevin to Aubry, May 20, 1906, AUG.
22. Dunne to Aubry, July 31, 1906, AUG.
23. Joseph Lemius to Aubry, Feb. 27, 1906, AUG.
24. Slevin to Aubry, May 20, 1906, AUG.
25. Aubry to Lenihan, May 23, 1906, AUG.
26. Aubry to Lemius, June 18, 1906, AUG.
27. Aubry to the Sacred Congregation of Religious, June 16, 1906, AUG.
28. Galvin to Stanislaus Duffey, March 23, 1906, AUT.

Chapter Fifteen

1. St. Julien Aubry to Angela Lincoln, June 19 and 28, 1906, AUG.
2. Aubry to Lincoln, July 4, 1906, AUG.
3. St. Peter's annals, Jan. 17, 1908, AUW.
4. Ibid., Jan 18, 1908.
5. Ibid.
6. *Great Falls Daily Tribune*, Saturday, Jan. 18, 1908, AUW.
7. Amadeus Dunne to Katharine Drexel, Dec. 23, 1908, ASBS.
8. St. Labre's annals, May 15, 1909, AUW.
9. St. Peter's annals, Oct. 30, 1909, AUW.
10. Francis Seibert to Irene Gill, March 1909, AUW.
11. Paris Gibson, *The Founding of Great Falls* (Great Falls, Mont.: Private Printing, 1914), AUW.
12. Irene Gill to Angèle de Notre Dame, March 1, 1912, AUG.
13. *Great Falls Daily Tribune*, Aug. 8, 1912.

Chapter Sixteen

1. Brian W. Dippie, *The Vanishing American: White Attitudes and U.S. Indian Policy* (Middletown, Conn.: Wesleyan University Press, 1982), 173.
2. Joseph Piet to William Ketcham, Jan. 1911, Series 1, Reel 66, BCIM.
3. Piet to Ketcham, March 15, 1909, Series 1, Reel 51, and Series 1, Reel 46, BCIM.
4. Holy Family Jesuit house diary, Dec. 12, 1912, Roll 9, JOPA/NWMC.
5. Joseph Bruckert to Ketcham, May 25 and Aug. 17, 1907, Series 1, Reel 37, BCIM.
6. Oct. 19, and Sept. 28, 1913, Series 1, Reel 71; Feb. 23, 1914, Series 1, Reel 75, BCIM.
7. Thomas Grant to George De la Motte, Feb. 15, 1911, Roll 14, JOPA/NWMC.
8. *Litterae Annuae*, 1910–1913, Roll 14, JOPA/NWMC.
9. Grant to De la Motte, March 2, 1911, Roll 14, JOPA/NWMC.
10. Grant to Scott, Feb. 11, 1911, Series 1, Reel 56, BCIM.
11. Louis Taelman to Ketcham, March 7, 1909, Series 1, Reel 46, BCIM.
12. Ursuline Sisters to Ketcham, Nov. 20, 1910, Series 1, Reel 50, BCIM.

13. De la Motte to Ketcham, 1910, Series 1, Reel 56, BCIM.

14. De la Motte to Cato Sells, quoted in Sells to Isidore Dockweiler, March 6, 1915, Series 1, Reel 75, BCIM.

15. St. Labre's annals, Jan. 1910, AUW.

16. Ibid., Feb. 1909.

17. Ibid.

18. Grant to Ketcham, Nov. 22, 1911, Series 1, Reel 56, BCIM.

19. St. Labre's annals, Jan. 1911, AUW.

20. Ketcham to Thecla Flood, Nov. 11, 1911, Series 1, Reel 56, BCIM.

21. Flood to Ketcham, Nov. 23, 1911, Series 1, Reel 56, BCIM.

22. James Yellow Hair to Ketcham, Feb. 25, 1912, Series 1, Reel 62, BCIM.

23. Ketcham to Mathias Lenihan, Oct. 16, 1912, Series 1, Reel 62, BCIM.

24. Paul Gallagher to Ketcham, Oct. 1908, Series 1 Reel 42, BCIM.

25. Ketcham to Lenihan, Oct. 16, 1912, Series 1, Reel 62, BCIM.

Chapter Seventeen

1. St. Julien Aubry to Irene Gill, May 16 and June 25, 1909, AUG.

2. Evangelist Holly to Gill, Feb. 15, 1910, AUG.

3. Amadeus Dunne to Angèle de Notre Dame, July 16, 1912, AUG.

4. Dunne to Edward O'Dea, Oct. 24, 1912, AAS.

5. Mathias Lenihan to Gill, Dec. 16, 1913, AUG.

6. Francis Seibert to de Notre Dame, Dec. 11, 1913, AUG.

7. Gill to de Notre Dame, Dec. 22, 1913, AUG.

8. John Van der Pol to O'Dea, Nov. 12, 1912, AAS.

9. de Notre Dame to Seibert, Dec. 29, 1914, AUG.

10. Dunne to Katharine Drexel, May 27, 1915, ASBS.

11. Angèle Fouyer to de Notre Dame, Jan 20. 1915, AUG; Evangelist Holly to de Notre Dame, March 20, 1915, AUG.

12. John Carroll, S.J., to de Notre Dame, Dec. 26, 1914, AUG.

13. O'Dea to de Notre Dame, Aug. 18, 1915, AUG.

14. de Notre Dame to Dunne, Sept. 21, 1915, AUG.

15. Dunne to de Notre Dame, Aug. 17, 1915, AUG.

16. Perpetua Egan to Regis McMahon, April 14, 1916; Lenihan to de Notre Dame, April 17, 1916, AUG.

17. Annals of the Ursulines of Toledo, AUT.

18. Fouyer to de Notre Dame, March 2 and June 24, 1917; Carroll to McMahon, June 17, 1917, AUG.

19. Concepta Brown to de Notre Dame, Nov. 29, 1917; Dunne to de Notre Dame, Aug. 28, 1917, AUG.

20. Dunne to Raphael Crimont, March 7, 1918, Crimont Collection: Alaska Ecclesiastical Superiors, JOPA/NWMC.

21. John Sifton to Crimont, Dec. 16, 1918, Crimont Collection: Alaska Ecclesiastical Superiors, JOPA/NWMC.

22. Sifton to Crimont, April 22, 1919, Crimont Collection: Alaska Ecclesiastical

Superior, JOPA/NWMC.

23. Dunne to de Notre Dame, Feb. 19, 1914, AUG.
24. Amata Dunne to de Notre Dame, July 8, 1919, AUG.
25. Egan to de Notre Dame, Oct. 15, 1919, AUG.
26. Egan to de Notre Dame, Nov. 25, 1919, AUG.

Chapter Eighteen

1. Thomas Grant to F. H. Abbott, Oct. 14, 1912, Series 1, Reel 62, BCIM.
2. Louis Taelman to William Ketcham, Sept. 9, 1913, Series 1, Reel 66, BCIM.
3. Grant to Ketcham, Feb. 24, 1912, Series 1, Reel 62, BCIM.
4. Taelman to Ketcham, July 7, 1919, Series 1, Reel 62, BCIM.
5. Francis Dillon to Taelman, Aug. 12, 1921, Roll 15, JOPA/NWMC.
6. Xavier Gavigan to Dillon, Aug. 16, 1921, Roll 15, JOPA/NWMC.
7. Ketcham to Dillon, Oct. 1, 1921, Roll 5, JOPA/NWMC.
8. Theresa Abair to Ketcham, June 29, 1916, Series 1, Reel 80, BCIM.
9. Thomas Stoeckel to Ketcham, Jan. 15, 1917, Series 1, Reel 80, BCIM.
10. Ketcham to Mathias Lenihan, March 4, 1918, Series 1, Reel 92, BCIM.
11. Abair to Ketcham, Feb. 17, 1912, Series 1, Reel 75, BCIM.
12. Hubert Post to Ketcham, Nov. 8, 1912, Series 1, Reel 62, BCIM.
13. Ketcham to Post, Sept. 13, 1912, Series 1, Reel 62, BCIM.
14. Aloysius Bailey to O'Brien, May 12, 1921, Series 1, Reel 97, BCIM.
15. St. Henry Perret, Nov. 13, 1931, AUW.
16. St. Paul's annals, July 1896, AUW.
17. Thomas Grant to Charles Lusk, Nov. 10, 1916, Series 1, Reel 80, BCIM.
18. Grant to Ketcham, Aug. 25, 1917, Series 1, Reel 84, BCIM.
19. Grant to Franciscan Missionaries of Mary, June 17, 1918, Series 1, Reel 88, BCIM.
20. *The Calumet*, Oct. 1939.
21. Holy Family annals, June 4, 1940, AUW.
22. Joseph Bruckert to Ketcham, Oct. 1, 1921, Series 1, Reel 97, BCIM.
23. Bruckert to Ketcham, Dec. 11, 1919, Series 1, Reel 92, BCIM.
24. Ambrose Sullivan to William Hughes, Feb. 20, 1922, Series 1, Reel 105, BCIM.
25. Hughes to Perpetua Egan, Feb. 23, 1922, Series 1, Reel 105, BCIM.
26. Egan to Hughes, Sept. 5, 1924, Series 1, Reel 117, BCIM.

Bibliographic Notes

Although I have been fortunate in having had a wealth of material to draw on as background for this narrative, there is very little published material dealing specifically with women missionaries in the Far West, and especially in Montana. Except for the biography of Amadeus Dunne, O.S.U., by her fellow missionary Angela Lincoln (*Life of the Reverend Mother Amadeus of the Heart of Jesus*, Paulist Press, 1923), Sister Genevieve McBride's interesting sourcebook (*The Bird Tail*, Vantage Press, 1974), Suzanne H. Schrems's recent study of Catholic missionary sisters in Montana (*Uncommon Women, Unmarked Trails: The Courageous Journey of Catholic Missionary Sisters in Frontier Montana*, Horse Creek Publications, 2003), and Anne Butler's essay on Mother Amadeus in *Portraits of Women in the American West* edited by Dee Garceau-Hagen (Routledge, 2005), there is no substantive published material. *Lady Blackrobes* is indebted almost entirely to archival sources. Consequently, it seemed appropriate to limit my bibliography to these sources, citing published material only when it was particularly apposite to my subject.

My primary indebtedness is to the archives of the Ursuline sisters, both in the United States and abroad. The Ursulines of Toledo provided all the essential documentation for the foundation and early years of the missions. The archives of the Western Province of the Ursulines of the Roman Union, presently housed in Great Falls, Montana, was, of course, my major source for the growth and development of the missions. Archives at the Roman Generalate of the Ursulines of the Roman Union were particularly helpful in providing documentation for the later years of Amadeus Dunne and her effort to establish missions in Alaska. The Ursulines of the Canadian Union, both at Québec and Trois Rivières, provided valuable correspondence covering the years that the Canadian Ursulines served on the Montana missions.

Three other archival sources have been invaluable. The archives of the Sisters of the Blessed Sacrament, located in Bensalem, Pennsylvania, provided correspondence between Mother Amadeus Dunne and Mother Katharine Drexel, whose philanthropy enabled many of the missions to continue their work. Since the Ursulines had worked in tandem with the Society of Jesus, I relied heavily on the Jesuit Oregon Province Archives, located at Gonzaga University, Spokane, Washington, containing the microfilm collection of Northwest Indian Missions. Another major source was the mission correspondence of the Bureau of Catholic Indian Missions, housed at Marquette University, Milwaukee, Wisconsin, and handily available through an online catalog.

For the correspondence of Bishops John Baptist Brondel, Richard Gilmour, Mathias Lenihan, and Edwin O'Dea, I am indebted to the archdiocesan archives of Cleveland, Ohio; Helena, Montana; Great Falls, Montana; and Seattle, Washington. The archives of the Catholic University of America, Washington, D.C., provided me with the diaries and correspondence of Father Eli W. J. Lindesmith.

Among the published sources that must be acknowledged in any study of the Rocky Mountain Missions is the work of Lawrence Palladino, S.J., *Indian and White in the Northwest: A History of Catholicity in Montana, 1831–1891* (J. Murphy and Company, 1894), a seminal work that remains today an indispensible tool for this period. The extensive work of Wilfred P. Schoenberg, S.J., is nonpareil. *Paths to the Northwest: A Jesuit History of the Oregon Province* (Loyola University Press, 1982) provided invaluable background on the development of the Jesuit missions in Montana, replete with details of daily living and vivid vignettes of the missionaries. My own work would be considerably poorer without Schoenberg's meticulous and engaging scholarship.

Index

323